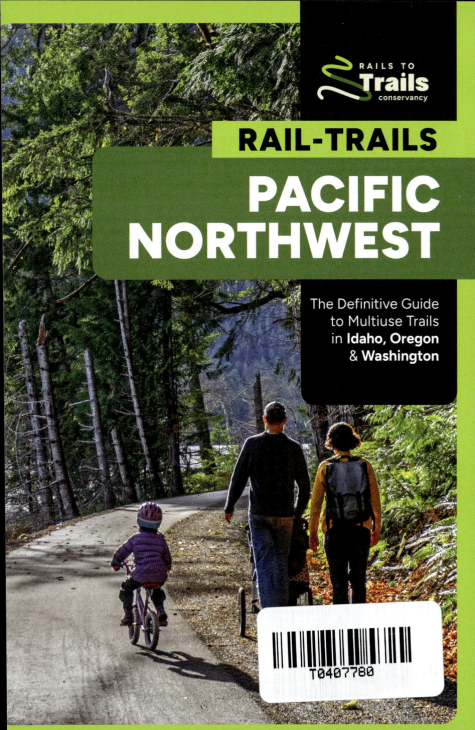

Rail-Trails: Pacific Northwest
Copyright © 2015, 2025 by Rails to Trails Conservancy
1st edition 2015, originally published as *Rail-Trails: Washington & Oregon*
2nd edition 2025
Cover and interior photographs copyright © 2025 by Rails to Trails Conservancy

Project editor: Kate Johnson
Content editors: Laura Stark and Amy Kapp
Maps: Derek Strout, Lohnes+Wright; map data © OpenStreetMap contributors
Cover design: Jonathan Norberg
Book design and layout: Annie Long
Proofreader: Emily Beaumont
Indexer: Frances Lennie

Cataloging-in-Publication Data is on file with the Library of Congress.
ISBN: 978-1-64359-117-9 (pbk.)
ISBN: 978-1-64359-118-6 (ebook)

Published by: **WILDERNESS PRESS**
   An imprint of AdventureKEEN
   2204 First Ave. S., Ste. 102
   Birmingham, AL 35233
   800-678-7006; fax 877-374-9016

Visit wildernesspress.com for a complete listing of our books and for ordering information. Contact us with questions or comments at our website, at facebook.com/wildernesspress1967, or at x.com/wilderness1967.

Manufactured in the United States of America
Distributed by Publishers Group West

Front cover photo: Washington's Olympic Discovery Trail (*see page 203*); photo by John Gussman
Back cover photo: Washington's Snoqualmie Valley Trail (*see page 233*); photo by Eli Brownell/courtesy King County Parks

All rights reserved. No part of this book may be reproduced in any form, or by any means, electronic, mechanical, recording, or otherwise, without written permission from the publisher, except for brief quotations used in reviews.

SAFETY NOTICE Although Wilderness Press and Rails to Trails Conservancy have made every attempt to ensure that the information in this book is accurate at press time, they are not responsible for any loss, damage, injury, or inconvenience that may occur to anyone while using this book. You are responsible for your own safety and health while in the wilderness. The fact that a trail is described in this book does not mean that it will be safe for you. Be aware that trail conditions can change from day to day. Always check local conditions, know your own limitations, and consult a map.

About Rails to Trails Conservancy

At Rails to Trails Conservancy, we believe in the joy and impact trails deliver for people, places, and the planet. That's why—as the nation's largest advocacy organization for trails, walking, and bicycling—we're working hard to make sure trails connect everyone, in every neighborhood across America. With a grassroots community more than 1 million strong, RTC is committed to ensuring a better future for America made possible by trails and the connections they inspire. Learn more at **railstotrails.org.**

Railways helped build America. Spanning from coast to coast, these ribbons of steel linked people, communities, and enterprises, spurring commerce and transforming the nation. Today, our focus is on the potential these corridors have to create public spaces that connect our communities and make it possible for millions of people to be active outside.

When RTC opened its doors in 1986, the rail-trail movement was in its infancy. At the time, many rail-trails were inspired by grassroots activism, where neighbors and friends saw the potential of a disused rail corridor to create a new space for outdoor recreation and conservation. RTC saw an opportunity to elevate these incredible community assets into the national conversation. With our headquarters in Washington, D.C., and field offices around the country, our staff is at the center of local, state, and national efforts to create, connect, and maintain America's trails.

Americans now enjoy nearly 26,000 miles of rail-trails, and they flock to the trails to connect with family and friends, enjoy nature, and access places in their neighborhoods and beyond. Building upon this foundation of rail-trails, connected trail networks—including all types of multiuse pathways and active-transportation routes—are being developed in every state in the nation. Year after year, RTC's efforts to protect and align public funding with trail and trail-network development helps to advance this work and sustain the growing enthusiasm for making walking and biking part of our everyday lives.

TrailLink™, the free trail-finder website and mobile app from RTC, can be used as a companion resource to the trails in this guidebook; it includes detailed descriptions, interactive maps, photo galleries, and firsthand ratings and reviews. When RTC launched the website in 2000, our organization was one of the first to compile such detailed trail information on a national scale. TrailLink continues to play a critical role in both encouraging and satisfying the country's growing need for opportunities to use trails for recreation or transportation.

iv Rail-Trails: **Pacific Northwest**

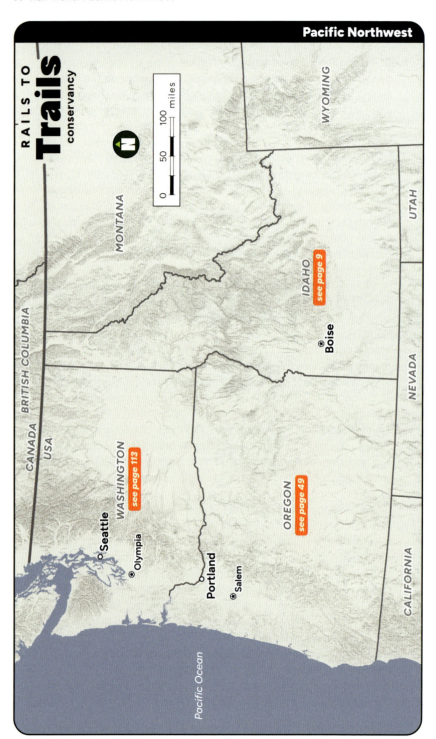

Table of Contents

About Rails to Trails Conservancy iii
Regional Locator Map . . . . opposite page
Foreword viii
Acknowledgments ix
Summary of Trails x
Introduction 1
How to Use This Book 3

IDAHO 9

1 Ashton-Tetonia Trail 11
2 Boise River Greenbelt 15
3 Canyon Rim Trail 19
4 Idaho Falls Greenbelt 21
5 Latah Trail 25
6 North Idaho Centennial Trail 29
7 Route of the Hiawatha 33
8 Trail of the Coeur d'Alenes 37
9 Weiser River National Recreation Trail 41
10 Wood River Trail 45

OREGON 49

11 Astoria Riverwalk 51
12 Banks-Vernonia State Trail 53
13 Bear Creek Greenway 57
14 Crown Zellerbach Trail 61
15 Deschutes River Trail (Bend) 65
16 Deschutes River Trail (Sherman County) 69
17 Fanno Creek Trail 73
18 Historic Columbia River Highway State Trail 77
19 I-205 Multi-Use Path 81

20	OC&E Woods Line State Trail	85
21	Rogue River Greenway	89
22	Row River Trail	91
23	Ruth Bascom Riverbank Path System	95
24	Springwater Corridor	97
25	Trolley Trail	101
26	Vera Katz Eastbank Esplanade	105
27	Westside Trail	109

WASHINGTON 113

28	Apple Capital Loop Trail	115
29	Appleway Trail	119
30	Bill Chipman Palouse Trail	121
31	Burke-Gilman Trail	125
32	Cascade Trail	129
33	Cedar River Trail	131
34	Centennial Trail	135
35	Chehalis Western Trail	139
36	Cowiche Canyon Trail	143
37	Cross Kirkland Corridor	147
38	Discovery Trail	151
39	East Lake Sammamish Trail	153
40	Elliott Bay Trail	157
41	Ferry County Rail Trail	163
42	Fish Lake Trail	165
43	Foothills Trail	169
44	Green River Trail	173
45	Interurban Trail (Bellingham)	177
46	Interurban Trail (North)	179

TABLE OF CONTENTS **vii**

47 Interurban Trail (South). 183
48 Issaquah-Preston Trail. 187
49 Karen Fraser Woodland Trail 191
50 Klickitat Trail 193
51 Lower Yakima Valley Pathway .197
52 Old Railroad Grade 199
53 Olympic Discovery Trail. 203
54 Palouse to Cascades State Park Trail. 211
55 Preston-Snoqualmie Trail. 219
56 Richland Riverfront Trail 221
57 Sammamish River Trail 225
58 Similkameen Trail. 229
59 Snoqualmie Valley Trail 233
60 South Bay Trail 237
61 Spokane River Centennial State Park Trail 239
62 Tommy Thompson Parkway 243
63 Willapa Hills State Park Trail 247
64 Yakima Greenway 251
65 Yelm–Rainier–Tenino Trail 255

Index. 257
Support Rails to Trails Conservancy. 265

Foreword

Welcome to the *Rail-Trails: Pacific Northwest* guidebook, a comprehensive companion for discovering the region's top rail-trails and multiuse pathways—spaces where you can run, hike, bike, and play. This book will help you uncover fantastic opportunities to get outside and experience adventure on more than 1,500 miles of trails in Idaho, Oregon, and Washington.

Rails to Trails Conservancy's mission is to build a nation connected by trails. We reimagine public spaces to create safe ways for everyone to walk, bike, and be active outdoors. We hope this book will inspire you to experience firsthand the joy and impact of trails. That feeling when you're first out on the trail and see the dew rise. Sharing the space with friends and family. Exploring nature, while connecting to the history and culture of a place.

Since its founding in 1986, RTC has been at the forefront of a growing movement where trails and trail networks are essential to people and places. Today, more than 42,000 miles of multiuse trails provide invaluable benefits for people and communities across the country. We hope you find this book to be a delightful and informative resource for discovering the many unique trail destinations throughout the region.

I'll be out on the trails, too, experiencing the thrill of the ride right alongside you. Be sure to say hello and share your #TrailMoments with us on social media. You can find us on Facebook at facebook.com/railstotrails and on Instagram @railstotrails. Or submit your stories about the ways trails have made a difference in your life at **trailmoments.org.** We want to hear from you!

Enjoy the journey,

Ryan Chao, President
Rails to Trails Conservancy

Acknowledgments

Special acknowledgment is owed to Laura Stark and Amy Kapp, editors of this guidebook, and to Derek Strout and Bart Wright (of Lohnes+Wright) for their work on the creation of the trail maps included in the book. Rails to Trails Conservancy also thanks Amy Ahn, Cindy Barks, Gene Bisbee, and Glenn Zinkus for their assistance in writing and editing content.

We also appreciate the following staff contributors, as well as local trail managers, who helped us ensure that the maps, photographs, and trail descriptions are as accurate as possible.

Quinton Batts	Willie Karidis
Kevin Belle	Mary Ellen Koontz
Ken Bryan	Maddie Krentz
Danielle Casavant	Joe LaCroix
Eduardo Coyotzi Zarate	Isabelle Lord
Ryan Cree	Cas Marburger
Peter Dean	Yvonne Mwangi
Cindy Dickerson	Lauren Swan
Kate Foster	Eileen Symons
Brandi Horton	Jesse Voremberg

Summary of Trails

Trail Number/Name	Page	Mileage	Walking	Cycling	Wheelchair Accessible	In-line Skating	Mountain Biking	Fishing	Horseback Riding	Cross-Country Skiing	Snowmobiling
IDAHO											
1 Ashton-Tetonia Trail	11	29.6	•				•	•	•	•	•
2 Boise River Greenbelt	15	46.1	•	•	•	•		•			
3 Canyon Rim Trail	19	8.2	•	•	•			•			
4 Idaho Falls Greenbelt	21	11.4	•	•	•	•					
5 Latah Trail	25	16.4	•	•	•	•				•	
6 North Idaho Centennial Trail	29	23	•	•	•	•			•	•	
7 Route of the Hiawatha	33	15	•				•				
8 Trail of the Coeur d'Alenes	37	73.2	•	•	•	•		•		•	•
9 Weiser River National Recreation Trail	41	85.5	•				•	•	•	•	
10 Wood River Trail	45	36.1	•	•	•	•		•		•	
OREGON											
11 Astoria Riverwalk	51	6.4	•	•	•			•			
12 Banks-Vernonia State Trail	53	21.2	•	•	•			•	•		
13 Bear Creek Greenway	57	20.6	•	•	•	•		•			
14 Crown Zellerbach Trail	61	23	•	•	•		•		•		
15 Deschutes River Trail (Bend)	65	12.5	•	•	•		•	•			
16 Deschutes River Trail (Sherman County)	69	18.6	•				•	•	•		
17 Fanno Creek Trail	73	9.2	•	•	•					•	
18 Historic Columbia River Highway State Trail	77	18.8	•	•							
19 I-205 Multi-Use Path	81	18.5	•	•	•	•					
20 OC&E Woods Line State Trail	85	109.2	•	•	•	•	•		•	•	
21 Rogue River Greenway	89	9.8	•	•	•	•		•			
22 Row River Trail	91	16.4	•	•	•	•			•	•	
23 Ruth Bascom Riverbank Path System	95	19.5	•	•	•	•		•			
24 Springwater Corridor	97	21	•	•	•	•			•		
25 Trolley Trail	101	6.9	•	•	•						
26 Vera Katz Eastbank Esplanade	105	1.5	•	•	•	•					
27 Westside Trail	109	11.2	•	•	•	•	•				

SUMMARY OF TRAILS

Trail Number/Name	Page	Mileage	Walking	Cycling	Wheelchair Accessible	In-line Skating	Mountain Biking	Fishing	Horseback Riding	Cross-Country Skiing	Snowmobiling
WASHINGTON											
28 Apple Capital Loop Trail	115	22	•	•	•	•				•	
29 Appleway Trail	119	5.8	•	•	•	•					
30 Bill Chipman Palouse Trail	121	7.1	•	•	•	•				•	
31 Burke-Gilman Trail	125	19.7	•	•	•	•					
32 Cascade Trail	129	22.9	•				•		•	•	
33 Cedar River Trail	131	17.4	•	•	•	•			•	•	
34 Centennial Trail	135	30.6	•	•	•	•			•		
35 Chehalis Western Trail	139	21.2	•	•	•	•			•	•	
36 Cowiche Canyon Trail	143	2.9	•				•		•	•	
37 Cross Kirkland Corridor	147	5.8	•	•	•						
38 Discovery Trail	151	8.3	•	•	•	•	•	•			
39 East Lake Sammamish Trail	153	11	•	•	•	•		•			
40 Elliott Bay Trail	157	3.9	•	•	•	•		•			
41 Ferry County Rail Trail	163	25	•	•	•	•	•	•	•	•	
42 Fish Lake Trail	165	7.6	•	•	•	•		•		•	
43 Foothills Trail	169	24.7	•	•	•	•		•			
44 Green River Trail	173	19.6	•	•	•	•		•		•	
45 Interurban Trail (Bellingham)	177	6.7	•	•	•		•		•		
46 Interurban Trail North	179	31.3	•	•	•	•			•		
47 Interurban Trail South	183	19.8	•	•	•	•					
48 Issaquah-Preston Trail	187	5.5	•	•	•				•		
49 Karen Fraser Woodland Trail	191	5.2	•	•	•	•					
50 Klickitat Trail	193	31	•				•		•	•	
51 Lower Yakima Valley Pathway	197	14	•	•	•	•				•	
52 Old Railroad Grade	199	3.6	•				•				
53 Olympic Discovery Trail	203	64.5	•	•	•	•		•	•		
54 Palouse to Cascades State Park Trail	211	245.6	•	•			•	•	•	•	•
55 Preston-Snoqualmie Trail	219	6.5	•	•	•	•			•		
56 Richland Riverfront Trail	221	7	•	•	•	•		•			

(continued on next page)

Summary of Trails (continued)

Trail Number/Name	Page	Mileage	Walking	Cycling	Wheelchair Accessible	In-line Skating	Mountain Biking	Fishing	Horseback Riding	Cross-Country Skiing	Snowmobiling
WASHINGTON *(continued)*											
57 Sammamish River Trail	225	10.3	•	•	•	•			•	•	
58 Similkameen Trail	229	4.9	•				•		•		
59 Snoqualmie Valley Trail	233	29.5	•	•					•	•	
60 South Bay Trail	237	2.5	•	•	•				•		
61 Spokane River Centennial State Park Trail	239	40	•	•			•		•	•	•
62 Tommy Thompson Parkway	243	3.3	•	•		•	•				
63 Willapa Hills State Park Trail	247	56	•	•			•			•	
64 Yakima Greenway	251	22.9	•	•	•			•			
65 Yelm–Rainier–Tenino Trail	255	14.5	•	•	•	•			•	•	

Introduction

Of the more than 2,400 rail-trails across the United States, more than 130 thread through Idaho, Oregon, and Washington. These routes relate a two-part story: The first speaks to the early years of railroading, while the second showcases efforts by Rails to Trails Conservancy, local organizations, and other trail supporters and volunteers to resurrect these unused railroad corridors as public-use trails. This guidebook highlights 65 of the region's top trails, offering you the insight to plan your perfect adventure.

From the forested and lake-laden north to the Snake River plain in the south, Idaho offers a variety of exceptional trails that are urban, rural, or a bit on the wild side. Especially notable are the Trail of the Coeur d'Alenes (see page 37) and Route of the Hiawatha (see page 33), nestled in the state's scenic panhandle. In the capital and largest city of Idaho, the Boise River Greenbelt (see page 15) provides a pleasant way to get around, connecting Boise State University, Zoo Boise, numerous parks, and other destinations through a tree-lined riparian corridor. In contrast, the state's longest rail-trail, the Weiser River National Recreation Trail (see page 41), journeys 85 miles through remote canyons, evergreen wilderness, and alpine meadows and across a whopping 62 historical railroad trestles.

Oregon's trails follow the Pacific coastline, trek through mountainous terrain, traverse the high-desert landscape, and wind through bustling downtowns. Similar to a rail-trail, the Historic Columbia River Highway State Trail (see page 77) has transformed a former roadway into a serene experience along rugged cliffs overlooking sapphire-blue water. Other highlights of the state are the Banks-Vernonia State Trail (see page 53), tucked into the towering forests of the Coast Range foothills; the charming Astoria Riverwalk (see page 51), near the mouth of the mighty Columbia River; and the Springwater Corridor (see page 97), connecting Greater Portland.

Washington boasts the Burke-Gilman Trail (see page 125), undoubtedly one of the busiest trails in the state, serving as the backbone to Seattle's expansive trail network. Two of the longest trails in this book are also located here: the Palouse to Cascades State Park Trail (see page 211), which crosses two-thirds of the state, and the Olympic Discovery Trail (see page 203), a developing 123-mile endeavor to connect Puget Sound to the Pacific Ocean.

A handful of the trails featured here are Hall of Fame designees, noted throughout the book with a special icon (see page 2). The Pacific Northwest also hosts the western terminus of the Great America Rail-Trail® (see page 2); trails that are part of this multiuse trail route stretching across the country between Washington state and Washington, D.C., are also noted.

No matter which trails you choose to explore from *Rail-Trails: Pacific Northwest*, you'll experience the unique history, culture, and geography of each, as well as the communities that have built and embraced them.

What Is a Rail-Trail?

Rail-trails are multiuse paths built along former railroad corridors that create public space for outdoor activity and transportation. Most often flat or following a gentle grade, they are suited to walking, running, cycling, mountain biking, wheelchair use, in-line skating, cross-country skiing, and horseback riding. RTC has been at the forefront of helping America create nearly 26,000 miles of rail-trails throughout the country.

These extremely popular recreation and transportation corridors traverse urban, suburban, and rural landscapes. Many preserve historical landmarks, while others serve as wildlife conservation corridors, linking isolated parks and establishing greenways in developed areas. Rail-trails also stimulate local economies by boosting tourism and promoting trailside businesses.

What Is a Rail-with-Trail?

A rail-with-trail is a public path that parallels a still-active rail line. Some run adjacent to fast-moving, scheduled trains, often linking public transportation stations, while others follow tourist routes and slow-moving excursion trains. Many share an easement, separated from the rails by fencing or other barriers. Nearly 450 rails-with-trails exist in 47 states across the country, plus the District of Columbia.

What Is Rails to Trails Conservancy's Hall of Fame?

In 2007, RTC began recognizing exemplary trails around the country through its Hall of Fame program. Inductees are selected based on merits such as scenic value, high use, trail and trailside amenities, historical significance, excellence in management and maintenance of facility, community connections, and geographic distribution.

The Pacific Northwest region boasts four Hall of Fame inductees: Idaho's Trail of the Coeur d'Alenes (see page 37) and Route of the Hiawatha (see page 33); Oregon's Springwater Corridor (see page 97); and Washington's Burke-Gilman Trail (see page 125). These trails are indicated in this book with a special icon. For the full list of Hall of Fame trails, visit **railstotrails.org/halloffame**.

What Is the Great American Rail-Trail?

The Great American Rail-Trail® is RTC's signature project to create the nation's first cross-country multiuse trail, stretching more than 3,700 miles between Washington, D.C., and Washington state. This trail is an iconic piece of American infrastructure that will connect thousands of miles of rail-trails and other multiuse trails, serving tens of millions of people living along the route, as well as those who visit the trail from around the country and the world. The Pacific Northwest is the western terminus of the Great American Rail-Trail, and many trails in this book are part of the route. These trails are indicated with a special icon. Learn more at **greatamericanrailtrail.org**.

How to Use This Book

Rail-Trails: Pacific Northwest provides the information you'll need to plan a rewarding trek on a rail-trail or other multiuse trail in the region. With words to inspire you and maps to chart your path, it makes choosing the best route a breeze. Following are some of the highlights.

Maps

You'll find three levels of maps in this book: an **overall regional map, state locator maps**, and **detailed trail maps**.

The trails are located in Idaho, Oregon, and Washington. Each chapter details a particular state's network of trails, marked on locator maps at the beginning of the chapter. Use these maps to find the trails nearest you, or select several neighboring trails and plan a weekend excursion. Once you find a trail on a state locator map, simply flip to the corresponding trail number for a full description. Accompanying trail maps mark each route's access roads, trailheads, parking areas, restrooms, and other defining features.

Key to Map Icons

 parking   drinking water   restrooms   trailhead featured trail connecting trail active railroad

Trail Descriptions

Trails are listed in alphabetical order within each state chapter. Each description begins with a summary of key facts about the trail, including possible uses, trail endpoints and mileage, a roughness rating, and the trail surface.

The map and summary information list the trail endpoints (a city, street, or more specific location), with suggested start and end points. Additional access points are marked on the maps and mentioned in the trail descriptions. The maps and descriptions also highlight available amenities, including parking; restrooms; and area attractions, such as shops, services, museums, and parks. Trail length is listed in miles, one way, and includes only completed trail; the mileage for any gaps in the trail will be noted in its description.

Each trail description includes a **roughness rating** from 1 to 3. A rating of 1 indicates a smooth, level surface that is accessible to users of all ages and abilities. A 2 rating means the surface may be loose and/or uneven and could pose a problem for road bikes and wheelchairs. A 3 rating suggests a rough surface that is recommended only for mountain bikers and hikers. Surfaces can range from asphalt or concrete to ballast, boardwalk, cinder, crushed stone, gravel, grass, dirt, sand, and/or wood chips. Where relevant, trail descriptions address alternating surface conditions.

All trails are open to pedestrians. Bicycles are permitted unless otherwise noted in the trail summary or description. The summary also indicates whether the trail is wheelchair accessible. Other possible uses include in-line skating, mountain biking, horseback riding, fishing, and cross-country skiing. While most trails are off-limits to motor vehicles, some local trail organizations do allow snowmobiles in winter.

Trail descriptions themselves suggest an ideal itinerary for each route, including the best parking areas and access points, where to begin, direction of travel, and any highlights along the way.

Each trail description also lists a local website for further information. Be sure to check these websites for updates and current conditions before you set out. **TrailLink™** is another great resource for updated content on the trails in this guidebook.

Parking Waypoints

In the Parking section for each trail, we've included GPS coordinates for the main parking waypoints. These latitude and longitude coordinates can be used on a GPS device or in online mapping programs to locate parking areas. If you have a smartphone, you can use this guidebook along with Rails to Trails Conservancy's TrailLink app, which provides driving directions at the tap of a waypoint.

Trail Use Guidelines

Rail-trails are popular destinations for a range of users, which makes them busy places to enjoy the outdoors. Following basic trail etiquette and safety guidelines will make your experience more pleasant.

➤ **Keep to the right,** except when passing.

➤ **Pass on the left, and give a clear, audible warning:** "On your left!"

➤ **Be aware of other trail users,** particularly around corners and blind spots, and be especially careful when entering a trail, changing direction, or passing so that you don't collide with traffic.

➤ **Respect wildlife and public and private property;** leave no trace and take out litter.

➤ **Control your speed,** especially near pedestrians, playgrounds, and congested areas.

➤ **Travel single file.** Cyclists and pedestrians should ride or walk single file in congested areas or areas with reduced visibility.

- ➤ **Cross carefully at intersections;** always look both ways and yield to through traffic. Pedestrians have the right-of-way.
- ➤ **Keep your headphone volume low** to increase your awareness of your surroundings.
- ➤ **Wear a helmet and other safety gear** if you're cycling or in-line skating.
- ➤ **Consider visibility.** Wear reflective clothing, use bicycle lights, and bring flashlights or helmet-mounted lights for tunnel passages or twilight excursions.
- ➤ **Keep moving and don't block the trail.** When taking a rest, pull off the trail to the right. Groups should avoid congregating on or blocking the trails. If you have an accident on the trail, move to the right as soon as possible.
- ➤ **Bicyclists yield to all other trail users.** Pedestrians yield to horses. If in doubt, yield to all other trail users.
- ➤ **Dogs are permitted on most trails,** but some trails through parks, wildlife refuges, or other sensitive areas may not allow pets; it's best to check the trail website before your visit. If pets are permitted, keep your dog on a short leash and under your control at all times. Remove dog waste and place in a designated trash receptacle.
- ➤ **Teach your children these trail essentials** and be diligent in keeping them out of faster-moving trail traffic.
- ➤ **Be prepared, especially on long-distance and rural trails.** Bring water, snacks, maps, a light source, matches, and other equipment you may need. Because some areas may not have good reception for mobile phones, know where you're going and tell someone else your plan.

E-Bikes

Electric bicycles, or e-bikes, feature a small electric motor to assist the rider by adding power to the wheels. A three-tiered system has been developed to classify e-bikes based on speed capacity and other factors; many states allow Class 1 (up to 20 mph; requires pedaling) and Class 2 (uses a throttle) e-bikes to operate on trails, but not Class 3 (up to 28 mph). However, these rules vary by local jurisdiction, so if you would like to ride an e-bike on one of the trails listed in this book, please visit the website listed for the trail or contact the local trail manager to determine whether the use of e-bikes is permitted. Learn more at **rtc.li/rtc-ebikes.**

Travel Precautions

When planning a trail excursion in the Pacific Northwest, check wildfire risk levels before you go. Visit the website listed for the trail or contact the local trail manager to see if there are any fire restrictions in the area you plan to visit. You can also check regional or national resources, such as the USDA Northwest Climate Hub (**rtc.li/usda-climate-hubs**), Bureau of Land Management (**blm.gov/programs/fire/fire-restrictions**), or National Weather Service (**weather.gov/fire**) for current wildfire assessments.

Another consideration in this region and elsewhere are encampments of unhoused individuals along some trails, particularly in urban centers. If you come across an encampment, please maintain a respectful distance and keep an eye out for individuals, pets, and wildlife that may be crossing the pathway from either side.

Wherever you explore, remember to #SharetheTrail (**railstotrails.org/share-the-trail**) and #RecreateResponsibly (**recreateresponsibly.org**), as multiuse trails are used by people of every age, ability, and mode. Together, we can help make every trip safe and fun for everyone.

Wildlife Tips

As many Pacific Northwest trails pass through habitat for cougars, bears, and other wildlife, we've included some safety tips. For more information, check out the National Park Service's website, **rtc.li/nps-wildlife.**

Washington's Olympic Discovery Trail overlooking Lake Crescent (*see Trail 53, page 203*)

HOW TO USE THIS BOOK **7**

➤ **Avoid hiking or biking trails at dawn or dusk,** when many animals are active.

➤ **Stay aware of your surroundings.**

➤ **Make noise every so often** (such as singing or using your bike bell) so that animals are aware of your presence.

➤ **Ensure that any food you bring is properly stored.**

➤ **Never approach or feed wild animals.**

➤ **Consider carrying bear spray** as a precaution.

Key to Trail Use Icons

Learn More

To learn about additional multiuse trails in your area or to plan a trip to an area beyond the scope of this book, visit **TrailLink™,** the free trail-finder website and mobile app from Rails to Trails Conservancy, with more than 42,000 miles of mapped rail-trails and multiuse trails nationwide.

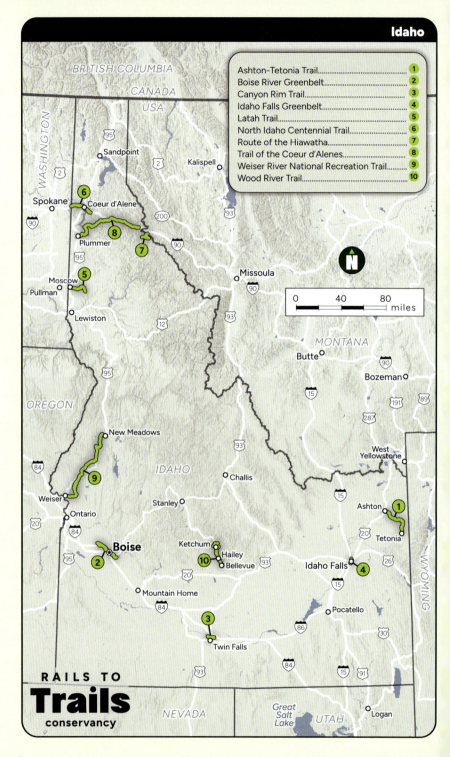

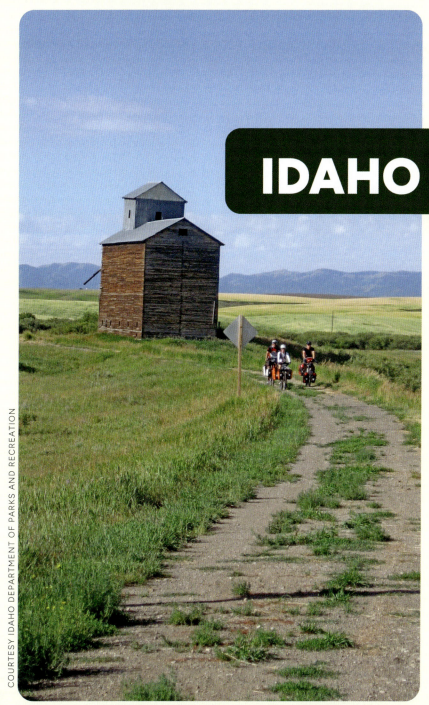

IDAHO

As you journey through eastern Idaho's agricultural landscapes on the Ashton-Tetonia Trail (*see next page*), you'll pass several grain elevators.

10 Rail-Trails: **Pacific Northwest**

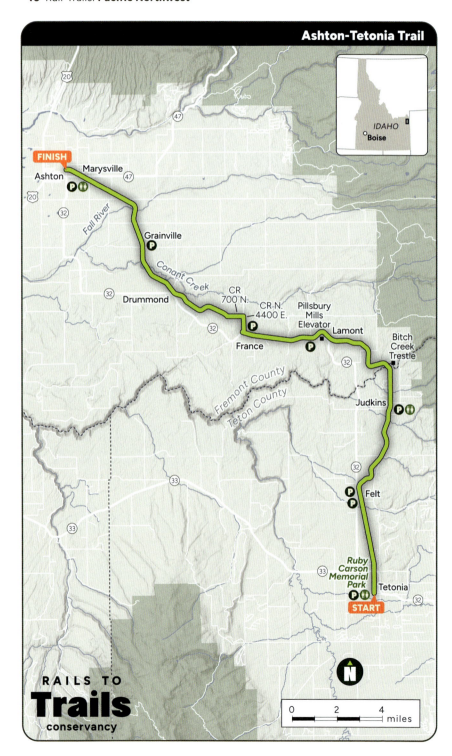

Ashton-Tetonia Trail

Officially opened in 2010, the Ashton-Tetonia Trail extends nearly 30 miles between the Idaho towns of Ashton and Tetonia. The trail occupies a former rail spur once operated by the Union Pacific Railroad (the Oregon Short Line) to transport livestock, peas, limestone, and grain (a theme of this trail). The line also carried tourists to Yellowstone and Grand Teton National Parks.

The Idaho Department of Parks and Recreation manages the dirt-and-gravel trail and received funding to provide significant improvements to it, including changing portions of the surface to asphalt between July and September of 2025. For the most recent project updates, visit the state park website, **rtc.li/id-ashton-tetonia-trail.**

Passing through riparian, pine forest, aspen, and agricultural landscapes, the trail includes three restored historical rail trestles spanning 600 feet in length and 130 feet

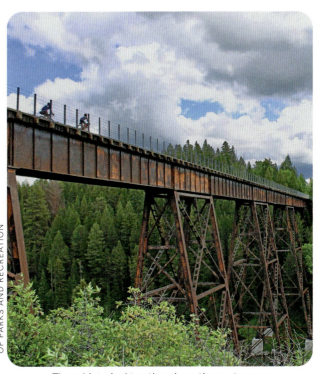

Three historical trestles along the route span Bitch Creek, Conant Creek, and the Fall River.

Counties
Teton, Fremont

Endpoints
Egbert Ave., 0.3 mile west of N. 3000 W. (Tetonia); N. 3600 E., between 1350 N. and ID 47/ E. 1300 Road N. (Ashton)

Mileage
29.6

Type
Rail-Trail

Roughness Rating
2–3

Surface
Dirt and Gravel

in height. The trail is part of the Greater Yellowstone Ecosystem, home to elk, deer, moose, bears, pronghorn, marmots, coyotes, wolves, foxes, bald eagles, mountain lions, Columbian ground squirrels, and more.

Horseback riding is allowed on the entirety of the trail, which is also open to skiers, snowshoers, and snowmobilers when there is enough snow to groom the trail. Mountain bikers and hikers might want to travel from Ashton south to Tetonia to enjoy views of the Teton Mountains and quicker access to two of the three trestle bridges, though this option involves an 800-foot elevation gain over the course of the trail. In addition, there is no official trail parking at the Ashton endpoint, although there are trailheads in both Ashton and Marysville.

If starting from the southern terminus in Tetonia, you'll pass Ruby Carson Memorial Park in just 0.1 mile. Head 10.5 miles north through the communities of Felt and Judkins before arriving at the impressive Bitch Creek Trestle. Continue west through the neighborhood of Lamont and past the historical Pillsbury Mills Elevator, one of several grain elevators along the trail.

From here, go 7.5 miles west to County Road North 4400 East, where you will take a 1.4-mile detour off the main rail line in Fremont County's France neighborhood to skirt private property. The detour heads north onto North 4400 East (a gravel road) and west onto CR 700 North (a doubletrack dirt road) before picking up the trail again and heading toward the city of Drummond.

The section from Drummond north to Ashton passes through the small Fremont County communities of Grainville and Marysville and includes two historical rail trestles spanning Conant Creek and Fall River. In Ashton, the Ashton Visitor Center, open daily from 9 a.m. to 5 p.m., lies 2 miles west of the trail's western terminus.

TRAIL 1 ASHTON-TETONIA TRAIL

The Ashton-Tetonia Trail is part of the Greater Yellowstone Trail, which is spearheaded by Wyoming Pathways. The developing 180-mile trail system will connect Jackson Hole, Wyoming, with West Yellowstone, Montana, via rail-trails traversing the Idaho cities of Victor, Driggs, Tetonia, Ashton, and Island Park.

CONTACT: rtc.li/id-ashton-tetonia-trail or idahofriends.org/ashton-tetonia-trail.html

PARKING

Parking areas are listed from south to north. *Indicates that at least one accessible parking space is available.*

TETONIA: Egbert Ave., 0.3 mile west of N. 3000 W. (43.8109, -111.1652); gravel lot.

FELT: McReynolds Ave., 0.3 mile east of ID 32 (43.8685, -111.1756).

JUDKINS: Idaho State Park Trailhead, Wells Ave., 0.1 mile east of Reece Road (43.9292, -111.1485).

LAMONT: ID 32 and N. 4700 E. (43.9696, -111.2189).

FRANCE: Old grain elevator at ID 32, 0.3 mile east of N. 4400 E. (43.9725, -111.2750).

GRAINVILLE: Grainville Road and Squirrel Road/E. 1000 N. (44.0280, -111.3684).

MARYSVILLE: ID 47/E. 1300 Road N., 300 feet west of 3675 E. (44.0716, -111.4221).

Boise River Greenbelt

2

The Boise River Greenbelt follows its namesake river among towering trees, connecting downtown Boise with suburban neighborhoods, the business district, and a popular series of riverside parks known as the Ribbon of Jewels. This cherished, award-winning community trail extends out of the city southeast to Lucky Peak State Park and northwest through Garden City and Eagle.

The trail (stretching roughly 25 miles on either side of the river) is one of the area's most popular for its scenic views, wildlife, and access to popular parks and recreation sites. There are many entry points along the trail, including spurs from various neighborhoods.

From the northwesternmost endpoint in Eagle at West State Street, head 1.6 miles east along ID 44 to the first trailhead. Dip south to hug the northern shore of the river, and continue another 0.9 mile east to a new bike-pedestrian bridge. (Alternatively, continue on the northeastern side for another 2.6 miles to the West Greenbelt Bridge.)

Cross the river at the bridge to access River Pointe Park in 1.5 miles on the river's southern side. (While you could continue on the eastern side to Riverside Park, there is a gap in the trail on the northern side that begins soon after the park.) From River Pointe Park, head 0.9 mile east to a fork in the river, which allows you to pick up the trail (left at the

County
Ada

Endpoints
W. State St./
S. Urban Gate Ave.
and W. State St./
ID 44 (Eagle);
Lucky Peak State
Park, E. Sandy
Point Road,
0.9 mile northeast
of ID 21 (Boise)

Mileage
46.1

Type
Greenway/
Rail-Trail

Roughness Rating
1

Surface
Asphalt, Concrete,
Crushed Stone

The trail connects a series of riverside parks known as Boise's Ribbon of Jewels.

fork) back on the northern side, as there is a small gap on the southern side. From the fork, head 0.4 mile east to enter Boise proper. Once in the city, there are many opportunities to cross the river.

You will pass an athletic complex shortly before a bridge at Veterans Memorial Parkway/North Curtis Road. Remain on the eastern side for a loop around Boise Cascade Lake, followed by Bernardine Quinn Riverside Park. The trail then heads safely under multiple roads and highways, including POW-MIA Memorial Highway/Boise Connector/US 26/US 20. Directly after the highway, a steel-truss bike-pedestrian bridge crosses the river. On the western side of the bridge, the trail passes Kathryn Albertson Park and Ann Morrison Park in quick succession.

The river cuts through downtown Boise, with a zoo and Julia Davis Park to the north and Boise State University to the south. The trail passes more parks, the Red Bridge, and a golf course before traveling through the Vernon neighborhood. *Note:* For a 3.5-mile stretch from Warm Springs Park to South Eckert Road, there are no safe bridge crossings.

At South Eckert Road, the trail merges into one until its terminus in Lucky Peak State Park, 4.6 miles later. The park offers swimming, picnicking, fishing, boating, biking, and more. Visit **parksandrecreation.idaho.gov/parks/lucky-peak** for more information.

Throughout Boise, the paved path is ADA accessible, except for a 1.5-mile section from Barber Park downstream. Due to the trail's proximity to the river, high river flows sometimes lead to closed trail sections in the spring. Anglers may access the Boise River at any point. Ample restrooms, water fountains, and bike air and repair stations are located throughout.

CONTACT: rtc.li/boise-greenbelt and totallyboise.com/boise-river-greenbelt

TRAIL 2 BOISE RIVER GREENBELT **17**

PARKING

Select parking areas are listed below, from northwest to southeast. For a detailed list of parking areas and other waypoints, as well as an interactive map showing all the neighborhood access points, go to **TrailLink™**. *Indicates that at least one accessible parking space is available.*

North/East of the river:

GARDEN CITY*: Riverside Park, 7559 W. Riverside Dr. (43.6632, -116.2821).

BOISE*: Willow Lane Athletic Complex, 4623 Willow Lane (43.6431, -116.2461).

BOISE*: Veterans Memorial Park, 930 Veterans Memorial Pkwy./ N. Curtis Road (43.6375, -116.2389).

BOISE*: Idaho Fallen Firefighters Memorial Park, 1791 Shoreline Dr. (43.6181, -116.2239).

BOISE*: Kristin Armstrong Municipal Park, 500 S. Walnut St. (43.6022, -116.1838).

South/West of the river:

GARDEN CITY*: River Pointe Park, 6015 N. Glenwood St. (43.6607, -116.2818); accessible parking is available at the library.

BOISE*: Ann Morrison Park, 1000 S. Americana Blvd. (43.6132, -116.2203).

BOISE*: Baggley Park, 1411 E. Parkcenter Blvd. (43.5830, -116.1654).

BOISE*: Barber Park, 4049 S. Eckert Road (43.5679, -116.1367).

ADA COUNTY*: Lucky Peak State Park, E. Sandy Point Road, 0.9 mile northeast of ID 21 (43.5299, -116.0586); entry fee required.

Canyon Rim Trail

3

The Canyon Rim Trail offers jaw-dropping views along the southern rim of the Snake River Canyon in the south-central Idaho community of Twin Falls. You don't need to bring your BASE jumping gear to enjoy the trail, but be prepared for some inclines where the trail travels in and out of the canyon. Pack plenty of water and sunscreen and consider starting out early, as there is no shade on the trail.

From the western terminus in Twin Falls, head 1.4 miles east to the Perrine Coulee—a tributary of the Snake River providing the first waterfall along the trail. The trail heads south, hugging the Perrine Coulee's western edge, before crossing it and heading north along the tributary's eastern edge.

Head 0.7 mile east on the trail as it parallels Canyon Springs Road. When the road curves south, you'll cross the street to pick up the trail, which heads north, on the other side. In another 0.4 mile, you'll reach the Twin Falls Visitor Center, followed by views of the Perrine Bridge. Towering a whopping 500 feet above the Snake River, the bridge is the only spot in the country that's open to year-round BASE

Shoshone Falls, nicknamed the Niagara of the West, is a popular attraction along the trail.

County
Twin Falls

Endpoints
E. 4200 Road N., 350 feet east of Parkview Dr. (Twin Falls); Quail Ridge Dr. and N. 3400 E. (Kimberly)

Mileage
8.2

Type
Greenway/
Non-Rail-Trail

Roughness Rating
1–2

Surface
Asphalt, Concrete

jumping. The trail heads under this iconic structure, continuing another mile to Pole Line Road East/East 4100 North. Continue 1.3 miles to the Evel Knievel Jumpsite, the spot of the world-famous daredevil's 1974 attempt to fly his "sky cycle" across the Snake River Canyon. The trail's next section, through Shoshone Falls Park, includes elevation changes, challenging hills, and hairpin turns.

Once at the park, you'll be rewarded with one of the country's largest natural waterfalls. Its flow varies seasonally and is usually best viewed during the spring when the snowpack begins to melt. At 212 feet tall and 900 feet wide, Shoshone Falls is commonly referred to as the Niagara of the West (it is actually the taller of the two). The park offers a parking area, restrooms, a drinking fountain, a picnic area, concessions, scenic overlooks, and a boat ramp/river access.

Next up is Dierkes Lake Park, but there's a 0.7-mile gap in the trail between the falls and the lake. Navigate this gap by taking Shoshone Falls Grade Road/Champlin Road from the Shoshone Falls parking lot for 0.4 mile until the road intersects East 3400 North, then turn left, following the signs to Dierkes Lake Park, which you'll reach in another 0.3 mile. Although these are low-speed roads, use caution as there is no bike lane or shoulder. Plan to spend some time at the park—a former apple orchard turned swimming hole. It offers fishing, volleyball, a playground, nonmotorized boating, a nature trail, hidden lakes, and rock climbing. The trail loops around the lake before heading roughly 0.4 mile south to the trail's easternmost endpoint in the city of Kimberly.

Though the trail is asphalt with partial railings, there are wide, deep cracks across the width of the trail, especially on the western end. Shoshone Falls itself is ADA accessible, with multiple places to view the falls without having to navigate any stairs.

CONTACT: tfid.org/486/parks-and-recreation

PARKING

Parking areas are listed from west to east. *Indicates that at least one accessible parking space is available.*

TWIN FALLS: Washington St. N. and Federation Road/E. 4150 Road N. (42.5991, -114.4793).

TWIN FALLS*: Twin Falls Visitor Center, 2015 Nielsen Point Pl. (42.5982, -114.4552).

TWIN FALLS: E. 4100 N. and Pole Lane Road E. (42.5917, -114.4402).

TWIN FALLS*: Shoshone Falls Park, dead end of Shoshone Falls Grade Road (42.5935, -114.4015); vehicle access fee required March–September.

KIMBERLY: Dierkes Lake Park at Dierkes Road (42.5940, -114.3917); vehicle access fee required March–September.

Idaho Falls Greenbelt

The Idaho Falls Greenbelt is a north–south connector through the city along both sides of the Snake River. The experience at the trail's northern end is more serene as the trail winds through patches of trees and open areas. Going south, the trail borders residential neighborhoods and then commercial areas beginning midtrail. There is some light industrial activity along the last leg.

The trail is organized into a series of loops. On its northern end, the 1-mile **Freeman Loop** circles Freeman Park, which features the Idaho State Vietnam Veterans Memorial, a playground, an osprey nest platform, disc golf, picnic shelters, restrooms, and water fountains. From there, the paved pathway heads south, safely whisking travelers beneath Rigby Freeway/Medal of Honor Highway/US 20. A path along the highway presents trail users with their first opportunity to cross from the east to the west side of the trail. A floating walkway connects Freeman Park to US 20 from June to October (for walkway status, call 208-612-8479).

South of US 20, you'll begin the 2.3-mile **Temple Loop,** the most heavily used trail section. Crossing the river to

County
Bonneville

Endpoints
Northwest corner of Idaho State University campus (Idaho Falls); Snake River Landing, 260 feet southeast of Snake River Pkwy. and Event Center Dr. (Idaho Falls); Ryder Park at W. Sunnyside Road/POW-MIA Memorial Hwy./US 26/I-15BL and Ryder Park Road (Idaho Falls)

Mileage
11.4

Type
Greenway/Non-Rail-Trail

Roughness Rating
1

Surface
Asphalt

Midtrail, a bridge over the Snake River provides access to the Japanese Friendship Garden.

TRAIL 4 IDAHO FALLS GREENBELT **23**

head counterclockwise on this loop, you'll soon approach Johns Hole Boat Ramp. Farther down is a diversion dam overlook, complete with a constructed 20-foot waterfall and wheelchair-accessible walkway. Following the dam overlook are a flower garden, a veterans memorial, and other historical markers. To complete the counterclockwise loop, take the pedestrian bridge at West Broadway Street/Business US 20/I-15BL. Back on the east side, heading north, you'll pass several memorials, monuments, kiosks, and other historical markers before arriving at Civitan Park, which offers a picnic shelter, playground, water fountain, and ball field.

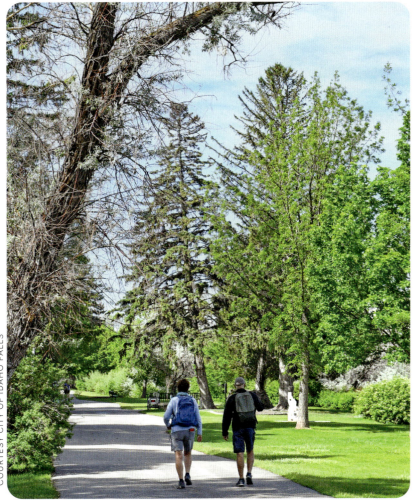
The greenway serves as a pleasant north–south connector through Idaho Falls.

South of the Temple Loop is the 1.4-mile **Memorial Loop,** from south of the West Broadway Street Bridge to Pancheri Drive. On the west side of the river are an overlook, a monument, and a bridge replica. On the east side is Sportsman Park, containing a gazebo, picnic tables, and a Japanese friendship garden. Following the park are the Art Museum of Eastern Idaho and South Capital Park. The next crossing comes at a bridge over Pancheri Drive. Cross here to reach Snake River Landing, a mixed-use development combining trails, parks, and a commercial area. Alternatively, head a mile east on Pancheri Drive/17th Street to intersect the 2.4-mile Idaho Falls Canal Trail.

Continuing southwest on the east side of the river is the 1.4-mile **Sunnyside Extension.** It includes South Tourist Park, where camping and a boat launch are available. South of the park, the trail crosses the river on West Sunnyside Road/POW-MIA Memorial Highway/US 26/I-15BL, ending on the west side at Ryder Park, a 1-acre fishing and wildlife area. The trail provides plenty of restrooms and drinking fountains and is easily accessed from the city's adjacent roads, though users have noted trail signage is somewhat limited.

CONTACT: rtc.li/idaho-falls

PARKING

Parking areas are located within Idaho Falls and are listed from north to south. Select parking areas for the trail are listed below; for a detailed list of parking areas and other waypoints, consult **TrailLink™**. *Indicates that at least one accessible parking space is available.*

FREEMAN PARK: Presto St. and Cultural Cir. (43.5155, -112.0541). There are several parking lots throughout the park; this one is the closest to the trail's northern endpoint.

JOHNS HOLE BOAT RAMP*: 1417 River Pkwy. (43.5050, -112.0502).

DIVERSION DAM OVERLOOK*: 547 River Pkwy. (43.4974, -112.0439).

VETERANS WAR MEMORIAL*: Memorial Dr. and D St. (43.4964, -112.0413); 2-hour parking limit.

SOUTH CAPITAL PARK*: 270 S. Capital Ave. (43.4892, -112.0458).

RYDER PARK: 2001 W. Sunnyside Road (43.4671, -112.0718).

Latah Trail

The Latah Trail connects Moscow, home of the University of Idaho, and Troy in the scenic Palouse region of northern Idaho. Developed by the Latah Trail Foundation, it was built on the former Moscow-Arrow rail line that carried both passengers and freight. Although the rail-trail parallels ID 8 between the two cities, you'll have picturesque views of the surrounding prairie and farmland as well as forested areas. While on the trail, it's common to see a variety of birds, rabbits, and other wildlife.

Although drinking water is limited along the trail, you'll find trailside restrooms, benches, and picnic tables, as well as interpretive panels on the area's history and flora and fauna. In the winter, the trail is also used for cross-country skiing and snowshoeing.

Begin on the eastern edge of Moscow, at Carmichael Road and ID 8, where you'll find a parking lot and nearby picnic shelter and restrooms. Head east from here to experience the Latah Trail, a paved and largely flat pathway.

Heading west from Carmichael Road would take you on the connecting Paradise Path, which traverses Moscow and nearly reaches the Idaho border. On its western end,

Approaching Troy on the west end of the trail, you'll travel through a forested area.

County
Latah

Endpoints
Paradise Path at Carmichael Road and ID 8 (Moscow); Bear Creek Canyon (southeast of Troy)

Mileage
16.4

Type
Rail-Trail

Roughness Rating
1

Surface
Asphalt

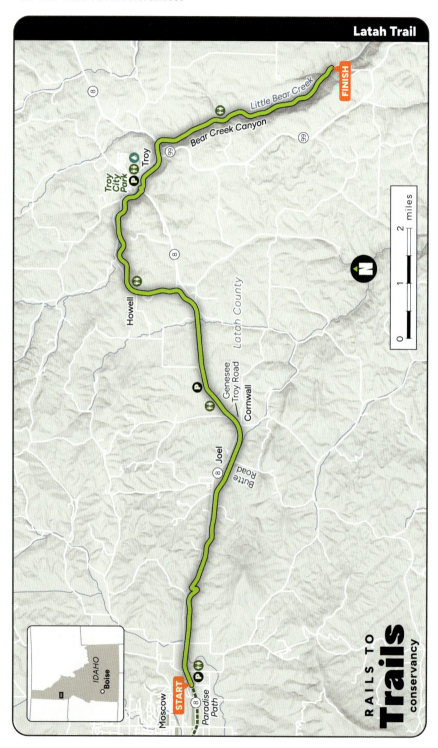

the Paradise Path connects with the Bill Chipman Palouse Trail (see page 121), which continues into Washington. Together, the three trails form a seamless route of more than 25 miles across two states.

Continuing on the Latah Trail, in 4.4 miles, you'll cross Butte Road—where tall silos abut the trail—and enter the unincorporated community of Joel. You'll pass the neighboring community of Cornwall 0.6 mile after that. Exiting Cornwall, you'll cross Genesee Troy Road and then reach restrooms in another 0.5 mile, followed by a tunnel under ID 8.

After the tunnel, the trail soon turns northward, and you'll reach more restrooms in 2.6 miles. From here, you'll travel through a densely forested area until you reach Troy and Troy City Park in 1.9 miles. The park offers play structures, athletic facilities, picnic tables, restrooms, and parking.

From the park, you'll head southeast through the city, crossing ID 99 in 0.7 mile. The adventurous (and prepared) can continue their journey on the rugged and more remote 4-mile section through Bear Creek Canyon, which winds along the forested creek and crosses the waterway a handful of times. Note that there's a steep descent into the canyon, which you will need to climb on the way back as there is no parking at trail's end. There is no drinking water along this stretch, so be sure to bring your own. Please respect private property and stay on the trail.

CONTACT: latahtrail.org and latahcountyid.gov/parks_rec

PARKING

Parking areas are listed from west to east. *Indicates that at least one accessible parking space is available.*

MOSCOW: Carmichael Road and ID 8 (46.7205, -116.9641).

TROY: ID 8, 0.8 mile northeast of Genesee Troy Road/Larson Road (46.7184, -116.8493).

TROY: City Park on ID 8, 450 feet west of Big Meadow Road (46.7367, -116.7756).

28 Rail-Trails: **Pacific Northwest**

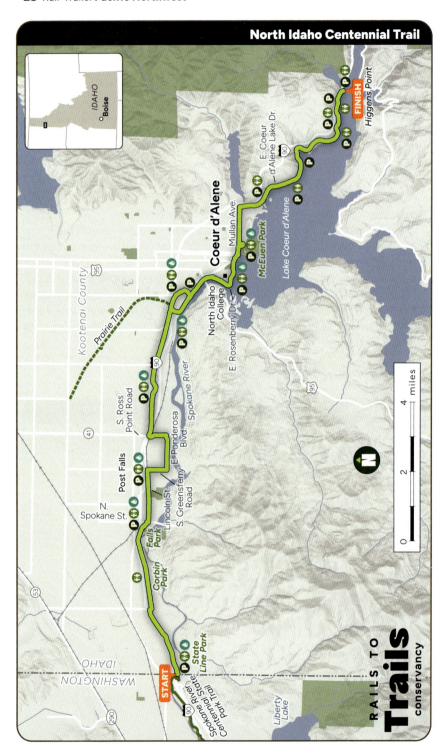

North Idaho Centennial Trail

Visitors to the North Idaho Centennial Trail are treated to breathtaking waterfront vistas of the Spokane River and Lake Coeur d'Alene. The trail extends east from the Idaho–Washington state line to Higgens Point in Coeur d'Alene Lake Parkway State Park, 6 miles past the city of Coeur d'Alene. There are ample opportunities for swimming, kayaking, and fishing along the way.

Development of the 23-mile paved trail started in the 1990s at about the same time as an adjoining trail in Washington state, commemorating 100 years of statehood in both states. Officially completed in 1995, the North Idaho Centennial Trail joins the Spokane River Centennial State Park Trail (see page 239) at the state line, adding another 40 miles to explore in Spokane and beyond.

The ADA-accessible route begins near the intersection of East Appleway Avenue and Spokane Bridge Road at a trailhead for the Liberty Lake Stateline Trail. Heading east for less than half a mile, you will cross a large pedestrian bridge over the Spokane River that boasts the North Idaho Centennial Trail name. The bridge is lit at night for safety. Within the first mile you'll experience more views of the river from State Line Park.

County
Kootenai

Endpoints
Washington–Idaho state line at the Spokane River Centennial State Park Trail, 0.3 mile east of Spokane Bridge Road and E. Appleway Ave. (Post Falls); Higgens Point on E. Coeur d'Alene Lake Dr. (Coeur d'Alene)

Mileage
23

Type
Rail-Trail/Rail-with-Trail

Roughness Rating
1

Surface
Asphalt

Near the Washington–Idaho state line, a pedestrian bridge over the Spokane River features the trail's name.

The first 2 miles of trail run parallel to I-90 through retail and business centers of Post Falls. After crossing Pleasant View Road, the trail veers away from the interstate and enters a residential area. It continues another 2 miles past Corbin Park and Falls Park along the Spokane River before crossing North Spokane Street at Mile 4.75. In a half mile, the trail crosses Lincoln Street and in another mile begins a 2.1-mile on-road route. Follow the bike lanes right onto South Greensferry Road, left onto East Ponderosa Boulevard, and left onto South Ross Point Road.

Turn right onto the trail again just before I-90, which the trail follows for 4.5 miles; be prepared for a steep climb in this section. At 3.9 miles, you'll cross Prairie Trail, which heads north-northwest about 4 miles. After the junction, the North Idaho Centennial Trail leaves I-90 and heads south, skirting the Spokane River for a couple of miles. At the North Idaho College campus, it runs along the shoulder of East Rosenberry Drive.

This section reveals your first views of Lake Coeur d'Alene, a popular summer vacation spot. The trail leaves East Rosenberry Drive and enters the city of Coeur d'Alene's lakeside McEuen Park. Here you'll find the Centennial Trail Monument, a Veterans Memorial, a waterfront concession stand, and a large playground and splash pad.

Leaving the park, the trail follows another on-road segment on the shoulder of Mullan Avenue for a mile to East Coeur d'Alene Lake Drive. Here it begins a nearly 6-mile stretch nestled between the lakeshore and the road, with many locations to enjoy the lake. There is a short, steep climb 3.3 miles into this segment before you arrive at the trail's end at Higgens Point in Coeur d'Alene Lake Parkway State Park.

CONTACT: nictf.org

TRAIL 6 NORTH IDAHO CENTENNIAL TRAIL **31**

PARKING

Parking areas are listed from west to east. For a detailed list of parking areas and other waypoints, consult **TrailLink™**. *Indicates that at least one accessible parking space is available.*

LIBERTY LAKE (WA): Liberty Lake Trailhead, E. Appleway Ave. and Spokane Bridge Road (47.6939, -117.0484).

POST FALLS: Millennium Skate Park, 300 N. Greensferry Road (47.7081, -116.9153).

POST FALLS*: Huetter Rest Area and Welcome Center, 6132 I-90 (47.7075, -116.8649).

COEUR D'ALENE*: 2250 W. Seltice Way (47.6982, -116.8075).

COEUR D'ALENE*: W. Fort Grounds Dr. and Northwest Blvd. (47.6747, -116.7872).

COEUR D'ALENE*: McEuen Park, 420 E. Front Ave. (47.6724, -116.7821).

COEUR D'ALENE*: E. Coeur d'Alene Lake Dr. and E. Potlatch Hill Road (47.6614, -116.7482).

COEUR D'ALENE*: 6400-6670 E. Coeur d'Alene Lake Dr., 0.1 mile south of S. Silver Beach Road (47.6479, -116.7355).

COEUR D'ALENE: Beacon Point Lake Access, E. Coeur d'Alene Lake Dr., 0.5 mile south of E. Wilma Road (47.6295, -116.7070).

COEUR D'ALENE: Coeur d'Alene Parkway State Park, E. Coeur d'Alene Lake Dr. (47.6297, -116.6885).

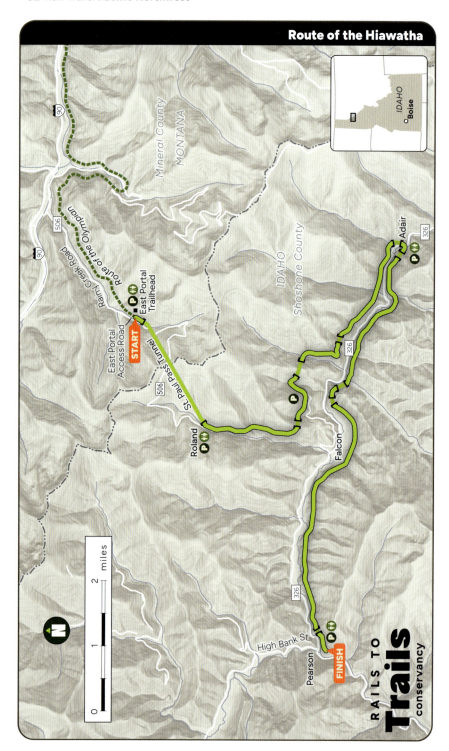

Route of the Hiawatha

7

Hall of Fame

Inducted into Rails to Trails Conservancy's Hall of Fame in 2010, along with the nearby Trail of the Coeur d'Alenes (see page 37), the exhilarating Route of the Hiawatha passes through nine tunnels and across seven lofty trestles over the course of 15 miles, from the trailhead at East Portal in Montana to Pearson in Idaho.

Lookout Pass Ski Area operates the trail, which is open seasonally from late May through mid-September. Note that trail users must obtain and display trail passes; find information about these (as well as details about shuttles and bike rentals) at **ridethehiawatha.com**.

As you glide through the forested trail, you'll have views of distant trestles, deep canyons with trout-filled creeks, cliffs, and wildlife. The 47 interpretive signs along the way provide historical, geographic, and environmental information. Whether starting from the East Portal or West Portal, your grade never exceeds a gentle 2% on a wide dirt-and-gravel railbed.

The groundwork for what is now the Route of the Hiawatha began at the turn of the 20th century by breaking

Counties
Mineral (MT); Shoshone (ID)

Endpoints
East Portal Trailhead at dead end of East Portal Access Road (East Portal, MT); Pearson Trailhead, 700 feet north of St. Joe River Road (Avery, ID)

Mileage
15

Type
Rail-Trail

Roughness Rating
2

Surface
Dirt and Gravel

You'll cross seven historical wooden trestles along the route.

through the Bitterroot Mountains, creating what was known as the most ruggedly beautiful stretch of railroad in the continental United States. Named for the Mohawk chief immortalized in the Henry Wadsworth Longfellow poem "The Song of Hiawatha," the highly stylized and futuristic passenger train fleet of the Chicago, Milwaukee, St. Paul, and Pacific Railroad (aka the Milwaukee Road) adopted the *Hiawatha* moniker during the 1930s. Beginning in 1947, the *Olympian Hiawatha* raced across the Midwest at speeds exceeding 100 mph before climbing the rugged Bitterroot Range en route to Tacoma, Washington. Despite being the coolest train in service, the *Olympian Hiawatha* was never financially successful and underwent several transformations until the Milwaukee Road mainline went bankrupt and became defunct in 1980. The Route of the Hiawatha first opened as a 13-mile rail-trail in 1998, expanding to include the iconic St. Paul Pass Tunnel in 2001.

The 15-mile rail-trail travels through nine tunnels.

TRAIL 7 ROUTE OF THE HIAWATHA

Begin at the East Portal Trailhead, where there is also a connection to the 31-mile Route of the Olympian rail-trail for more exploring. A highlight of the Route of the Hiawatha will appear in 0.3 mile: a journey through the longest of the trail's tunnels, the St. Paul Pass Tunnel (also called the Taft Tunnel), a 1.66-mile-long passageway that takes you from Montana into Idaho. Because the Route of the Hiawatha is open only during the warmer months, this section will feel shockingly cool on most days, as the tunnel temperature averages 47°F. Be prepared with a coat for what can be a cool, wet, and dark experience, as well as high-lumen lights to penetrate the darkness, see the trail, and be visible to others.

Most people will complete the full length of the trail and then wait at the bottom in Pearson to catch one of the shuttles going back to the top on the West Portal side of the St. Paul Pass Tunnel. Note that there is a fee for this service. Trail users should also note that the second trail tunnel shares the road with these shuttle buses; it's just over 3 miles into the route when coming from the East Portal. Incoming shuttle buses will honk before they enter the tunnel.

Note: Lookout Pass Ski Area, which manages the trail, allows the use of adaptive devices or other manual or electric mobility aids. Bollards placed at various spots along the trail to block motor vehicle access can be removed (with advance notice) to allow for mobility devices more than 38 inches wide. Call 208-744-1234 or email info@skilookout.com.

CONTACT: ridethehiawatha.com

PARKING

Parking areas are listed from north to south. *Indicates that at least one accessible parking space is available.*

EAST PORTAL (MT): East Portal Trailhead at the dead end of East Portal Access Road (47.3969, -115.6348).

WEST PORTAL (ID): Roland Summit Trailhead on NF 506 (47.3773, -115.6683).

AVERY (ID): Moss Creek Trailhead on Cliff Creek Road/NF 506 (47.3615, -115.6536).

AVERY (ID): Turkey Creek Trestle on Loop Creek Road (47.3388, -115.6078); follow the trail 0.8 mile west of the parking area to reach the trestle.

AVERY (ID): Pearson Trailhead, 700 feet north of St. Joe River Road (47.3500, -115.7363).

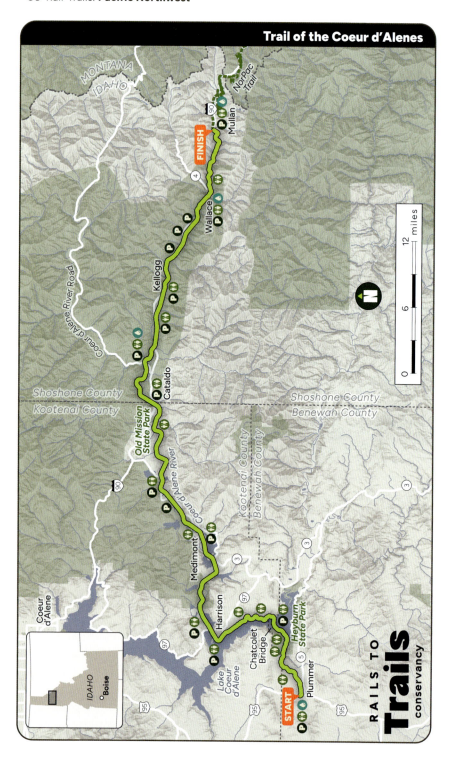

Trail of the Coeur d'Alenes

8

The **popular Trail of the Coeur d'Alenes** covers 73 paved miles through Idaho's Panhandle, boasting spectacular scenery; unique local attractions; and a rich and colorful mining, railroading, and Native American history. Immerse yourself in a diverse mix of Palouse Prairie habitats, from rolling foothills and valleys to mixed conifer forests, wetlands, farmland, small-town streetscapes, cottonwood groves, and deep water.

Between the cities of Plummer and Harrison, the trail covers just over 15 miles and skirts the shoreline of sparkling Lake Coeur d'Alene. (If going the opposite direction, note that there is an incline from Harrison to Plummer, including a 600-foot incline from Heyburn State Park to Plummer.) Stop for a refreshing swim at Heyburn State Park (for parking fees and other information, visit **parksandrecreation.idaho.gov/parks/heyburn**).

One of the most popular trail sections is the ride from the 3,100-foot Chatcolet Bridge (located in Heyburn State Park) to Harrison. Crossing the southern end of Lake Coeur d'Alene, the bridge has a stair-step ramp that eases the uphill climb and makes for an exhilarating, roller-coaster-like downhill ride. In the 10 miles between Harrison and

Between Plummer and Harrison, the trail skirts the shoreline of Lake Coeur d'Alene.

LISA JAMES

Counties
Benewah, Kootenai, Shoshone

Endpoints
Annie Antelope Road, 350 feet west of US 95 (Plummer); River St./I-90 and N. Second St. (Mullan)

Mileage
73.2

Type
Rail-Trail

Roughness Rating
1

Surface
Asphalt

Medimont, the trail passes through Idaho's chain-of-lakes region (15 small lakes and marshes linked by the Coeur d'Alene River). Watch for wildlife, including coyotes, foxes, otters, beavers, river otters, turtles, muskrat, white-tailed deer, elk, moose, and even black bears. Birders will also have opportunities to see great blue herons, western pelicans, eagles, osprey, and other birds of prey. Fishing is allowed anywhere on the trail that is not private property.

Heading east from the chain-of-lakes, it's a 16-mile trip from Medimont to Cataldo. The trail follows the Coeur d'Alene River through the Silver Valley, once one of the country's most productive silver mining areas. Approaching Cataldo, it's a worthwhile side trip to nearby Old Mission State Park, which involves a few miles of on-road riding; in return, cyclists are admitted for free. From Cataldo, the trail follows the main Coeur d'Alene River, then along its south fork, where the mountains become more forested. In another 12 miles, you'll reach Kellogg, the largest city along the trail, which offers plenty of places to eat. Next up, in 11 miles, is Historic Wallace, the Silver Capital of World, a mining town jam-packed with cafés, restaurants, and historical attractions.

From Wallace, the trail climbs 600 feet over 6 miles past historical mine sites to Mullan, where this trail ends and the NorPac Trail begins. Both trails are part of the Great American Rail-Trail® (**greatamericanrailtrail.org**), which spans the United States between Washington, D.C., and Washington state. The

A popular feature on the trail is the 3,100-foot Chatcolet Bridge, built in 1921 across the southern reaches of Lake Coeur d'Alene.

NorPac Trail runs to Taft, Montana, only 2.5 miles from the scenic Route of the Hiawatha (see page 33) and St. Paul Pass (also known as the Taft Tunnel), burrowing more than 8,700 feet under the Bitterroot Mountains. Both the 15-mile Route of the Hiawatha and the Trail of the Coeur d'Alenes were inducted into Rails to Trails Conservancy's Hall of Fame in 2010.

The Trail of the Coeur d'Alenes was created through a partnership among the Coeur d'Alene Tribe, Union Pacific Railroad, the U.S. government, and the state of Idaho. As the project is part of an environmental cleanup effort due to heavy metal contamination from the area's early mining activities, users are advised to remain on the trail, wash their hands and faces before eating, eat at designated picnic areas, and carry their own water for drinking and washing. Bike-friendly businesses along the way will happily refill water bottles.

Ample signage and 20 trailheads are provided throughout the trail, which is groomed in the winter for Nordic skiers and snowshoers. Snowmobiles are allowed from Wallace to Mullan in the winter.

CONTACT: rtc.li/coeur-d-alenes and friendsofcdatrails.org

PARKING

Parking areas are listed from west to east. Select parking areas for the trail are listed below. For a detailed list of parking areas and other waypoints, go to **TrailLink™**. *Indicates that at least one accessible parking space is available.*

PLUMMER*: Annie Antelope Road, 350 feet west of US 95 (47.3408, -116.8903).

PLUMMER: Chatcolet Bridge, Chatcolet Lower Road and Upper Chatcolet Road (47.3740, -116.7626).

MEDIMONT: Medimont Trailhead, S. Medimont Road and S. Ruddy Duck Road (47.4753, -116.6019).

CATALDO*: Bull Run Trailhead, Brewer Road/W. Bull Run Road and S. Bull Run Road (47.5343, -116.4754).

CATALDO*: Cataldo Trailhead, 40052 Riverview Road (47.5487, -116.3299).

KINGSTON: Enaville Trailhead, Coeur d'Alene River Road, 230 feet northeast of Pipe Line Road (47.5601, -116.2515).

PINEHURST*: Pinehurst Trailhead, E. Fork Pine Creek Road, 0.1 mile northeast of the Exit 45 ramp off I-90 (47.5492, -116.2240).

KELLOGG: W. Station Ave. and S. Division St. (47.5365, -116.1219).

WALLACE*: Historic Wallace Trailhead (under I-90), 300 feet north of Pine St. and Sixth St. (47.4740, -115.9236).

MULLAN*: Mullan Trailhead, 115 Second St. (47.4692, -115.8002).

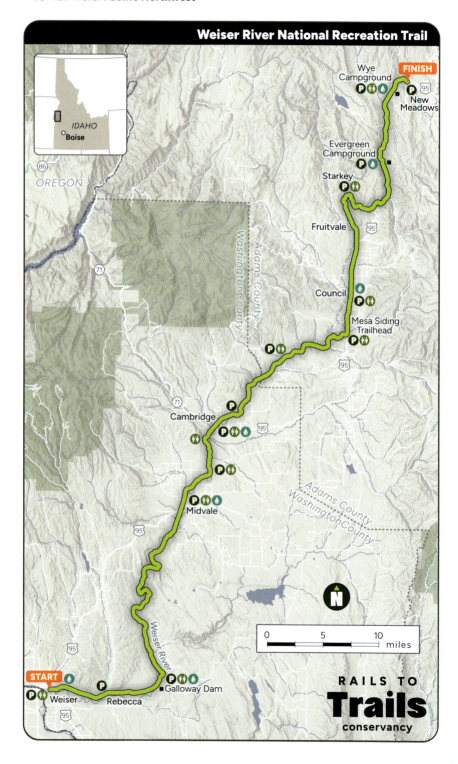

Weiser River National Recreation Trail

9

The Weiser River National Recreation Trail, the longest rail-trail in Idaho, is a feast of desert canyons, evergreen forests, and alpine meadows following the former right-of-way of a Union Pacific Railroad line from Weiser to north of the Tamarack lumber mill. The southern end consists mainly of rolling hills and open canyons, while the northern end is more densely forested.

Highlights of the trail include 62 historical rail trestles and wildlife such as deer, waterfowl, quail, turkeys, herons, eagles, coyotes, bears, and even mountain lions. If you like to fish, bring a pole and drop a line for rainbow trout in the Weiser River, which the trail follows for much of its route. Fishing is allowed wherever the trail is adjacent to the river, assuming no fences are present.

You can access the Weiser River Trail in dozens of places along its 85.5-mile route. Four communities along the trail provide services, including Weiser (the largest, with many restaurants, motels, and shops); Midvale; Cambridge; and Council. There is approximately 1 mile of asphalt through each town; between towns, the surface is an unpaved mix of ballast and gravel. Because there are large swaths of trail

Counties
Adams, Washington

Endpoints
Weiser Community Fishing Pond at E. Fourth St. and E. Washington St. (Weiser); Old Hwy. 95 and S. Pine Dr. (New Meadows)

Mileage
85.5

Type
Rail-Trail

Roughness Rating
1–3

Surface
Asphalt, Ballast, Gravel

A range of habitats—including riparian, desert, forest, and alpine meadow—can be enjoyed along the trail.

MIKE BEAVERS

between towns—and plenty of sections with no cell service—be sure to pack plenty of water and spare tubes.

Trail managers conduct winter grooming for cross-country, snowshoe, and dog-sledding users. In the spring and fall, the trail hosts annual bike rides, a 50K running event, and a four-day wagon train event from Weiser to Council. Horses and horse-drawn wagons are permitted on the full length of the trail, including the asphalt portions. While horse trailer parking is allowed at most of the parking lots, the biggest lots are at the Presley and Glendale Bridge Starkey Trailheads.

Beginning at the southern end of the old railroad corridor, the trail has its roots in the city of Weiser. Starting at the Weiser Community Fishing Pond, you'll head east about 11 miles, following the Weiser River to the Presley Trailhead, where you'll find parking (including horse trailer parking), restrooms, and river access. From there, the trail takes a more northerly route. Between Weiser and the small city of Midvale, you will have views of canyons lining the banks of the Weiser River. Galloway Dam is part of the lower canyon and is a popular fishing spot.

Horses, mules, and wagons are allowed on the entire trail.

Eight miles north of Midvale is the city of Cambridge. The city is one of the access points to the southern entrance of Hells Canyon; straddling the borders of northeastern Oregon and western Idaho, it's the deepest gorge in North America (note that the canyon is a 45-minute drive from here). The small community of Council is 60 miles north of Weiser. The surrounding valley is a beautiful open green space with wooded hills, farms, and ranches.

North of Council, you'll pass through several small communities. Directly adjacent to the trail, just off US 95, is Evergreen Campground. Run by the U.S. Forest Service, it includes an informational kiosk, signs, a small parking area (not suitable for horse trailers), and a short path connecting to the Weiser River Trail.

About 5 miles north of here is the Tamarack lumber mill, and just north of that is the Wye Campground, offering paid overnight camping. Slightly farther north is the trail's terminus on Old Highway 95, past Rubicon and about 5 miles northwest of New Meadows.

CONTACT: weiserrivertrail.org

PARKING

Parking areas are listed from south to north. Select parking areas for the trail are listed below. For a detailed list of parking areas and other waypoints, go to **TrailLink™**. *Indicates that at least one accessible parking space is available.*

WEISER: Weiser Community Fishing Pond, E. Fourth St. and E. Washington St. (44.2425, -116.9638); dirt pullout with limited parking spaces.

WEISER*: Weiser Trailhead, E. Main St., 400 feet east of E. Commercial St. (44.2457, -116.9446).

REBECCA: Unity Lane, 0.3 mile south of E. Park St./Weiser River Road (44.2406, -116.8571); small gravel lot.

PRESLEY: Presley Trailhead, E. Park St./Weiser River Road (44.2643, -116.7657); gravel lot.

MIDVALE: US 95/Railroad St. and Bridge St. (44.4706, -116.7355).

CAMBRIDGE*: Washington County Fairgrounds, US 95/E. Central Blvd. and N. Railroad St. (44.5717, -116.6745).

COUNCIL: Mesa Siding Trailhead, US 95/Little Weiser Road, 0.7 mile south of Cottonwood Road (44.6812, -116.4487).

COUNCIL: N. Railroad St./Hornet Creek Road, 250 feet east of Brady St. (44.7307, -116.4420).

STARKEY: Glendale Bridge Starkey Trailhead on Fruitvale Glendale Road (44.8456, -116.4436).

TAMARACK: Wye Campground, 3604 ID 95 (44.9670, -116.3718). Paid overnight camping May–October, including four horse corrals with adjacent water; for more information, visit **weiserrivertrail.org/wye-campground**.

44 Rail-Trails: **Pacific Northwest**

Wood River Trail

Known to locals simply as "the bike path," the Wood River Trail (WRT) was conceptualized by a group of visionary residents and realized by Blaine County Recreation District (BCRD). The WRT follows the northern periphery of what was once a railroad grade owned by Union Pacific Railroad. Interpretive signs along the way connect trail users with the community's history—one encompassing gold and silver mining, sheep ranching, and "ski-trains" that ferried passengers to a winter sports resort featuring the world's first chairlift.

With a central spine spanning more than 20 miles and a loop with additional spurs at its northern end, the trail now serves as an important connector for cities in the Wood River Valley, including Bellevue, Hailey, Ketchum, and Sun Valley. Many use the WRT as a form of active transportation, claiming it can be faster than driving between cities in the valley. Visitors can find lodging, restaurants, and other services readily available along the trail, which is often praised for the quality of its paving and general maintenance.

The paved, nonmotorized, multiuse pathway offers spectacular recreational opportunities year-round amid the equally spectacular scenery of central Idaho, nestled among

County
Blaine

Endpoints
Gannett Road, 440 feet southeast of ID 75/ S. Main St. (Bellevue); Trail Creek Road/Sun Valley Road/County Road 408, 0.3 mile north of Trail Creek Cabin Road (Sun Valley); W. Sage Road and ID 75 (north of Ketchum); Warm Springs Road/CR 227 and Gates Road (Ketchum)

Mileage
36.1

Type
Rail-Trail

Roughness Rating
1

Surface
Asphalt

Nestled in the Rocky Mountains of central Idaho, the trail offers spectacular scenery and year-round recreation.

DEV KHALSA/COURTESY BLAINE COUNTY RECREATION DISTRICT

the Rocky Mountains. In summer, walking, jogging, biking, and in-line skating are popular trail activities. In winter, the trail is groomed for Nordic skiing and snowshoeing. While horseback riding is permitted on the entire trail, none of the parking areas have designated horse trailer parking.

There are many access points to the trail. One recommended out-and-back route starts at the southernmost endpoint at Bellevue. Following a slight, gradual incline north, trail users can tour Sun Valley before heading back on a slightly easier return trip.

Head north 4.7 miles from Bellevue to a trailhead in Hailey at the Hailey Native Plant Arboretum. From here, head 6.3 miles to the Gimlet Pegram Truss Railroad Bridge, which takes you across the Big Wood River. Head another 4.1 miles to cross the river again on the Big Wood River Bridge.

A truss bridge over the Big Wood River south of Ketchum

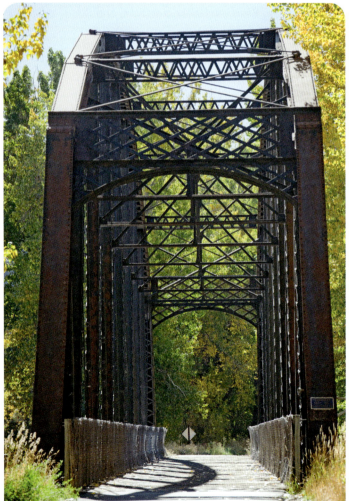

Head a half mile north to River Lane/Elkhorn Road and ID 75, at which point a 9.2-mile loop begins. Following the loop counterclockwise, head east onto the Sun Valley Trail (counted in the mileage of the WRT), which parallels River Lane/Elkhorn Road to Dollar Road/Saddle Road. The loop passes a golf club, Elkhorn Village, and a day lodge; crosses over Trail Creek to Sun Valley Lodge; and heads back over ID 75 and south to the loop's starting point.

Three spurs branch off this loop, leading to the WRT's three northern endpoints. The easternmost spur follows Trail Creek Road/Sun Valley Road/CR 408 to Boundary Campground at the northern tip of Sun Valley. The middle spur heads north along ID 75 to West Sage Road. The westernmost spur parallels Warm Springs Road/CR 227 to Warm Springs Lodge.

Pocket parks and tunnels dot the trail, but there is little shade (though the trail cools off a bit by the river) and few water fountains along the way, so pack accordingly. Free maps and trail guides—including ones showing public river access and BCRD-maintained fishing access—are available at trailheads, chambers of commerce, BCRD's offices in Hailey, and local sports stores.

CONTACT: rtc.li/wood-river

PARKING

Parking areas are listed from south to north. Select parking areas for the trail are listed below; for a detailed list of parking areas and other waypoints, go to **TrailLink.com™**. *Indicates that at least one accessible parking space is available.*

BELLEVUE: Gannett Road, 250 feet southeast of ID 75/S. Main St. (43.4557, -114.2560).

HAILEY*: Kiwanis Park, Laurelwood Dr. and Briarwood Dr. (43.5037, -114.2925).

HAILEY: Hailey Native Plant Arboretum, ID 75/S. Main St. and Fox Acres Road (43.5132, -114.3024).

HAILEY: Ohio Gulch Road and ID 75 (43.5813, -114.3379).

HAILEY: Ritzau Park at dead end of Audubon Pl., across from Gimlet Pegram Truss Railroad Bridge (43.5989, -114.3460).

HAILEY*: Broadway Run, 300 feet south of ID 75 (43.6462, -114.3490).

KETCHUM*: Serenade Lane, 95 feet west of ID 75/Main St. (43.6721, -114.3613).

KETCHUM*: Serenade Lane and Third Ave. N. (43.6708, -114.3660).

SUN VALLEY*: Hemingway Memorial at Trail Creek Road/Sun Valley Road/CR 408, 0.3 mile north of Golf Lane (43.7126, -114.3404).

KETCHUM: W. Sage Road and ID 75 (43.7178, -114.3781).

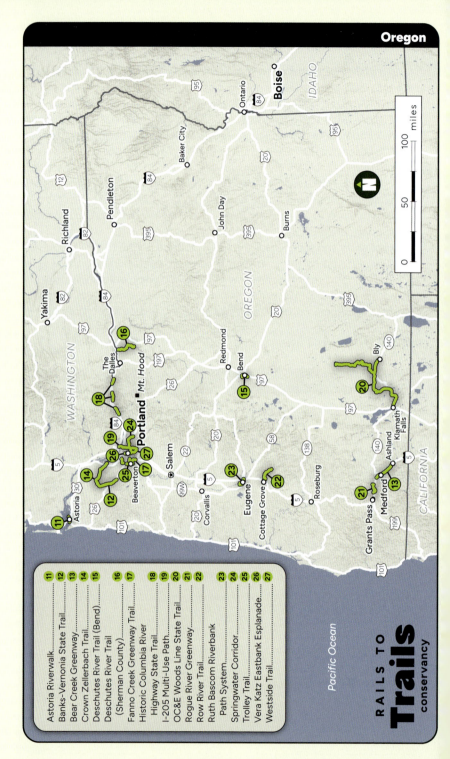

OREGON

In Cascade Locks, the Historic Columbia River Highway State Trail (*see Trail 18, page 77*) begins under the Bridge of the Gods.

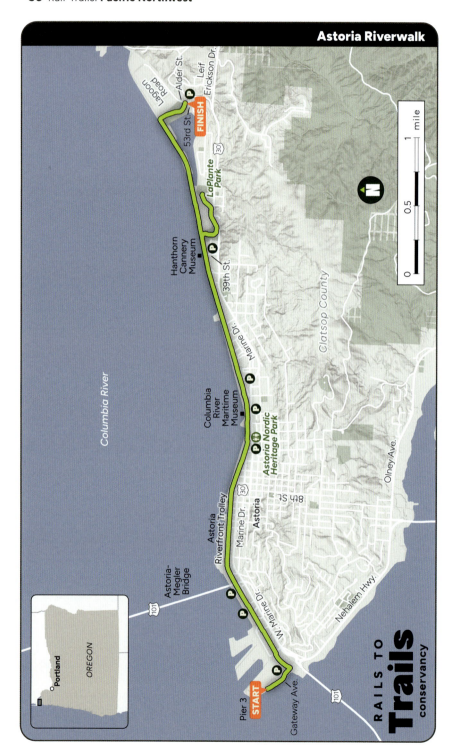

Astoria Riverwalk

11

Located near the mouth of the Columbia River as it empties into the Pacific Ocean, Astoria's working waterfront is a hub of activity. Boats that empty the day's catch dock next to the elegant cruise ships that take visitors down the historic Columbia River. Workers at the various seafood processing centers and canneries walk among the tourists, who are eager to explore the town where many of their favorite movies were filmed. In short, the Astoria Riverwalk is a perfect way to immerse yourself in the quintessential Pacific Northwest experience.

Heading east from the northwest point of Astoria at Pier 3, the trail largely follows the former Astoria & Columbia River Railroad. For almost the entire 6.4-mile journey, it parallels the tracks of the historic Astoria Riverfront Trolley, which operates from late March through the end of October. Pay special attention when the trolley is operating: The trail often shares the same bridge as the trolley, and you'll have multiple crossings on the trolley tracks, which can be slippery when wet. Trail users on wheels should cross the tracks at a 90-degree angle to prevent falls.

Enjoy views of the Columbia River as you follow the former Astoria & Columbia River Railroad route.

JOE LACROIX

County
Clatsop

Endpoints
Gateway Ave. and Pier 3 (Astoria); Alder St./Lagoon Road/53rd St., 0.2 mile northeast of Ash St. (Astoria)

Mileage
6.4

Type
Rail-Trail/Rail-with-Trail

Roughness Rating
1

Surface
Asphalt, Boardwalk

About 1 mile into the trip, the trail crosses under the Astoria-Megler Bridge, the longest continuous-truss bridge in North America. Travel another 2 miles to find two unique sites directly off the trail: Astoria Nordic Heritage Park educates visitors on the city's rich Nordic heritage, with cute yet funky trolls setting the mood. Two blocks away lies the Columbia River Maritime Museum, which delves into the fishing, shipping, and military history of the area.

A true gem along the trail lies another 1.3 miles east. Take a left on the wooden bridge on 39th Street to find a vibrant commercial area that includes the donation-only, self-guided Hanthorn Cannery Museum. Inside, visitors will find a fascinating variety of information on the history of the city's canning industry.

While there, look up at the hillside to the right. Movie fans of a certain age may recognize a white house with red trim. It's the iconic house that needed to be saved in the 1980s classic *The Goonies*. Astoria has embraced its film history, and signage along the Riverwalk highlights locations from other popular films, such as *Kindergarten Cop, Short Circuit,* and *Free Willy*.

From here to the end of the trail at Alder Street, if you stop to take in the sights along the Columbia River and adjacent wetlands, you will be rewarded with spottings of native wildlife, including seals, eagles, cormorants, and herons.

CONTACT: astoriaparks.com/riverwalk.aspx

PARKING

Parking areas are located within Astoria and are listed from west to east. Select parking areas for the trail are listed below; for a detailed list of parking areas and other waypoints, go to **TrailLink™**. *Indicates that at least one accessible parking space is available.*

PIER 3*: Western terminus of Gateway Ave. at Pier 3 (46.1846, -123.8628).

PORT OF ASTORIA LOT: Basin St. and W. Marine Dr. (46.1883, -123.8525); find parking information at **portofastoria.com/parking-information**.

MARITIME MEMORIAL: Bay St. and W. Marine Dr. (46.1898, -123.8494).

COLUMBIA RIVER MARITIME MUSEUM*: 1792 Marine Dr. (46.1895, -123.8235).

PORT OF ASTORIA LOT*: 36th St. and Leif Erikson Dr. (46.1938, -123.8039); find parking information at **portofastoria.com/parking-information**.

EASTERN TERMINUS: Alder St./Lagoon Road/53rd St., 0.2 mile northeast of Ash St. (46.1981, -123.7753).

Banks-Vernonia State Trail

12

The Banks-Vernonia State Trail is a scenic 21.2-mile paved trail that runs through lush Oregon forests and farmlands in Columbia and Washington Counties. It was the first rails-to-trails state park in the state and is recognized as a National Recreation Trail.

Although the entire trail is asphalt, many places where large tree roots have cracked the surface could present challenges for trail users with mobility concerns, as could several lips between boardwalk bridges and the trail, which are navigable but bumpy. Oregon State Parks is working on improving the trail surface. A paralleling gravel pathway is also available for equestrian use in many areas along the route.

The trail starts in the small town of Vernonia, located just an hour northwest of Portland. The first trailhead is at Vernonia Lake Park, which features an ice-cream shop next to the trailhead kiosk, restrooms, a water fountain, and fishing access. From the trailhead, you can head northwest and take a 1-mile loop around the lake or take the main route by heading southwest from the parking lot.

In 1.2 miles, you'll reach Anderson Park, where signage will point you to the nearby Crown Zellerbach Trail (see page 61)

Buxton Trestle, 3 miles south of the trail's midpoint

JOSHUA ZHU

Counties
Columbia, Washington

Endpoints
Vernonia Lake Park (Vernonia); Banks Trailhead at NW Sellers Road and NW Banks Road (Banks)

Mileage
21.2

Type
Rail-Trail

Roughness Rating
1–2

Surface
Asphalt, Boardwalk

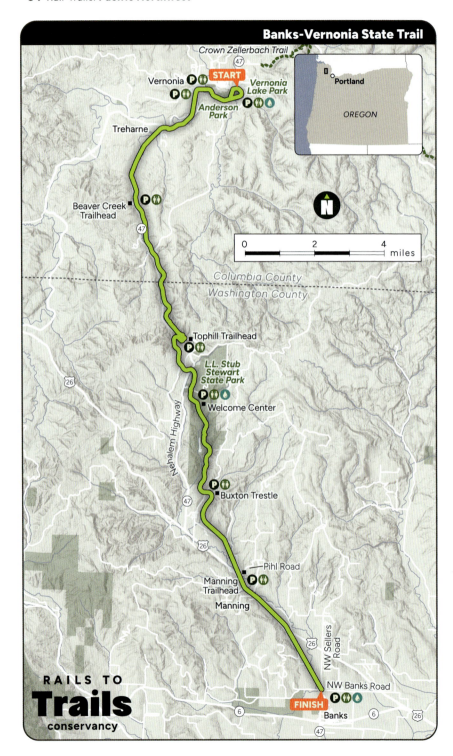

for more exploring. *Note:* At Adams Avenue, on the north end of the park, there is a quick blind turn in the trail, where you should watch for oncoming traffic.

From Anderson Park, you'll reach Beaver Creek Trailhead in 4.3 miles. It features interpretive signage, a gravel lot, and pit toilets. In this stretch, there are frequent driveways and rural road crossings, but each is well marked. From the Beaver Creek Trailhead, in 2.4 miles, you'll see a sign denoting your entrance into Washington County. After that point, the trail begins a steady low-grade climb.

In another 2 miles, you will see a SLOW sign. Please heed this warning, as the trail heads down a set of steep, tight switchbacks as it descends to a crossing of Nehalem Highway. On the other side of the highway, you'll reach Tophill Trailhead and another set of steep switchbacks.

From the Tophill Trailhead, it's 1.7 miles to L.L. Stub Stewart State Park; here you will feel the change to a significant downhill grade, which continues for the second half of the trail. Within the park, there is frequent signage to connect to hiking trails. At roughly the trail's midpoint, the trail crosses the state park's main entrance road. Just a short (but steep) ride up the road is the park's welcome center, as well as parking options, restrooms, and drinking water.

South of the welcome center, the trail continues its pleasant downhill grade. About 3 miles after the state park entrance, the trail approaches its most scenic point, the Buxton Trestle. The trail crosses this historical bridge, but you

The rail-trail winds through lush forests in the foothills of Oregon's Coast Range.

can also head down to the trailhead here and check out a side path that goes underneath the bridge for a unique perspective or photo op.

As the trail heads south and leaves the state park, it becomes less and less forested. From the Buxton Trestle, you'll reach Pihl Road in 2.8 miles. After this point, the trail is surrounded by open farmland. In 4 miles, it ends at the intersection of NW Sellers Road and NW Banks Road in the town of Banks. The trailhead here is well developed, with a bike repair station, signage, restrooms, and water.

CONTACT: rtc.li/banks-vernonia

PARKING

Parking areas are listed from north to south. *Indicates that at least one accessible parking space is available.*

VERNONIA*: Vernonia Lake Park, 1001 E. Bridge St. (45.857, -123.1746).

VERNONIA: Beaver Creek Trailhead, 300 feet north of 56039 Nehalem Hwy. S./OR 47 (45.8107, -123.2312).

BUXTON: Tophill Trailhead, Nehalem Hwy. S./OR 47, 0.75 mile south of Johnson Road (45.7584, -123.2015).

BUXTON*: Banks-Vernonia State Trail Midpoint, L.L. Stub Stewart State Park entrance off Nehalem Hwy. S./OR 47 (45.7378, -123.1953).

BUXTON*: Buxton Trailhead, 24600 NW Bacona Road, 1 mile north of Buxton (45.6985, -123.1837).

BANKS*: Manning Trailhead, NW Pihl Road, 200 feet from US 26/OR 47 (45.6650, -123.1637).

BANKS*: Banks Trailhead, NW Sellers Road and NW Banks Road (45.6223, -123.1142).

Bear Creek Greenway

At just over 20 miles, the Bear Creek Greenway connects five communities in southern Oregon's Rogue River Valley. Some sections are beautiful and bucolic, some are urban, and a few miles parallel I-5 and OR 99. The paved pathway gently gains elevation over its entire length, from its northern trailhead at approximately 1,220 feet in Central Point to its southern terminus in delightful Ashland at 1,750 feet.

Restrooms are available along the trail, as is drinking water in trailside parks. Throughout the route, there are also opportunities to venture just a short distance off the trail for refreshments in the surrounding communities. The trail is most popular around Medford's Lithia & Driveway Fields on its northern half, and between Blue Heron Park in Phoenix and Ashland Dog Park on the southern half.

There's a section designated for equestrian use around Central Point, from the trail's northern terminus at the Dean Creek Road Trailhead to the Central Point–Medford city line on the north side of Table Rock Road. On the trail's southern half, in Talent, there's another designated area for equestrian use, from Lynn Newbry Park to Wrangler's Arena.

The trail is also popular with birders in Central Point's wetland areas south of Pine Street and the ponds north and south of the Jackson County Expo; in Talent between Lynn

The Bear Creek Greenway traverses southern Oregon's Rogue River Valley.

County
Jackson

Endpoints
Dead end of Dean Creek Road (Central Point); W. Nevada St. and Almeda Dr. (Ashland)

Mileage
20.6

Type
Greenway/Non-Rail-Trail

Roughness Rating
1

Surface
Asphalt

58 Rail-Trails: **Pacific Northwest**

Newbry Park and Valley View Road, where the trail closely follows Bear Creek; and in Ashland along Bear Creek.

In Medford, an attraction for railroad enthusiasts is accessible via a connecting bike/pedestrian bridge that leads to the Medford Railroad Park on Berrydale Avenue. The park—open the second and fourth Sundays of each month from April through October—offers railroad equipment, smaller-scale train rides, and model trains.

From Phoenix through Talent, the trail is once again green after fire ravaged this section in 2020, burning many of the trees through the greenway corridor. Businesses that burned to the ground are back and better than ever, with restaurants and cafés providing welcome respite. Note that there are still ongoing maintenance activities that periodically close short forested sections of the trail to remove burned trees and other debris.

Long-term plans call for the greenway to link with the nearby Rogue River Greenway (see page 89), which runs east from Grants Pass. Together, the trails would span approximately 50 miles, connecting eight cities and two counties.

CONTACT: rtc.li/jackson-county and bearcreekgreenway.com

PARKING

Parking areas are listed from north to south. Select parking areas for the trail are listed below; for a detailed list of parking areas and other waypoints, consult TrailLink™. *Indicates that at least one accessible parking space is available.*

CENTRAL POINT*: Dean Creek Road Trailhead, dead end of Dean Creek Road, 0.9 mile southeast of Blackwell Road (42.3992, -122.9312).

CENTRAL POINT: Jackson County Expo, 1 Peninger Road (42.3878, -122.9137); paid parking lot.

CENTRAL POINT: Pine Street Trailhead, E. Pine St. and Peninger Road (42.3792, -122.8989).

MEDFORD*: Bear Creek Park, Siskiyou Blvd., 0.1 mile west of Highland Dr. (42.3205, -122.8522).

MEDFORD*: Lithia & Driveway Fields (formerly U.S. Cellular Park), Lowry Lane, 0.4 mile east of OR 99/S. Pacific Hwy. (42.2994, -122.8382).

MEDFORD*: Blue Heron Park, S. Pacific Hwy./OR 99/S. Main St. and Oak St. (42.2724, -122.8117).

TALENT*: Lynn Newbry Park, W. Valley View Road and Siskiyou View (42.2444, -122.7745).

TALENT: Wrangler's Arena, S. Pacific Hwy./OR 99 and Talent Ave. (42.2281, -122.7513).

ASHLAND: Ashland Dog Park, Perozzi St. and Sander Way (42.2126, -122.7121).

60 Rail-Trails: **Pacific Northwest**

Crown Zellerbach Trail

14

The Crown Zellerbach Trail, more commonly referred to as the Crown Z Trail, makes use of the former route of the Portland and Southwestern Railroad, which became a logging road when the tracks were removed in the 1940s. Now designated as a National Recreation Trail, this peaceful and secluded trail runs just over 23 miles, from Vernonia to Scappoose. Along the way, more than two dozen kiosks explain the area's geology and wildlife, as well as provide historical information provided by the Columbia County Museum Association.

The western starting point, Holce Trailhead, is located about an hour's drive from downtown Portland. There are no amenities at this trailhead, but restrooms and water can be found at Vernonia Lake Park, located 1.4 miles southwest. At the park, trail enthusiasts can also connect to the Banks-Vernonia State Trail (see page 53).

Those who are more accustomed to the typical rail-trail experience and enjoy low grades and well-packed gravel or pavement will want to be prepared for a more adventurous day. This trail is tailor-made for people who appreciate challenging terrain, including steep uphills and downhills (close

DANIELLE CASAVANT

Dense tree cover provides a secluded feeling despite the proximity of the Scappoose Vernonia Highway.

County
Columbia

Endpoints
Holce Trailhead on E. Knott St., 0.6 mile east of Nehalem Hwy. (Vernonia); Chapman Landing, 0.5 mile south of E. Columbia Ave. and Dike Road (Scappoose)

Mileage
23

Type
Rail-Trail

Roughness Rating
1–3

Surface
Asphalt, Gravel

to 20% grade at some points), as well as regular surface changes. Cyclists would be advised to have wider tires, as more than half of the trail is gravel and some portions have larger, looser stones. For a less challenging experience, head to the southern end of the trail in Scappoose, which is ADA compliant from the Trtek Trailhead to the Chapman Landing Trailhead. Equestrian use is permitted along the entirety of the trail.

As you depart the Holce Trailhead, the trail is paved for about a quarter of a mile, then abruptly changes to loose stone. The first 1.5 miles are uphill, with an elevation gain of about 450 feet. After this initial ascent, which is not shaded, you enter deep forest and enjoy a mostly shaded journey for the first 13 miles.

Birds and other wildlife are abundant along the trail. Although the trail runs mostly parallel with the Scappoose Vernonia Highway and alongside the Nehalem River and Scappoose Creek, the dense tree cover gives an isolated feel. About 5 miles in, the hilly and winding path narrows significantly as you approach a bridge that takes you over Hawkins Creek at the Floeter Trailhead. This trailhead offers a vault toilet, a picnic table, and a kiosk about the logging history of the area. Up to this point, the trail has ascended 522 feet and descended 509 feet.

The next 7.5 miles of trail ascend 607 feet and descend 659 feet to the Ruley Trailhead, where there is a bike repair station, vault toilets, a covered picnic area, and more interpretive signage. After the Ruley Trailhead, the trail is mostly flat as you make your way into Scappoose. It is no longer a logging road, but the surface is intermittent with packed gravel. The dense trees give way to lower shrubs and abundant raspberry bushes. Shortly before you cross US 30 in Scappoose (a signaled, high-traffic intersection), there is a trailhead with informational signage, another repair station, and restrooms.

After crossing US 30, the trail passes through marshy wetlands with many bird varieties and through dense vegetation. The trail continues out of Scappoose to the Trtek Trailhead, which has ample parking and restrooms. While this is a significant trailhead, the trail continues an additional 2 miles through farmland, with a termination point at Chapman Landing, which has restrooms, picnic tables, benches, and scenic views of the Columbia Channel.

CONTACT: columbiacountyor.gov/crownz-trail

TRAIL 14 CROWN ZELLERBACH TRAIL **63**

PARKING

Parking areas are listed from northwest to southeast. *Indicates that at least one accessible parking space is available.*

VERNONIA: Holce Trailhead, E. Knott St., 0.6 mile east of Nehalem Hwy. (45.8667, -123.1609).

VERNONIA: Wilark Trailhead, Pebble Creek Mainline and Scapoose Vernonia Hwy. (45.8693, -123.1237).

SCAPPOOSE: Floeter Trailhead, Scappoose Vernonia Hwy., 200 feet southeast of Hawkins Road (45.8442, -123.0926).

SCAPPOOSE: Nehalem Divide Trailhead, Pisgah Lookout Road and Scappoose Vernonia Hwy. (45.8315, -123.0465).

SCAPPOOSE: Ruley Trailhead, Scappoose Vernonia Hwy., 0.3 mile east of Chapman Grange Road (45.8249, -122.9667); horse trailer parking available.

SCAPPOOSE: Bonnie Falls Trailhead, Scappoose Vernonia Hwy. and Walker Road (45.8065, -122.9383).

SCAPPOOSE: Pisgah Trailhead, Scappoose Vernonia Hwy., 480 feet north of Wikstrom Road (45.7838, -122.9030).

SCAPPOOSE: Trtek Trailhead, 33920 Crown Zellerbach Road (45.7605, -122.8670).

SCAPPOOSE: Chapman Landing Trailhead, E. Columbia Ave. and Dike Road (45.7501, -122.8438).

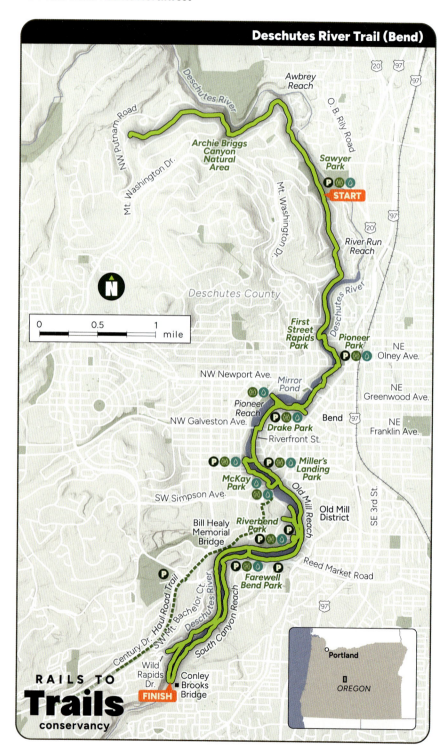

Deschutes River Trail (Bend)

The Deschutes River Trail (DRT) provides a fantastic way to explore the river through Bend, from the wild canyons of the north side to the urban parks of the center and the forested canyons in the south. There are five city-managed segments within Bend: (from north to south) the Awbrey Reach, River Run Reach, Pioneer Reach, Old Mill Reach, and South Canyon Reach. Restrooms are available throughout the trail, and drinking fountains are available at the parks. The **Awbrey Reach,** on the northern end of the trail, offers a wild out-and-back stretch through northwestern Bend. The best place to begin your adventure is Sawyer Park, where the only parking area for this section of trail is located. The park spans both sides of the river and provides restrooms and drinking water in addition to parking. From the park, you'll cross the Deschutes River to access the trail on the west bank, then head northwest following a gently rolling arc around Awbrey Butte. In 1.7 miles, you'll reach the Archie Briggs Canyon Natural Area, where you can reach a stunning river canyon vista via a set of stairs. From the natural area, you'll travel 1 more mile to reach the north end of the trail at Northwest Kirkaldy Court, then retrace your steps back to

County
Deschutes

Endpoints
NW Kirkaldy Ct., 0.1 mile northeast of NW Putnam Road (Bend); Wild Rapids Dr., 225 feet east of SW Mt. Bachelor Ct. (Bend)

Mileage
12.5

Type
Greenway/Non-Rail-Trail

Roughness Rating
1–2

Surface
Asphalt, Concrete, Dirt, Gravel

The trail provides access to a handful of parks in the urban heart of Bend.

Sawyer Park. As you head south from Sawyer Park, there is a steep climb up to the intersection with Mt. Washington Drive. The Awbrey Reach section—and the next section through First Street Rapids Park—is crushed gravel.

The **River Run Reach** extends 1.5 miles south from Sawyer Park to Pioneer Park. This riverside portion of the trail is dominated by wetlands that attract bird and animal life. The trail runs between the river and the base of a canyon wall, climbs a short but steep slope, and passes through the River's Edge golf course and adjacent neighborhoods. There is river access and recreation at First Street Rapids Park.

Begin **Pioneer Reach** at Pioneer Park and traverse Bend's riverside neighborhoods along NW Riverfront Street down to Miller's Landing Park. This section of the trail is paved and follows the banks of the city's placid Mirror Pond. On the eastern shore of the Deschutes River, the trail joins an interesting boardwalk over the river, hugs the shoreline, and passes under the Northwest Newport Avenue bridge to the lower reaches of Mirror Pond. There is easy access into downtown Bend from this section of the trail, and it also ties together the exciting whitewater action at Pioneer Park, Drake Park, Miller's Landing Park, and McKay Park.

Pine and juniper trees line the northern half of the trail as it winds through wide canyons.

The **Old Mill Reach** is a popular stretch of the trail along the riverbank through Bend's revitalized Old Mill District, a hot spot of shops, restaurants, galleries, and entertainment. Two lumber mills grew Bend into a business hub early in the 20th century, bringing the railroads through central Oregon. The Old Mill Reach consists of two loops: Mill A Loop (1.5 miles) and Logger Loop (1.3 miles). Three bike/pedestrian bridges connect both sides of the river through this section. The trail continues upriver to Farewell Bend Park and Riverbend Park.

The **South Canyon Reach** is a wilderness section located south of Reed Market Road, winding through ponderosa pine forests and over a canyon rim where the river gushes through narrow flumes and over boulder-strewn rapids. Bicycles are not allowed on the west side of the trail section in the South Canyon Reach, but there is an alternative bike route that connects the Bill Healy Bridge to the Haul Road Trail along Century Drive. The DRT is narrow, rocky, and challenging along the east side of the river. It continues to the Conley Brooks Bridge and crosses the river to create a loop.

CONTACT: bendparksandrec.org/parks-trails

PARKING

Parking areas are located within Bend and are listed from north to south. Select parking areas for the trail are listed below; for a detailed list of parking areas and other waypoints, consult **TrailLink™**. *Indicates that at least one accessible parking space is available.*

SAWYER PARK: Oatman Cir. and Angels Flight Road (44.0865, -121.3100).

PIONEER PARK*: 1525 NW Wall St. (44.0653, -121.3093).

MILLER'S LANDING PARK*: 55 NW Riverside Blvd. (44.0517, -121.3214).

RIVERBEND PARK*: SW Columbia St. and SW Shevlin Hixon Dr. (44.0432, -121.3198).

FAREWELL BEND PARK: SW Reed Market Road, 0.1 mile west of Brookswood Blvd. (44.0408, -121.3205).

FAREWELL BEND PARK*: SW Reed Market Road, 400 feet west of Alderwood Cir. (44.0408, -121.3248).

SKYLINE PARK*: Mountaineer Way, 0.2 mile southwest of Mt. Washington Dr. (44.0382, -121.3403).

68 Rail-Trails: **Pacific Northwest**

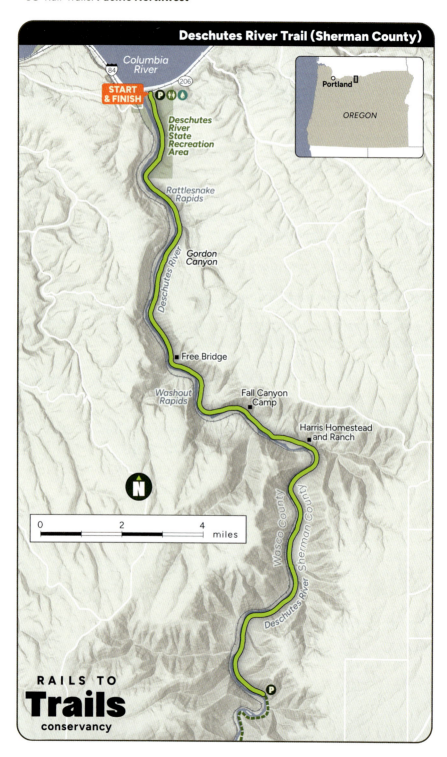

Deschutes River Trail
(Sherman County)

This exhilarating trail above the east banks of the Lower Deschutes River, a federally designated Wild and Scenic River, brings users across a ruggedly beautiful riverscape set in Oregon's high desert. Sagebrush blankets the canyon slopes, and towering basalt columns line the canyon rim. Home to fantastic trout and steelhead fishing, this canyon also has mule deer, elk, bighorn sheep, wild horses, and cougars, as well as chukars and small game.

The trail is best suited for hiking and mountain biking. Equestrians are also allowed March 1–June 30 and can use the first 11 miles of the trail. Reservations are required and can be made through the website listed on page 71.

As the entire Lower Deschutes Canyon is high-desert country, it's important to be prepared for this trail. Bring lots of water and be ready for high summer temperatures, especially during the months of June–August. Winds typically build and blow upstream on many afternoons during the warmer months, so you may also encounter headwinds on the return trip. The most popular months on the trail are April and May.

The trail winds along a federally designated Wild and Scenic River in Oregon's high desert.

County
Sherman

Endpoints
Deschutes River State Recreation Area at OR 206/ Biggs Rufus Hwy. (Wasco); 7 miles north of Macks Canyon Campground (Grass Valley)

Mileage
18.6

Type
Rail-Trail

Roughness Rating
2

Surface
Dirt, Gravel

As there is little to no cell phone coverage a couple of miles into the canyon, it's best to also bring a first aid kit, lights, and a bike repair kit. Tires here are especially vulnerable: Puncturevine, a noxious weed also known as goat's head, easily punctures tires. Tubeless tire setups help mitigate this potential problem. Keep in mind that the desert is also home to things that sting: spiders, scorpions, and rattlesnakes, so keep an eye out. The trailhead to the Deschutes River Trail, which heads south along the east side of the river, originates near the entrance to the Deschutes River State Recreation Area, a grass-covered expanse with campsites, parking, and day-use areas that provide a comfortable place to embark on a day trip up the canyon. Almost all users take this trail as an out-and-back.

The first 2 miles of the trail are in the state recreation area, after which you'll come to trail segments managed by the Oregon Department of Fish and Wildlife and the US Bureau of Land Management. Although almost all the old railroad features were destroyed by the 2018 Substation Fire, a wooden trestle still exists about 5 miles into the trail.

The first visible river feature is Rattlesnake Rapids, where you'll find big waves, a rock garden, and washing machine–like currents. Continue another mile, and you'll make a sharp descent into Gordon Canyon and then back up to

Sagebrush blankets the canyon slopes, and towering basalt columns line the Lower Deschutes Canyon rim.

the original railroad grade. Trains used to travel on a high trestle across this canyon, but it no longer exists. Once back on the railroad grade, you'll pass beside some beautiful lichen-covered basalt cliffs.

At 6.6 miles along the trail, you'll see the remaining remnants of a piece of Deschutes River history, the remains of Free Bridge. This bridge was first constructed as a toll bridge, a common means to pass difficult obstacles during pioneer times. Wasco County purchased the bridge in 1887, eliminating the toll to provide free passage over the river. This bridge was later sabotaged—blown up by dynamite in 1914 by competing toll bridge operators. Farther up the trail are the more recently formed Washout Rapids, the result of a 1995 flash flood that deposited boulders here.

At 10.1 miles, a trail leads down to Fall Canyon Camp, a good spot to camp if you're backpacking or bike-packing. (Note that equestrian users may not camp overnight.) One of the first natural turnaround points is what remains of the Harris Homestead and Ranch and the spur trail winding up Harris Canyon, located just past mile 11. Much of the ranch, ravaged by the Substation Fire, is now nothing more than charred posts in the ground. The old railroad water tower near mile 11.4 is now neatly piled planks.

The main trail beyond Harris Canyon becomes rockier, with a few more bumps over the next 7-plus miles, ending at mile 18.6. Fewer trail users continue this far. For the more intrepid, the trail departs from the railbed and narrows at mile 18.6 to a faint game trail along the canyon walls all the way to Macks Canyon. There is vehicle access at Macks Canyon, so a one-way trip is possible.

CONTACT: rtc.li/deschutes-sra

PARKING

Parking areas are located within Wasco and are listed from north to south.
Indicates that at least one accessible parking space is available.

DESCHUTES RIVER STATE RECREATION AREA: OR 206/Fulton Canyon Road, 0.4 mile east of Old Moody Road (45.6343, -120.9080).

DESCHUTES RIVER STATE RECREATION AREA*: 0.4 mile south of OR 206/Fulton Canyon Road (45.6293, -120.9078).

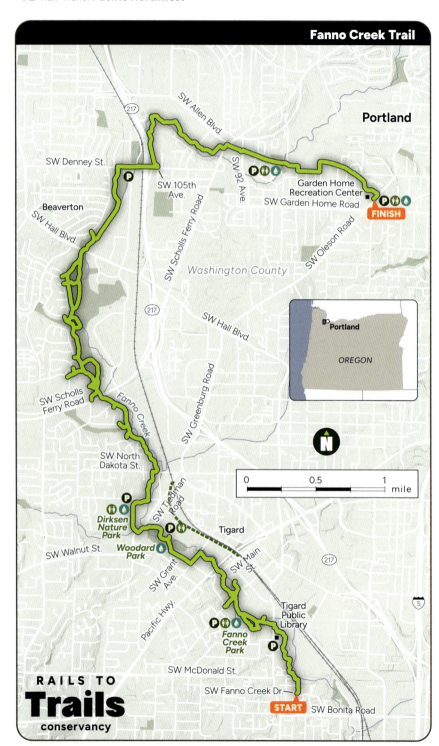

Fanno Creek Trail

17

The Fanno Creek Trail meanders for nearly 10 miles through the cities of Tigard and Beaverton, west of Portland, largely following Fanno Creek. Overall, it's well shaded, with dozens of neighborhood entry points and ample opportunities to leave the trail for a restaurant and additional sightseeing. With its parklike settings and wetlands, the trail is a nature lover's destination for birding and wildlife viewing.

The trail begins in Tigard, on Southwest Fanno Creek Drive, just north of Southwest Bonita Road. (As there's no parking here, you could begin your journey 0.5 mile north at the Tigard Public Library, which has a large parking lot.) You'll experience a few sharp turns and some short steep hills as the narrow trail winds its way to the library. To your left is the Colony Creek subdivision; to your right, the lush greenery along Fanno Creek.

Throughout Tigard, the trail runs through a system of parks, natural areas, and greenways. As you head north from the library, you'll enter Fanno Creek Park, where you'll find parking, drinking fountains, restrooms, and wildlife viewing. There's a well-marked road crossing at Southwest Main

The trail largely follows—and often crosses—Fanno Creek as it meanders through Tigard and Beaverton.

County
Washington

Endpoints
SW Fanno Creek Dr., 0.3 mile northwest of SW Bonita Road (Tigard); SW Oleson Road, 485 feet northeast of SW Garden Home Road (Portland)

Mileage
9.2

Type
Greenway/Non-Rail-Trail

Roughness Rating
1

Surface
Asphalt

Street, which you'll reach 1 mile after the library; then the trail continues under Pacific Highway/OR 99 W and reaches Southwest Grant Avenue in 1 block. This starts a 0.3-mile on-road section that follows Southwest Grant Avenue west, then turns north onto Southwest Johnson Street to reach Woodard Park. The park offers vault toilets, drinking water, playground equipment, and a covered picnic shelter.

After crossing Southwest Tiedman Road, the Fanno Creek Trail continues into Dirksen Nature Park with its sports fields, wildlife viewing areas, restrooms, drinking water, picnic shelters, and playgrounds. There's a large parking lot west of the trail just before it crosses Southwest Tigard Street and dips into a more heavily wooded area.

At the next road crossing, Southwest North Dakota Street (in 0.2 mile), take a right to travel on-road 200 feet before rejoining the trail on the north side of the street. The trail continues to wind behind neighborhoods and through parklands with a good amount of shade cover as you approach the halfway point

The Fanno Creek Trail includes many scenic viewing areas, including this unique bridge in Tigard's Dirksen Nature Park.

and go under Southwest Scholls Ferry Road. (*Note:* There is the potential for flooding in this area after heavy rains.)

In 1.8 miles, there's a major road crossing where Southwest Denney Street encounters the on- and off-ramp traffic for OR 217; there are traffic signals, but it's a very busy area. After the crossing, turn right to follow the broad sidewalk along Denney Street 0.3 mile to Southwest 105th Avenue. Turn left on Southwest 105th Avenue, taking an on-road route of 0.2 mile to a cul-de-sac in an office park, where the trail resumes.

You'll follow the tree-lined path 0.8 mile to Southwest Scholls Ferry Road in Beaverton. Turn right at its intersection with Southwest Allen Boulevard, and follow the boulevard on-road to Southwest 92nd Avenue in 0.1 mile, where you'll pick up the trail again. It cruises through the neighborhoods of Beaverton, with dense foliage cover, until you arrive at the trail's end at the Garden Home Recreation Center, which offers parking, restrooms, water, sports facilities, and a community center.

When all of its planned segments are completed, the Fanno Creek Trail will span about 20 miles, with a route extending east from Beaverton into Portland via a connection to the proposed Red Electric Trail. It will also continue south to Tualatin and link into the Tualatin River Greenway.

CONTACT: thprd.org/parks-and-trails/fanno-creek-trail and rtc.li/tigard

PARKING

Parking areas are listed from south to north. Select parking areas for the trail are listed below; for a detailed list of parking areas and other waypoints, consult **TrailLink™**. *Indicates that at least one accessible parking space is available.*

TIGARD*: Tigard Public Library, 13500 SW Hall Blvd. (45.4222, -122.7648).

TIGARD*: Woodard Park, dead end of SW Katherine St., 0.2 west of SW Tigard St. (45.4335, -122.7828).

TIGARD*: Dirksen Nature Park, 10562 SW Tigard St. (45.4361, -122.7862).

BEAVERTON*: Denney Road Trailhead, SW Denney Road and SW 111th Ave. (45.4691, -122.7900).

PORTLAND*: Vista Brook Park, 6697 SW 88th Ave. (45.4712, -122.7673).

PORTLAND*: Garden Home Recreation Center, SW Oleson Road and SW Garden Home Road (45.4672, -122.7521).

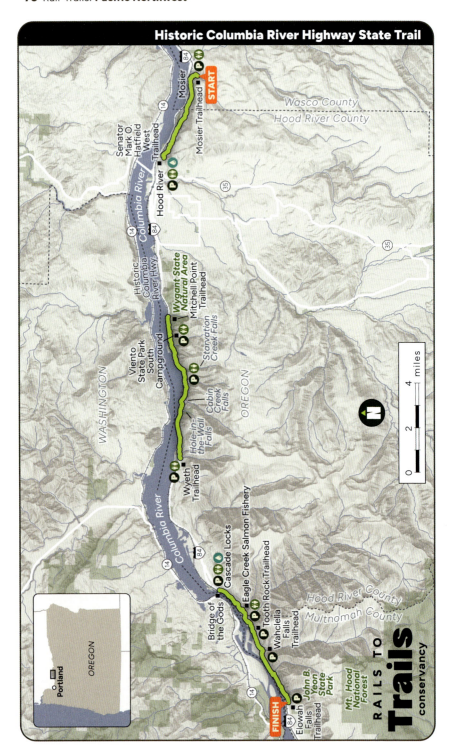

Historic Columbia River Highway State Trail

18

The Historic Columbia River Highway State Trail is a road-to-trail conversion built on former US 30—the first highway in the United States built for scenic purposes. It currently consists of three disconnected segments along northern Oregon's Columbia River Gorge, designated a National Scenic Area in 1986. Part of this act, which protected 85 miles of ancient volcanic corridor, also included the establishment of this recreational trail that today parallels I-84, which is also signed as the modern-day US 30 route.

A good place to begin your journey is Mosier, at the easternmost end of the trail. While the western gorge is filled with deep, misty forests and an abundance of waterfalls, the 4.7-mile trail segment between Mosier and Hood River runs through rolling farmlands, grasslands, and rocky outcroppings.

There is a day-use fee at the Mosier Trailhead, where you'll find a parking lot and restrooms. Almost immediately from the parking lot, the trail starts a significant climb. In 0.8 mile, there's a viewpoint bump-out overlooking the gorge, and 0.4 mile after that you'll encounter the most scenic attraction along this segment of trail, the Mosier Twin Tunnels. The first tunnel features a craggy roof with small

Counties
Hood River, Multnomah, Wasco

Endpoints
Rock Creek Road, 0.7 mile southwest of US 30/Historic Columbia River Hwy. (Mosier); Senator Mark O. Hatfield West Trailhead (Hood River); Wygant State Natural Area, adjacent to I-84 and Perham Creek (Cascade Locks); Wyeth Trailhead (Cascade Locks); Wa Na Pa St. and Bridge of the Gods entrance (Cascade Locks); Elowah Falls Trailhead in John B. Yeon State Park (Cascade Locks)

Mileage
18.8

Type
Greenway/Non-Rail-Trail

Roughness Rating
1

Surface
Asphalt

Viewpoints look out over the Columbia River Gorge National Scenic Area.

MADDIE KRENTZ

windows that provide light and glimpses of the gorge. The second tunnel starts just a few feet after and has a more industrial look.

After reaching the tunnels, the trail largely has a downhill grade, with some rolling hills throughout. As you head west, the landscape changes to shady pine forests. You'll reach another viewpoint bump-out 0.9 mile after the tunnels, and then the trail coasts downhill to the Senator Mark O. Hatfield West Trailhead, which offers parking and restrooms.

An 8.5-mile gap precedes the next segment of trail. The only way to navigate the gap is to take I-84. Bikes are allowed on this highly trafficked road, but it may not be suitable for less experienced riders and is not suited for pedestrians. The best way, for now, to get between these sections is to drive to Viento State Park South Campground and continue riding from there. The majority of this 7.2-mile segment heads west from the campground, but 1.5 miles of newly constructed trail head back east, dead-ending adjacent to I-84. This part of the trail will eventually continue all the way to the Mitchell Point Trailhead, with the connection expected by 2026–2027.

Head west from Viento State Park South Campground to continue along the main trail route. This section also has some rolling hills. While it is paved, the asphalt is older, with some cracks and bumps. After 1.3 miles, the trail reaches Starvation Creek Falls, where a short, paved spur leads to a waterfall viewing point. Be sure to look up at the viewing point, or you might miss the falls high up in the trees.

In 0.4 mile, the trail reaches Cabin Creek Falls and then Hole-in-the-Wall Falls, which is a short distance off the trail. The final portion of this segment largely runs alongside I-84, with surrounding views of the gorge. There is a 7.3-mile gap before the next segment begins.

This last segment of trail, spanning 6.9 miles, starts at Cascade Locks, right underneath the Bridge of the Gods, which crosses the Columbia River and provides access into Washington. The trail heads southwest from the bridge, paralleling a narrow road along I-84. In 1.1 miles, you'll reach a tunnel that takes you under the interstate. You will have a short, quick climb in elevation before an even steeper downhill that would be difficult to climb in the opposite direction.

The trail returns to the roadside at Eagle Creek Salmon Fishery, 1.1 miles after the interstate tunnel. A short on-road section leads to a steep set of stairs (an accessible detour to avoid the stairs is not available). Just after climbing these stairs, stop at the final scenic viewpoint. Along the way, you will also be able to spot the old stones and markings of the historic highway. After this, the trail passes the Wahclella Falls Trailhead, where hiking trails head deeper into the gorge. The trail ends at the Elowah Falls Trailhead in John B. Yeon State Park.

CONTACT: rtc.li/hcrhst

TRAIL 18 HISTORIC COLUMBIA RIVER HIGHWAY STATE TRAIL

PARKING

Parking areas are listed from east to west. *Indicates that at least one accessible parking space is available.*

MOSIER*: Rock Creek Road, 0.7 mile southwest of US 30/Historic Columbia River Hwy. (45.6802, -121.4090); day-use fee.

HOOD RIVER*: Senator Mark O. Hatfield West Trailhead, Old Columbia River Dr., 1 mile from OR 35 (45.7038, -121.4868); day-use fee.

CASCADE LOCKS*: Viento State Park Campground South, I-84 Exit 56 (45.6961, -121.6687); day-use fee.

CASCADE LOCKS*: Starvation Creek State Park, I-84 Exit 55 (45.68844, -121.6903); day-use fee.

CASCADE LOCKS*: Wyeth Trailhead, Wyeth Road, I-84 Exit 51 (45.6896, -121.7736); day-use fee.

CASCADE LOCKS*: Bridge of the Gods Trailhead, Wa Pa Na St. and Bridge of the Gods (45.6618, -121.8983).

CASCADE LOCKS*: Tooth Rock Trailhead, Star Route, I-84 Exit 40 (45.6346, -121.9481); day-use fee.

CASCADE LOCKS*: Wahclella Falls Trailhead, I-84 Exit 40 (45.6305, -121.9539); day-use fee.

CASCADE LOCKS*: Elowah Falls Trailhead, John B. Yeon State Park, NE Frontage Road, I-84 Exit 37 (45.6124, -122.0043).

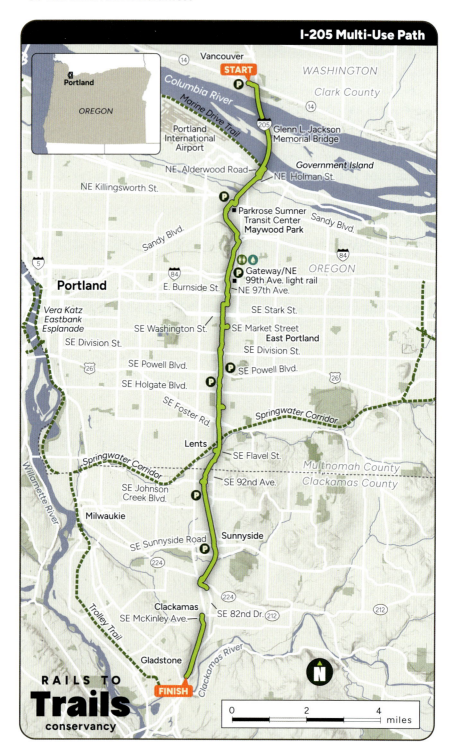

I-205 Multi-Use Path

19

Visitors to the I-205 Multi-Use Path, part of the Intertwine trail network, will experience the full scope of Greater Portland's connectivity and transportation options on this 18.5-mile trail that connects Vancouver, Washington, and Clackamas County to central Portland, Oregon.

The trail begins in the wooded neighborhood of Old Evergreen Highway in Vancouver and runs parallel to WA 14. As the trail unites with I-205, it ascends to Glenn L. Jackson Memorial Bridge into Oregon via a heavily protected trail in the center lane of the highway. The bridge crosses over Government Island, a protected nature area in the Columbia River known for its wildlife, including a great blue heron colony.

After descending the bridge, the trail connects to the Marine Drive Trail for further exploration of the scenic Columbia River. Follow the I-205 trail to the right after the bridge to continue into Portland along Northeast Holman Street before crossing Northeast Alderwood Road. Shortly

TRAILLINK USER DAN ROKOSZ

Although the trail parallels the interstate, wildflowers and native vegetation beautify route.

Counties
Clackamas, Multnomah (OR); Clark (WA)

Endpoints
I-205 and WA 14/Lewis and Clark Hwy. (Vancouver, WA); 82nd Dr. and I-205 Gladstone Interchange (Gladstone, OR)

Mileage
18.5

Type
Greenway/Rail-with-Trail

Roughness Rating
1

Surface
Asphalt

after the intersection, the trail continues a short distance from I-205; here, wildflowers and native vegetation greet visitors through the spring and summer.

As the trail approaches Sandy Boulevard, proceed through the signalized intersection with caution and head west. In a few hundred feet, the trail turns south to resume its route along I-205. At the Parkrose/Sumner Transit Center, visitors and commuters alike can choose to continue along the trail or take advantage of the MAX Light Rail service. Day parking is available at the station.

The trail continues through the city of Maywood Park, where it is popular with joggers and dog walkers. Just south of Maywood Park, visitors encounter Gateway Green, a park that's open from 7 a.m. to 10 p.m. and is well equipped with restrooms, water fountains, picnic tables, and a skills park.

South of Gateway Green, visitors and commuters have another opportunity for a transit connection at the Gateway/Northeast 99th Avenue light rail and transit station. Shortly after the transit station, the trail crosses Northeast Glisan Street at a signalized crossing before turning left and immediately right just before Northeast 97th Street. Here, the trail runs between I-205 and Northeast 97th Street. Approaching East Burnside Street, another signalized crossing directs visitors across the road and to the left, where the trail resumes its course on the west side of the interstate.

As it continues through East Portland, the trail has two more signalized crossings in quick succession, across Southeast Stark Street and Southeast Washington Street. Half a mile from East Burnside Street, the trail intersects with the Southeast Pedestrian Trail, which crosses under I-205 to connect the adjacent neighborhoods to the Southeast Main Street transit station. Additional parking is available at this station.

As the I-205 trail continues south, use caution crossing Southeast Market Street, one of the few instances where the trail does not have a signalized crossing for trail users. The trail soon approaches the SE Powell Boulevard transit station, complete with an above-grade trail connection or at-grade path crossing the roadway. From here, the trail traverses the Lents neighborhood and connects to the renowned Springwater Corridor (see page 97) in 1.7 miles.

At Southeast Flavel Street, continue straight through the intersection along Southeast 92nd Avenue before the trail turns back along Southeast Flavel Street and veers right to reconnect with the light rail right at the Southeast Flavel Street station. Approximately 1 mile later, follow the trail to the left as it approaches Southeast Johnson Creek Boulevard via a trail underpass, or take advantage of a signalized crossing by following the trail to the right. Shortly, the Southeast Fuller Road MAX light-rail stop offers a reprieve with some shade trees and a large parking lot.

In Sunnyside (1.5 miles south of the Southeast Fuller Road station), the trail crosses Southeast Sunnyside Road and then Southeast Sunnybrook Boulevard. While these intersections are signalized, use caution when traversing high-traffic roads, paying careful attention to the turning lanes. The trail continues south, weaving over and under roads, until Southeast Enoch Court, after which there is a gap of a few blocks.

The trail resumes in Clackamas at the intersection of Southeast McKinley Avenue and OR 212. Confident cyclists who feel comfortable crossing major roadways can traverse this gap on-road. To do so, follow Southeast 82nd Drive to OR 212; cross OR 212, then turn right, paralleling the southern side of the highway on the sidewalk. You'll cross over I-205 and resume the trail on the western side of the I-205 on-ramp. The I-205 Multi-Use Path terminates at 82nd Drive in Gladstone.

CONTACT: portland.gov/parks/nature/trails

PARKING

Parking areas are listed from north to south. *Indicates that at least one accessible parking space is available.*

VANCOUVER: 11307 SE 23rd St. (45.6044, -122.5560).

SUMNER*: Parkrose/Sumner Transit Center, 9481 NE Sandy Blvd. (45.5590, -122.5637).

GATEWAY NORTH*: Gateway North Transit Center, NE Pacific St. and NE 99th Ave. (45.5297, -122.5625).

POWELL*: SE Powell Blvd. Park & Ride, 3618 SE 92nd Ave. (45.4952, -122.5664).

HOLGATE*: SE Holgate Blvd. Park & Ride, 9669 SE Holgate Blvd. (45.4908, -122.5667).

CLACKAMAS: Clackamas Town Center, 9225 SE Sunnyside Road (45.4344, -122.5681).

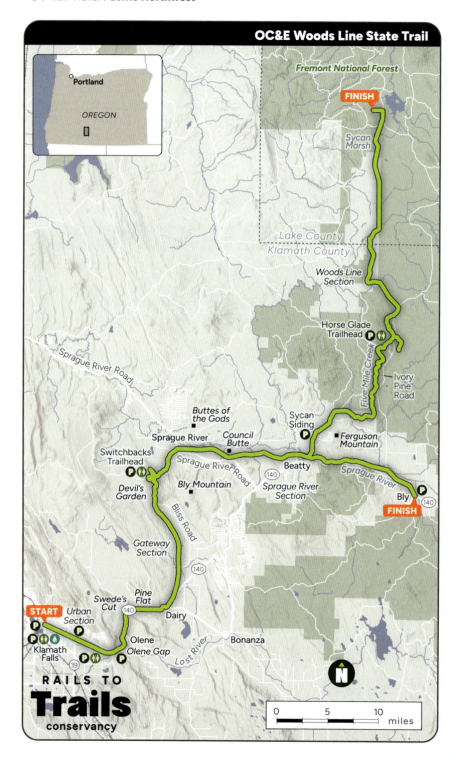

OC&E Woods Line State Trail

20

Spanning 109 miles, the OC&E Woods Line State Trail is one of the country's longest rail-trails. It gets its name from the Oregon, California, and Eastern Railroad (OC&E), on which it was built. The pathway connects south-central Oregon's largest community, Klamath Falls, to the agricultural, ranching, and forest lands to the east. Beginning in Klamath Falls, the trail extends east for more than 63 miles to Bly. Between these two communities, a 46-mile spur of the trail begins in Beatty and meanders north along spring-fed creeks past the Sycan Marsh.

The trail is paved and accessible for 9 miles from Klamath Falls to Olene, and the remainder is dirt and gravel. Much of the OC&E trail east of Klamath Falls is in Oregon's outback, with long distances between towns for food, water, and restrooms—so be prepared.

First envisioned by pioneer, author, and publicist Robert E. Strahorn, the OC&E began as the Klamath Falls Municipal Railway. Construction began in July 1917, first reaching the town of Sprague River in 1923 and eventually reaching its easternmost terminus in Bly in 1929. The separate

Counties
Klamath, Lake

Endpoints
Washburn Way, 0.2 mile south of S. Sixth St. (Klamath Falls); OR 140/Klamath Falls–Lakeview Hwy., 0.2 mile southeast of Edler St. (Bly); 1 mile northwest of NF 288 (Lake County)

Mileage
109.2

Type
Rail-Trail

Roughness Rating
1–3

Surface
Asphalt, Ballast, Cinder, Dirt, Gravel

The trail winds through open sage and grassland areas, as well as agricultural and ranching lands.

Weyerhaeuser Woods line operated from Beatty to a point 46 miles north past the Sycan Marsh, transporting logs from camps in what is now the Fremont National Forest to the mills along the main OC&E. Spurring growth and industry from Klamath Falls to Bly, the OC&E thrived, bringing enormous ponderosa pine logs—millions of board feet of lumber each year—to the four mills in the region. Operations peaked in the late 1970s but diminished during the 1980s and ceased in 1990. The railway owner, Weyerhaeuser Corporation, railbanked the right-of-way to Oregon Parks and Recreation.

This trail is divided into four distinct sections:

URBAN SECTION: Klamath Falls to Olene (7.6 miles)
This paved section is the most popular because of its proximity to the urban center of Klamath Falls. After passing OR 39 outside Klamath Falls, you'll traverse farms and forests and sweep through the Olene Gap, a glen just wide enough for OR 140, the OC&E trail, and the adjacent Lost River to pass through. At Olene, you'll go through a gate and continue your journey on a dirt-and-gravel surface for the remainder of the trail.

GATEWAY SECTION: Olene to Sprague River (31.2 miles)
The trail starts off rough but improves over a short distance. If cycling, this section is best suited for mountain and gravel bikes. The trail crosses OR 140, zigzags along the side of a ridge, and then diverges from the highway and turns along the western edge of a valley. The trail curves into Swede's Cut and drops into Pine Flat, then crosses under OR 140 for a descent into Dairy. From Dairy, the trail ascends the foot of Bly Mountain, skirting the Devil's Garden, an open sage and grasslands area. At Bly Mountain, a double switchback was used to split trains to get them over the mountain (plans to construct a tunnel during the early days of the railroad never materialized); this was the last railway double switchback, used until 1990. From Bly Mountain, the trail drops into the Sprague River Valley and into the town of Sprague River.

SPRAGUE RIVER SECTION: Sprague River to Bly (24.3 miles)
The trail leads east along the Sprague River, past Council Butte and Buttes of the Gods toward Beatty. Just past Beatty, a spur heads north from the junction of the main east–west OC&E route at the site of the old Sycan Siding. The Sycan Siding area in Beatty was the primary yard and place for maintenance shops for the OC&E line. East of here, the main OC&E line enters a small canyon, crossing the Sprague River over numerous trestles toward Bly.

WOODS LINE SECTION: Beatty to west of Thompson Reservoir (46.1 miles)
(*Note:* This spur is currently closed. While there isn't a firm reopening date, it is expected to reopen in 2026.)

The Woods Line section of the trail turns north from the Sycan Siding site, climbing the base of Ferguson Mountain. It then follows the course of pristine, spring-fed Five Mile Creek, crossing it several times over wood trestles.

At mile 19 from the junction in Beatty, the trail crosses NF 27 (Ivory Pine Road) and passes the Horse Glade Trailhead, where camping and restrooms are available. Shortly afterward, you'll reach a Y-juncture; continue straight (north). The 400-foot-long Merritt Creek trestle once stood past Horse Glade at mile 27 but was destroyed in the 2021 Bootleg Fire. The Woods Line section ends at the Sycan Marsh. The land, owned by The Nature Conservancy, is a great area for bird-watching.

CONTACT: rtc.li/oce

PARKING

Parking areas are listed from west to east. *Indicates that at least one accessible parking space is available.*

KLAMATH FALLS*: Crosby Trailhead, 400 feet north of Crosby Ave. and Avalon St. (42.2073, -121.7520).

KLAMATH FALLS*: Wiard Park Trailhead, Wiard St., 250 feet north of Hilyard Ave. (42.2003, -121.7278).

KLAMATH FALLS*: 39 Trailhead, OR 39/OR 140, 0.1 mile south of Booth Road (42.1905, -121.6984).

KLAMATH FALLS*: Reeder Road/Pine Grove Trailhead, 5015 Reeder Road (42.1810, -121.6687).

OLENE: Olene Trailhead, OR 140, 0.5 mile west of the bridge from Crystal Springs Road/S. Poe Valley Road (42.1714, -121.6270).

SPRAGUE RIVER: Switchbacks Trailhead, NF 22, just west of NF 11/Bliss Road (42.4146, -121.5487).

BEATTY: Sycan Siding Parking, Ferguson Mountain Road, 0.1 mile northwest of Medicine Dr. (42.4755, -121.2388).

BLY: Bly Trailhead, OR 140, 0.6 mile north of Axel St. (42.4096, -121.0483).

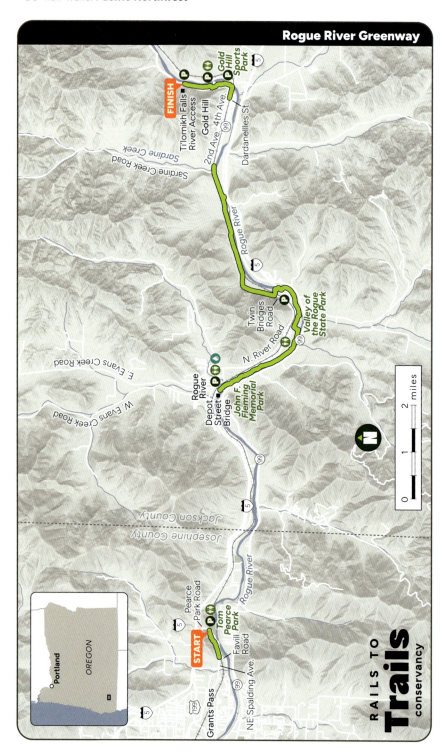

Rogue River Greenway

21

This scenic, paved trail along Oregon's Rogue River is currently open in three disconnected segments totaling nearly 10 miles between Grants Pass and Gold Hill. Long-term plans call for the Rogue River Greenway to link with the nearby Bear Creek Greenway (see page 57), which runs through the Medford area. Together, the two trails would span approximately 50 miles, connecting eight cities and two counties.

Begin on the trail's western end in Tom Pearce Park on the outskirts of Grants Pass. Just under a mile of trail traverses the park along the densely forested northern bank of the Rogue River. Restrooms, picnic areas, and parking are available in the park.

After a gap of 6 miles, the longest stretch of the trail—spanning 7.5 miles—picks up in the city of Rogue River at the Depot Street Bridge. The trail begins on the north side of the bridge, but you can easily cross it to reach John F. Fleming Memorial Park, where there are restrooms and parking, on the southern bank of the Rogue River. Although the trail parallels I-5 as it heads southeast from the bridge, it's pleasantly tucked into a wooded corridor along the river

Counties
Jackson, Josephine

Endpoints
Dead end of NE Spalding Ave./SE N St., 0.1 mile east of Favill Road (Grants Pass); Pearce Park Road in Tom Pearce Park (Grants Pass); Depot Street Bridge (Rogue River); Second Ave. and Sardine Creek Road (Gold Hill); Dardanelles St. and Fourth Ave. (Gold Hill); Ti'lomikh Falls River Access and Parking Area, 0.2 mile north of OR 234/Rogue-Umpqua Scenic Hwy. (Gold Hill)

Mileage
9.8

Type
Greenway/
Rail-with-Trail

Roughness Rating
1

Surface
Asphalt

In addition to biking and walking, you'll have opportunities to camp, fish, and picnic in Valley of the Rogue State Park.

over mildly rolling terrain. There are benches along the trail, with many providing views of the riverscape.

In 2 miles, you'll exit the woods to broad meadows and mountain vistas as you enter Valley of the Rogue State Park. A series of paths traverse the state park, including a gravel pedestrian path that skirts the water; camping, fishing, and picnicking opportunities are also available here.

After the state park, the trail swings away from the river and under I-5. From the underpass you'll pop out along Twin Bridges Road, which you'll follow until it meets North River Road in 0.2 mile. You'll parallel this quiet roadway for 2.7 miles—with the views becoming more agricultural—until its end at OR 99/OR 234. You'll continue along this connecting highway to the western outskirts of Gold Hill. This trail segment ends at a bridge over Sardine Creek.

After a gap of 1.6 miles, the final stretch of trail begins in downtown Gold Hill at the corner of Dardanelles Street and Fourth Avenue. This 1.4-mile section runs along Fourth Avenue and the railroad tracks, within easy reach of restaurants and businesses. In 0.3 mile, you'll reach the Rogue River and turn north, passing through the Gold Hill Sports Park, which offers restrooms, parking, and athletic facilities. The trail ends at Ti'lomikh Falls River Access.

CONTACT: roguerivergreenway.org

PARKING

Parking areas are listed from west to east. Select parking areas for the trail are listed below; for a detailed list of parking areas and other waypoints, consult **TrailLink™**. *Indicates that at least one accessible parking space is available.*

GRANTS PASS: Tom Pearce Park, 3700 Pearce Park Road (42.4328, -123.2725).

ROGUE RIVER*: John F. Fleming Memorial Park, 8898 Rogue River Hwy. (42.4312, -123.1718).

ROGUE RIVER*: Valley of the Rogue State Park, I-5 Exit 45B (42.4116, -123.1286).

GOLD HILL*: Gold Hill Sports Park, OR 234, 0.3 mile north of Fourth Ave. (42.4347, -123.0426).

GOLD HILL: Ti'lomikh Falls River Access and Parking Area, OR 234, 1 mile north of Fourth Ave. (42.4454, -123.0439).

Row River Trail

22

Located 22 miles south of Eugene, the Row River Trail spans 16.4 miles from its start in the center of Cottage Grove to its end at Culp Creek. Along the way, the trail skirts sections of the Row River and rolls past the shores of Dorena Lake. It's also part of the 37-mile Lane County Covered Bridges Bikeway and includes two covered bridges, with another just a short distance past the eastern terminus.

Note that Dorena Lake and the Row River itself (in the Row River Nature Park) offer some good fishing. Both are stocked with trout by the Oregon Department of Fish and Wildlife during the spring season. Equestrians are allowed year-round; there is a dirt-and-gravel path adjacent to the paved trail for equestrian use, and the Mosby Creek Trailhead offers trailer parking.

The Oregon and Southeastern Railroad (O&SE), also nicknamed the "Old Slow and Easy," was built to serve the Bohemia mining district, a productive gold and silver mining area from the 1860s to the 1920s along the western foothills of the Cascade Range. Once the tracks were laid, sawmills sprang up along the railroad, igniting the growth of other

The Harms Park Trestle over Mosby Creek was featured in *Emperor of the North* and *Stand by Me*.

County
Lane

Endpoints
Trailhead Park, S. 10th St. and E. Main St. (Cottage Grove); Culp Creek Trailhead, Row River Road (Culp Creek)

Mileage
16.4

Type
Rail-Trail

Roughness Rating
1

Surface
Asphalt

92 Rail-Trails: **Pacific Northwest**

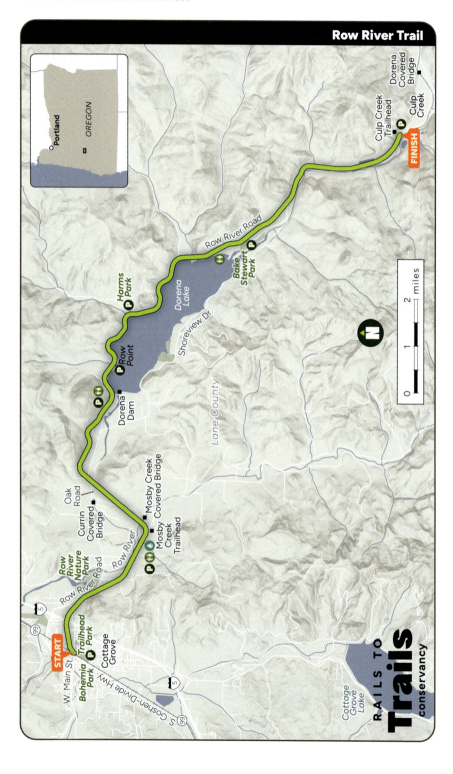

light manufacturing, such as the Cottage Grove Manufacturing Company. To this day, their windows and doors adorn houses and businesses around the trailhead. The O&SE was purchased by the Pacific & Eastern Railroad in 1914 and shortened to the 16.4 miles that now comprise the Row River Trail.

The trail begins at Cottage Grove's Trailhead Park; although there is no parking here, a large parking lot is available at Bohemia Park, 0.1 mile south of the trail's terminus. From the charming heart of Cottage Grove, the Row River Trail unfolds along a flat pathway, largely paralleling Mosby Creek Road, until it reaches the Mosby Creek Trailhead in 3.2 miles. The trail then begins a gentle ascent toward the serene waters of Dorena Lake. Just past the Mosby Creek Trailhead, the first covered bridge, the Mosby Creek Covered Bridge, becomes visible from the trail while passing over a trestle spanning the creek.

Roughly 4.5 miles into the trail, the eye-catching red-and-white Currin Covered Bridge is visible to the left when traversing the Row River. Accessible via a side road (Oak Road) branching off from the trail just before the crossing over the Row River, it presents an enticing opportunity for exploration.

Around 5 miles from Cottage Grove, the terrain begins a soft incline, with an average slope of 2%, reaching its zenith before mile 7. Here, the trail levels as it skirts along the eastern shore of Dorena Lake, offering captivating views of the waterscape from lakeside picnic tables and benches. There are trailheads at Dorena Dam, Row Point, Harms Park, and Bake Stewart Park along the lake. The trail continues past Bake Stewart Park about 4 miles to the endpoint at the Culp Creek Trailhead.

CONTACT: blm.gov/visit/row-river-trail

PARKING

Parking areas are listed from west to east. Select parking areas for the trail are listed below; for a detailed list of parking areas and other waypoints, consult **TrailLink™**. *Indicates that at least one accessible parking space is available.*

COTTAGE GROVE*: Bohemia Park, S. 10th St. and E. Adams Ave. (43.7955, -123.0581).

COTTAGE GROVE*: Mosby Creek Trailhead, Jenkins Road, 150 feet northwest of Layng Road (43.7775, -123.0073).

DORENA: Row Point, 35423 Row River Road (43.7887, -122.9442).

DORENA*: Harms Park, 36101 Row River Road (43.78267, -122.9236).

DORENA: Bake Stewart Park, 36898 Row River Road (43.7469, -122.8924).

CULP CREEK: Culp Creek Trailhead, 37811 Row River Road (43.7050, -122.8489).

94 Rail-Trails: **Pacific Northwest**

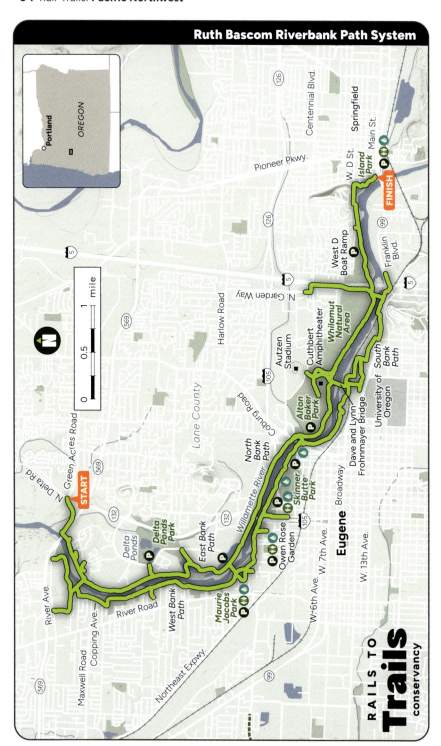

Ruth Bascom Riverbank Path System

23

Ruth Bascom, Eugene's forward-thinking mayor who served from 1993 to 1996, promoted the development of bicycle and pedestrian infrastructure to improve quality of life in the bike-centric city. This paved multiuse path that bears her name connects Eugene and Springfield, providing a nearly 20-mile scenic waterfront experience in the Southern Willamette Valley.

There are four seamlessly connected trail segments: the East Bank Path and the West Bank Path on the northern portion of the trail, and the North Bank Path and South Bank Path along the southeast portion. Five dedicated bike/pedestrian bridges connect these paths, giving trail users the ability to customize their routes and distances. Accessible from many neighborhoods, the riverbank path system serves as a launching point for numerous outdoor activities.

Beginning on the East Bank Path from the trail's northern end at North Delta Road and Green Acres Road, you'll arrive at Delta Ponds, a popular spot for bird-watching, in

This gem in the Southern Willamette Valley connects a handful of parks and natural areas.

County
Lane

Endpoints
N. Delta Road and Green Acres Road (Eugene); Island Park (Springfield)

Mileage
19.5

Type
Greenway/Non-Rail-Trail

Roughness Rating
1

Surface
Asphalt, Concrete

2.2 miles. In another 2.8 miles, you'll reach Alton Baker Park, a beautiful urban park adjacent to the University of Oregon. It's a perfect place for a picnic and outdoor recreation, including fishing, canoeing, and BMX, as well as outdoor concerts at the Cuthbert Amphitheater.

From there, the trail winds through the Whilamut Natural Area, an oasis with native plantings along the Willamette River, in 0.8 mile. Cross the river on the Dave and Lynn Frohnmayer Bridge and head northwest along the river's south bank to reach Skinner Butte Park in 1.6 miles. It offers views of downtown Eugene and the Willamette Valley, the Coburg Hills, and (in the distance) the Cascades. Rock climbing on the basalt columns defines Skinner Butte, which is also crisscrossed by miles of hiking trails. From the park, enjoy a pleasant, tree-lined route heading north along the western bank of the river back to your start.

There are several sections of the path system that require a short ride or walk off the trail along a road: On the far southeast portion of the North Bank Path, there is a short 0.2-mile section heading east along quiet West D Street in Springfield to Island Park. On the southeast portion of the South Bank Path, there is an on-road section along Garden Avenue and Riverfront Parkway, and at the north end of the West Bank Path, there is a 0.3-mile on-road ride along quiet Copping Avenue.

CONTACT: eugene-or.gov/324/park-and-trail-maps

PARKING

Parking areas are listed from north to south. Select parking areas for the trail are listed below; for a detailed list of parking areas and other waypoints, consult **TrailLink™**. *Indicates that at least one accessible parking space is available.*

EUGENE*: Delta Ponds Park, Goodpasture Island Road and Wimbledon Ct. (44.0823, -123.1115).

EUGENE*: Maurie Jacobs Park, Fir Lane and Lombard Lane (44.0655, -123.1151).

EUGENE*: Owen Rose Garden, 307 N. Jefferson St. (44.0624, -123.1018).

EUGENE*: Campbell Park, Cheshire Ave. and Skinner Butte Loop (44.0608, -123.0958).

EUGENE*: Skinner Butte Park, Skinner Butte Loop and W. Third Ave. (44.0580, -123.0923).

EUGENE*: Alton Baker Park, 413 Day Island Road (44.0560, -123.0804).

SPRINGFIELD: West D Boat Ramp, dead end of Aspen St. (44.0479, -123.0437).

SPRINGFIELD*: Island Park, W. B St. (44.0461, -123.0266).

Springwater Corridor

24

Hall of Fame

Stretching 21 miles from end to end, the popular Springwater Corridor runs south alongside the Willamette River in Portland before following Johnson Creek east. The trail winds through parks, wetlands, farmland, residential neighborhoods, and industrial areas. In 2011, it joined Rails to Trails Conservancy's Hall of Fame.

The trail is part of the regional 40 Mile Loop vision, inspired by John Charles Olmsted's 1903 plan for a network of parks connected by parkways. The trail provides connections to trails such as the Vera Katz Eastbank Esplanade (see page 105), the I-205 Multi-Use Path (see page 81), the Gresham-Fairview Trail, and the Trolley Trail (see page 101) in Milwaukie.

Before the trail existed, Springwater Corridor was occupied by the Springwater Division Line, ferrying passengers and produce into Portland from the east. The line opened in the early 1900s, ceased passenger service in 1958, and was acquired by the City of Portland in the 1990s to make way for the trail. Today, trail users can follow the same route the trains once plied, from Portland through Gresham and into Boring. Horseback riders can use the trail east of I-205.

As you ride east along the trail, the snowy peak of Mount Hood rises in the distance.

DANIELLE CASAVANT/COURTESY PORTLAND PARKS AND RECREATION

Counties
Clackamas, Multnomah

Endpoints
SE Fourth Ave. and SE Ivon St. (Portland); OR 212 and SE Richey Road (Boring)

Mileage
21

Type
Rail-Trail/Rail-with-Trail

Roughness Rating
1

Surface
Asphalt

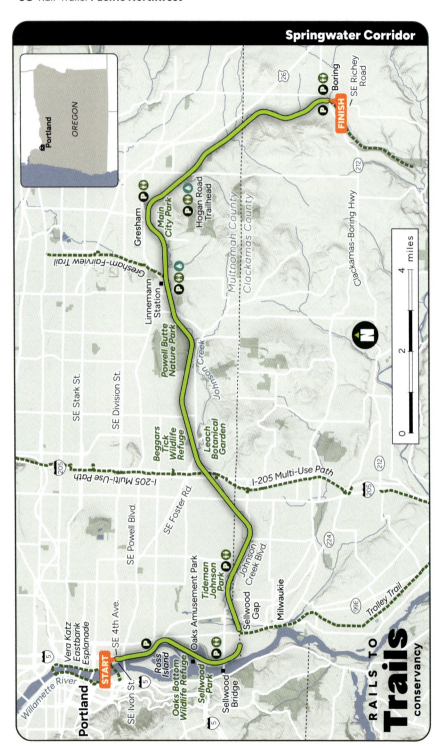

The westernmost segment of the trail sits on the banks of the Willamette River, just south of the Eastbank Esplanade. A gateway at Southeast Ivon Street and Southeast Fourth Avenue marks the start of the trail, which parallels an active railroad for over 3 miles. The urban industrial context quickly gives way to a vegetated corridor offering refreshing glimpses of the Willamette River and Ross Island through the trees and grassy meadows, as well as the ponds and wetlands of the Oaks Bottom Wildlife Refuge, a birding hot spot. If you are driving, there is parking available at Sellwood Park. Another highlight of this section is the Oaks Amusement Park.

South of the Sellwood Bridge, you will come to an on-road section, called the Sellwood Gap, between 13th and 19th Avenues. While there are plans to complete the trail in this section, you can navigate to the next segment of the trail by turning left on Southeast 13th Avenue, then taking a right on Southeast Linn Street in one block. Continue east on Southeast Linn Street 0.4 mile, where you will reconnect with the pathway. A succession of three bridges carries trail travelers over Johnson Creek, McLoughlin Boulevard, and the Union Pacific Railroad lines. Verdant shrubbery closely hems the trail in on both sides.

Located near mile 6, Tideman Johnson Park is another bird-watcher's paradise, boasting dozens of species, including bushtits, warblers, chickadees, owls, and woodpeckers. Even if you're not a birder, it's worth a detour into the park to explore the riparian woodland. A short boardwalk trail just off the main route takes you through the natural area.

East of Johnson Creek Boulevard, the trail crosses numerous streets and driveways, and while they are marked or signalized, it's always important to remain vigilant at crossings.

The trail continues, providing access to natural areas such as the 20-acre Beggars Tick Wildlife Refuge, a serene green haven in an industrial part of east Portland; the Leach Botanical Garden, with its aerial tree walk and pollinator garden; and the 612-acre Powell Butte Nature Park, with its maze of hiking, mountain biking, and equestrian trails wandering through meadows and mixed forests.

Linnemann Station at milepost 14 was one of the remaining stations on the Springwater Division Line, but the depot building burned down in 1995. The trailhead features a replica of the old depot, and interpretive signage offers historical photos and narratives. Just off the trail in Gresham is Main City Park, featuring a picturesque Japanese garden. As you head east, the snowy peak of Mount Hood rises in the background, creating a postcard-perfect scene.

Five more miles through rolling farmland gets you to the trail's conclusion in Boring. This easternmost stretch tends to have the least trail traffic. Despite the abundant plant life lining much of the Springwater Corridor, it's mostly exposed to the sun, so prepare accordingly and hydrate on your trip.

CONTACT: portland.gov/parks/springwater-corridor

PARKING

Parking areas are listed from west to east. *Indicates that at least one accessible parking space is available.*

PORTLAND*: Sellwood Riverfront Park, 1221 SE Oaks Park Way (45.4658, -122.6629).

PORTLAND*: Johnson Creek Blvd. Trailhead, SE Johnson Creek Blvd., 400 feet north of SE Brookside Dr. (45.4618, -122.6175).

GRESHAM*: Linnemann Station Park, 3804 Powell Loop (45.4885, -122.4698).

GRESHAM*: Main City Park, 219 S. Main Ave. (45.4955, -122.4315).

GRESHAM*: Hogan Road Trailhead, SE Hogan Road, 0.3 mile south of SE Palmquist Road (45.4822, -122.4142).

BORING*: Boring Station Trailhead Park, 28008 SE Dee St. (45.4316, -122.3748).

BORING: SE Wally Road, 200 feet west of OR 212 (45.4303, -122.3752); limited spaces.

Trolley Trail

25

The Trolley Trail is a nearly 7-mile multiuse path connecting Milwaukie and Gladstone in Clackamas County. It occupies the former corridor of the Portland Traction Company's Oregon City Line streetcar, which served the Portland suburbs of Milwaukie and Gladstone between 1893 and 1968. The rail-trail got underway in 2001 when Metro (a regional government agency serving portions of Clackamas, Multnomah, and Washington Counties) and the North Clackamas Parks & Recreation District acquired the right-of-way. The trail opened in 2012.

The Trolley Trail is part of a planned 20-mile loop connecting the Springwater Corridor (see page 97) and the I-205 Multi-Use Path (see page 81). At both ends of this trail, you'll be rewarded with scenic river views: the Willamette River at the north end and the Clackamas River at the south end.

The best place to begin your journey is Milwaukie Bay Park on the trail's north end. The 8.5-acre waterfront park provides parking, restrooms, and scenic river views, whetting your appetite for the rest of the journey. (The trail technically begins 1.3 miles farther north at Southeast 17th

A portion of the trail parallels the MAX light rail line and provides access to the SE Park Avenue station.

County
Clackamas

Endpoints
SE 17th Ave. and SE Ochoco St. (Milwaukie); Charles Ames Memorial Park at Portland Ave. and W. Clackamas Blvd. (Gladstone)

Mileage
6.9

Type
Rail-Trail

Roughness Rating
1

Surface
Asphalt, Concrete

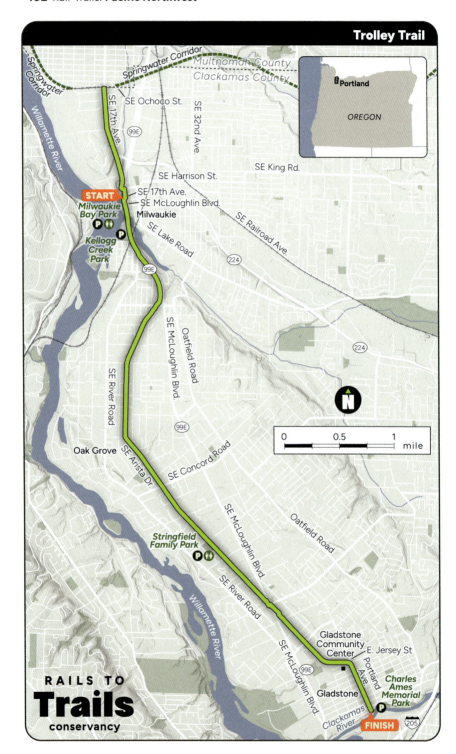

TRAIL 25 TROLLEY TRAIL **103**

Avenue and Southeast Ochoco Street, but there are no amenities there, so it's best to begin at the park. If you bike to the northernmost endpoint, you'll be able to connect to the Springwater Corridor at Southeast Ochoco Street.) There are other paths within the park, but the Trolley Trail is the one that runs adjacent to McLoughlin Boulevard, first as wide concrete pavement, then quickly transitioning to asphalt.

Not far from the park, the trail ducks under a railroad turned pedestrian bridge that connects across McLoughlin Boulevard to Kellogg Creek Park and the Kronberg Park Multiuse Trail. You'll soon encounter the first of many road crossings along this path. On busier streets, the crossings are signalized, whereas on quieter streets, stop signs and crosswalks suffice. The trail then parallels the MAX light rail line for about half a mile, providing bike and pedestrian access to the MAX station along Park Avenue. Ample signage provides wayfinding directions and keeps you abreast of your progress.

The rail-trail follows the route of the Oregon City Line streetcar, which once served Portland's suburbs of Milwaukie and Gladstone.

The trail continues within a vibrant green corridor, passing through residential neighborhoods boasting historic homes across various eras and trends. It is clearly a treasured community amenity; you will observe neighbors pouring onto the trail on their daily jogs, pushing strollers, or walking their dogs.

A 0.7-mile section of the route through downtown Oak Grove runs on-road along Southeast Arista Avenue, from Southeast Courtney Avenue almost to Southeast Creighton Avenue, but it is a low-speed street. In Oak Grove's commercial district, eateries tempt you off the trail. These establishments feature names that reflect both the area's railroad history and its present-day trail culture.

With 2.5 miles remaining, you will rejoin the off-street portion of the trail, which passes through residential areas and by Stringfield Family Park, which offers a playground and restrooms. In another 0.7 mile, the trail reaches Southeast McLoughlin Boulevard, where signage guides you safely across the major artery to continue on the route.

The trail portion ends adjacent to Gladstone Community Center, but you can continue the Trolley Trail route on-road by traveling southeast on Portland Avenue another 0.3 mile through downtown Gladstone, where you'll be able to reach eateries, shops, and ultimately the Charles Ames Memorial Park on the Clackamas River.

CONTACT: ncprd.com/parks/trolley-trail

PARKING

Parking areas are listed from north to south. *Indicates that at least one accessible parking space is available.*

MILWAUKIE*: Milwaukie Bay Park, 11211 SE McLoughlin Blvd. (45.4414, -122.6426).

OAK GROVE*: Stringfield Family Park, 3614 SE Naef Road (45.3993, -122.6251).

GLADSTONE: Charles Ames Memorial Park, Portland Ave. and W. Clackamas Blvd. (45.3778, -122.5926).

Vera Katz Eastbank Esplanade   26

Situated along the east bank of the Willamette River, the Vera Katz Eastbank Esplanade is a 1.5-mile trail featuring public art, native plants and wildlife, and iconic views of downtown Portland.

Although the trail begins at the intersection of Southeast Caruthers Street and Southeast Second Place, where a colorful mural adorns the street, you may prefer to start your journey at the parking lot adjacent to Portland Fire and Rescue Station 21 along Madison Avenue, under I-5. (To extend your trip, you can also connect to the Springwater Corridor, a Rails to Trails Conservancy Hall of Fame trail, just 0.5 mile farther south; see page 97.) The trail continues north to the Southeast Main Street access point with a water fountain and benches where you can stop and enjoy the native plants and shade trees that have helped restore the banks of the Willamette River and treat runoff from nearby I-5.

At Southeast Belmont Street, you can access a ramp up to the Morrison Bridge to cross the Willamette River.

County
Multnomah

Endpoints
SE Caruthers St. and SE Second Pl. (Portland); Steel Bridge, OR 99 W./Pacific Highway W., near N. Steel Bridge and N. Interstate Ave. (Portland)

Mileage
1.5

Type
Greenway/Non-Rail-Trail

Roughness Rating
1

Surface
Boardwalk, Concrete

106 Rail-Trails: **Pacific Northwest**

At the Southeast Belmont Street access point, trail users can access a ramp up to the Morrison Bridge or continue north along the trail to another rest area shaded with evergreens. In the spring and summer, this section of trail is populated with flowering plants native to the Pacific Northwest.

Several pieces of public art created by a group of local artists guide the trail north toward the Southeast Ash Street marker. These sculptures pay homage to Portland's rich industrial heritage and connection to the river.

At the Southeast Ash Street marker, the trail bears left to traverse under the Burnside Bridge via a ramp to the floating boardwalk that offers an opportunity to observe wildlife on the river. When the water level is low, the connection from the pathway to the floating boardwalk may be steep. Use caution and proceed slowly.

As the trail continues toward the Steel Bridge on dry land, it returns to higher ground and a concrete surface. From the terminus at the Steel Bridge, you can exit to nearby Peace Memorial Park or continue onto the bridge and cross the Willamette River to Waterfront Park on the western bank.

CONTACT: portland.gov/parks/eastbank-esplanade

PARKING

Parking is available near the southern terminus of the trail underneath I-5. *Indicates that at least one accessible parking space is available.*

PORTLAND*: 5 SE Madison St. (45.5131, -122.6682).

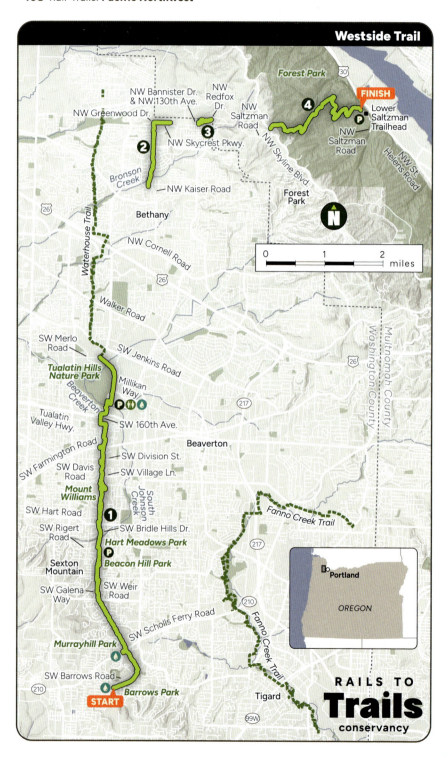

Westside Trail

27

The developing Westside Trail in Portland's western suburbs will one day be a 25-mile multiuse path between the Willamette River and the Tualatin River. Currently, the trail is open in four short, disconnected sections that weave through a Bonneville Power utility corridor and several Beaverton neighborhoods. It's perfect for those looking for challenging climbs and breathtaking descents.

SECTION 1

The southern and most significant segment of the trail spans 6.5 miles. Begin on its southern end at Beaverton's Barrows Park. Heading northeast, you will cross two low-volume roads before crossing Southwest Barrows Road at a signalized crossing. Here, the trail unites with the utility corridor that you'll follow for the duration of the trail. The first half mile along the park is accessible to all users before the trail begins a series of steep turns north of Southwest Barrows Road.

The trail ascends the first climb across Southwest Scholls Ferry Road toward Murrayhill Park and Sexton Mountain. This neighborhood park has a place to rest, refill water bottles, and even play tennis. A long series of switchbacks begins at this park as the trail continues toward Southwest Weir Road 2 miles into the trail. After crossing Southwest Galena

The trail largely follows a Bonneville Power utility corridor through several Beaverton neighborhoods.

Counties
Washington, Multnomah

Endpoints
Segment 1 (Beaverton): Barrows Park, Barrows Road; Merlo Road/158th Ave. Transit Station, Merlo Road
Segment 2 (Bethany): Kaiser Road, between Purvis Road and Banff Dr.; Skycrest Pkwy., north of Greenwood Dr. *Segment 3 (Bethany):* Bannister Dr. and 130th Ave.; Redfox Dr. and Ally Elizabeth Ct. *Segment 4 (Forest Park):* Dead end of Saltzman Road and Skyline Blvd.; Lower Saltzman Trailhead, dead end of Saltzman Road

Mileage
11.2

Type
Greenway/Non-Rail-Trail

Roughness Rating
1–3

Surface
Asphalt, Boardwalk, Gravel

Way, the first descent begins with a series of tight turns through native plants and wildflowers to Beacon Hill Park. Remember to share the trail on this popular neighborhood route.

As you approach Southwest Rigert Road, the trail continues through the corridor and past another tennis court. North of Hart Meadows Park, the trail connects with Summercrest Park Trail before crossing South Johnson Creek and Southwest Bridle Hills Drive. On the northern side of Southwest Hart Road, more switchbacks begin on the approach to Mount Williams. Through the shade of a wooded area, a series of quick turns lead to Southwest Davis Road, across which the descent continues past Southwest Village Lane and Southwest Division Street.

At Southwest Farmington Road, the trail turns left to allow a safe crossing at the signalized Southwest 160th Avenue intersection. In half a mile, the trail has a short on-road section. Follow Southwest Blanton Street west to Southwest 160th Avenue, where you will turn before crossing the road. The path continues north to Southwest Tualatin Valley Highway, across which the trail resumes. A short distance later at Millikan Way, the route follows the sidewalk for 0.1 mile.

Just after Beaverton Creek, the trail turns to the right toward Tualatin Hills Nature Park and continues 0.7 mile to Southwest Merlo Road after again intersecting with Southwest Millikan Way at the park entrance. Tualatin Hills Nature Park makes a natural stopping point for this section of the trail and is well equipped with amenities, including parking, restrooms, a nature center, and more walking paths.

SECTION 2

If you wish to continue, the trail resumes 5 miles north on Northwest Kaiser Road along the same utility corridor. Here, the 1.3-mile section begins with a boardwalk along the Bronson Creek wetlands. For approximately 1 mile, the trail ascends through prairie meadows toward the Rock Creek Trail. After a third residential road crossing at Northwest Wendy Lane, the trail joins Rock Creek Trail and turns right to its end just past Northwest Skycrest Parkway.

SECTION 3

Across a hilly residential neighborhood, a 0.4-mile section of the Westside Trail resumes at the intersection of Northwest Bannister Drive and Northwest 130th Avenue. A quick series of switchbacks carries visitors through another meadow that's full of wildflowers in spring and summer before this section of trail ends several yards past Northwest Redfox Drive.

SECTION 4

For the adventurous, a final section of the Westside Trail runs through Forest Park, beginning along the discontinued portion of Northwest Saltzman Road and traveling through the temperate forests for which the Pacific Northwest is known. With the rough terrain and steep switchbacks of this section, it's recommended only for mountain biking or hiking. Access the trail from Northwest

Skyline Boulevard. Note that there is no trailhead or parking at this west end of the trail segment; look for the brown FOREST PARK sign to find the entrance. Although the trail is not well marked, its wider width compared to the single-track trails in the park makes it relatively easy to follow. The 3-mile trail ends at the Lower Saltzman Trailhead, where parking is available along the road. From here, Northwest Saltzman Road takes a steep and narrow course to connect to US 30/Northwest St. Helens Road.

CONTACT: thprd.org/parks-and-trails/westside-trail

PARKING

Parking areas are located within Beaverton and are listed from south to north. Additional parking is available along residential streets throughout the trail. *Indicates that at least one accessible parking space is available.*

HART MEADOWS PARK: SW Rigert Road, between SW 160th Ave. and SW 159th Pl. (45.4602, -122.8411); on-street parking.

TUALATIN HILLS NATURE PARK*: 15655 SW Millikan Way (45.4978, -122.8389).

LOWER SALTZMAN TRAILHEAD: 6086 NW Saltzman Road (45.5664, -122.7534).

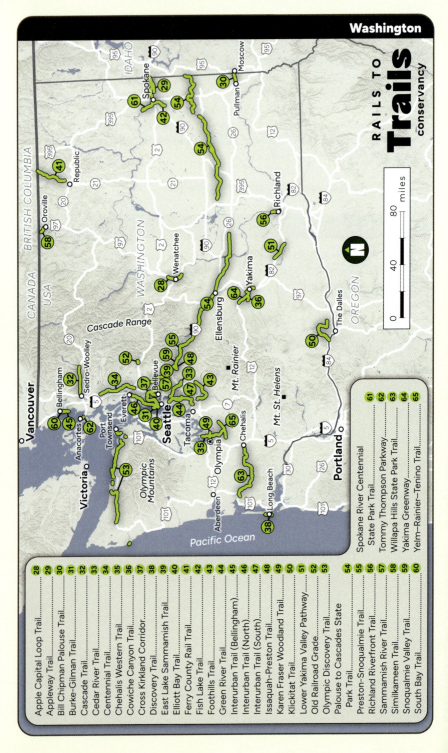

WASHINGTON

On the Preston-Snoqualmie Trail, a series of switchbacks climbs out of the Raging River ravine back to the railroad grade (*see page 219*).

GENE BISBEE

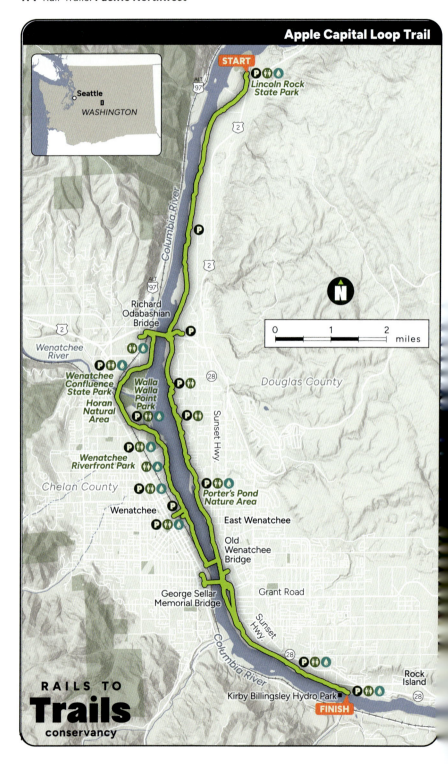

Apple Capital Loop Trail

28

Central Washington's Apple Capital Loop Trail offers scenic views of snowcapped mountains, shrub-steppe hillsides, lush orchards, and calm waters as it links parks, beaches, and playgrounds along the Columbia River in Wenatchee and East Wenatchee. The trail consists of a 10-mile loop encircling the Columbia River in Wenatchee and two lengthy spurs that head 5 miles north to Lincoln Rock State Park and 4 miles south to Kirby Billingsley Hydro Park. Additional short spurs bring the mileage total to 22 and provide connections to dining and shopping opportunities, including downtown Wenatchee.

The wide, paved trail is ADA accessible and perfect for all kinds of recreational activities, including cross-country skiing and snowshoeing in the winter. Several parks and trailheads offer restrooms, water fountains, and parking lots. There are also sheltered picnic areas, benches, bike racks, and pet waste stations placed along the trail. During the summer months, be sure to carry plenty of water and have sun protection as there is not much shade for long stretches.

Numerous informational panels also share information about the area's geological history, flora, and fauna. The trail

Counties
Chelan, Douglas

Endpoints
Lincoln Rock State Park, Lincoln Rock Park Road, 0.3 mile north of US 2 (East Wenatchee); Kirby Billingsley Hydro Park (East Wenatchee)

Mileage
22

Type
Greenway/Non-Rail-Trail

Roughness Rating
1

Surface
Asphalt, Concrete

The trail offers views of mountains, shrub-steppe hillsides, lush orchards, and the Columbia River.

traverses several different habitats, and there is a variety of wildlife to observe, including bald eagles and other birds of prey, yellow-bellied marmots, beavers, river otters, ducks, swans, loons, and swallowtail butterflies.

Start at Lincoln Rock State Park, which offers plenty of parking, restrooms, water fountains, a boat launch, a swimming area, sports facilities, picnic areas, and camping. (Note that a Discover Pass is required; day and annual passes are available for purchase online at **discoverpass.wa.gov**.) Heading south along the paved spur, the river is on your right, and orchards and shrub-steppe hillsides are on your left. Passing under the Richard Odabashian Bridge, the northern spur ends and you'll join the loop.

Crossing the Richard Odabashian Bridge via a protected bike/pedestrian lane takes you to the western bank of the river. Following the trail south along the western bank, the river will be on your left. The trail soon meanders through Wenatchee Confluence State Park, which offers parking, restrooms, water fountains, a boat launch, a swimming area, sports facilities, picnic areas, and camping. (A Discover Pass is required.) The trail crosses the Wenatchee River via a bike/pedestrian bridge and runs along the western edge of the Horan Natural Area, a wetland nature preserve. The trail very briefly passes through a somewhat industrial area before meandering through Walla Walla Point Park, which offers restrooms, picnic shelters, water fountains, a swimming area, sports facilities, and parking. Continuing south along the Columbia River, downtown Wenatchee is on your right and easily accessible from the trail. A switchback provides access to the bike/pedestrian Old Wenatchee Bridge, which crosses the river to form the southern part of the loop.

After crossing the river, you can head north to complete the loop or take the spur south to Kirby Billingsley Hydro Park. Heading north along the east bank of the river, the trail briefly parallels WA 28/Sunset Highway. Curving away from the highway and following the river, the trail passes through Porter's Pond Nature Area, which offers some shade along this mostly shade-free section. Heading north back toward the Richard Odabashian Bridge takes you along the bluffs with a few tight turns and 6% grades. A few short spurs lead to trailheads and offer connections to residential areas. At the Richard Odabashian Bridge, you've completed the loop.

Alternatively, from the Old Wenatchee Bridge on the east side of the river, you can head south along the spur to Kirby Billingsley Hydro Park. Several short spurs provide connections to East Wenatchee. A protected bike/pedestrian lane along the George Sellar Memorial Bridge crosses the river and offers another link to downtown Wenatchee on the west bank. The main spur continues south through Kirby Billingsley Hydro Park, which runs along the east bank of the river and has restrooms, water fountains, picnic shelters, a boat launch, a swimming area, sports facilities, and parking.

CONTACT: chelanpud.org/parks-and-recreation/our-parks/apple-capital-loop-trail

TRAIL 28 APPLE CAPITAL LOOP TRAIL

PARKING

Parking areas are listed from north to south. Select parking areas for the trail are listed below; for a detailed list of parking areas and other waypoints, consult **TrailLink™**. *Indicates that at least one accessible parking space is available.*

EAST WENATCHEE*: Lincoln Rock State Park, Lincoln Rock Park Road, 0.3 mile north of US 2 (47.5393, -120.2816); multiple parking lots; Discover Pass required (**discoverpass.wa.gov**).

EAST WENATCHEE*: 37th St. NW, 0.3 mile west of NW Cascade Ave. (47.4712, -120.3083).

WENATCHEE*: Wenatchee Confluence State Park, 333 Olds Station Road (47.4618, -120.3244); multiple parking lots; Discover Pass required (**discoverpass.wa.gov**).

WENATCHEE: 27th St. Trailhead, 27th St. NW, 600 feet west of NW Empire Ave. (47.4505, -120.3096).

WENATCHEE*: 19th St. Trailhead, 19th NW St., 700 feet east of NW Cascade Ave. (47.4341, -120.3017).

WENATCHEE*: Walla Walla Point Park, 1351 Walla Walla Ave. (47.4434, -120.3177); multiple parking lots.

WENATCHEE*: Wenatchee Riverfront Park, Riverside Dr. between E. Island View St. and Fifth St. (47.4336, -120.3135); multiple parking lots.

EAST WENATCHEE*: Kirby Billingsley Hydro Park, south of WA 28 (47.3834, -120.2483); multiple parking lots.

Appleway Trail

29

The Appleway Trail provides an important transportation route across Spokane Valley and into neighboring Liberty Lake following a former Chicago, Milwaukee, St. Paul, and Pacific Railroad (aka Milwaukee Road) right-of-way. The first segment of the corridor was built in 2015, and today the paved pathway spans 5.8 miles. Loosely paralleling and located just south of Sprague Avenue, a major thoroughfare, the trail provides access to commercial areas, neighborhoods, schools, Spokane Valley City Hall, and more.

On its western end, the trail begins at South Farr Road and East Appleway Boulevard. (Although there's no parking here, there are designated spaces for trail users 0.7 mile east, in the parking lot on the northeast corner of South University Road and East Appleway Boulevard.) As the trail closely follows East Appleway Boulevard through a suburban setting, it provides a useful commuter route but is not especially scenic in this section. Also be prepared for little shade along the trail.

At South University Road, East Appleway Boulevard ends. The trail continues on the east side of University, where you'll find a trailside bathroom and drinking fountain, as well

County
Spokane

Endpoints
S. Farr Road and E. Appleway Blvd. (Spokane Valley); E. Appleway Ave. and E. Broadway Ave. (Liberty Lake)

Mileage
5.8

Type
Rail-Trail

Roughness Rating
1

Surface
Asphalt

The Appleway Trail connects users with shops, recreational areas, and schools.

QUINTON BATTS

as a more parklike setting with trees occasionally lining the corridor. As the trail continues east, the surroundings become more residential.

In 2 miles, you'll reach a trailhead parking lot, restrooms, and a drinking fountain at South Best Road and East Second Avenue. The next trailhead with these facilities appears in another 1.8 miles at South Tschirley Road and Sprague Avenue, after which the trail becomes more utilitarian again, closely following East Appleway Avenue until trail's end in 1.3 miles at Ridgeline High School in Liberty Lake.

As of fall 2024, construction is underway to connect the trail to the Spokane Valley Library and adjacent Balfour Park (105 N. Balfour Road), located 0.2 mile north of the trail at its west end. Newly opened in 2024, the park includes a soccer field, an events plaza, restrooms, and parking.

CONTACT: spokanevalleywa.gov/585/appleway-trail

PARKING

Parking areas are located within Spokane Valley and are listed from west to east. *Indicates that at least one accessible parking space is available.*

BALFOUR PARK*: 105 N. Balfour Road (47.6580, -117.2659).

UNIVERSITY ROAD TRAIL ACCESS: S. University Road and E. Appleway Blvd. (47.6554, -117.2611); look for the designated Appleway Trail parking signs in the southwest corner of the lot.

BEST ROAD TRAIL ACCESS*: S. Best Road and E. Second Ave. (47.6554, -117.2125).

TSCHIRLEY ROAD TRAIL ACCESS*: S. Tschirley Road and Sprague Ave. (47.6569, -117.1689).

Bill Chipman Palouse Trail

30

The Bill Chipman Palouse Trail connects the college towns of Pullman, Washington (home of Washington State University), and Moscow, Idaho (home of the University of Idaho). The 7.1-mile paved trail crosses Paradise Creek a dozen times as it follows a relatively flat route through the picturesque hills of the fertile wheat-growing Palouse region.

Named in memory of Pullman businessman Bill Chipman, the 10-foot-wide trail follows the corridor of a railroad first built in 1885 by the Columbia & Palouse Railroad and later acquired by the Union Pacific Railroad. The railroad helped local farmers reach new markets for their crops and provided passenger service, especially for college sporting events between the local rivals. When the former Union Pacific and another railroad consolidated operations onto another railbed in 1996, the historic Union Pacific rail line became available for the long-awaited trail, which opened two years later.

In Pullman, the trail begins just across East Main Street from the sprawling university campus. Parking is available

The pathway provides a link between Washington State University and the University of Idaho.

Counties
Whitman (WA), Latah (ID)

Endpoints
SE Bishop Blvd., 0.1 mile south of E. Main St. (Pullman, WA); Perimeter Dr. and ID 8/W. Pullman Road (Moscow, ID)

Mileage
7.1

Type
Rail-Trail

Roughness Rating
1–2

Surface
Asphalt, Concrete

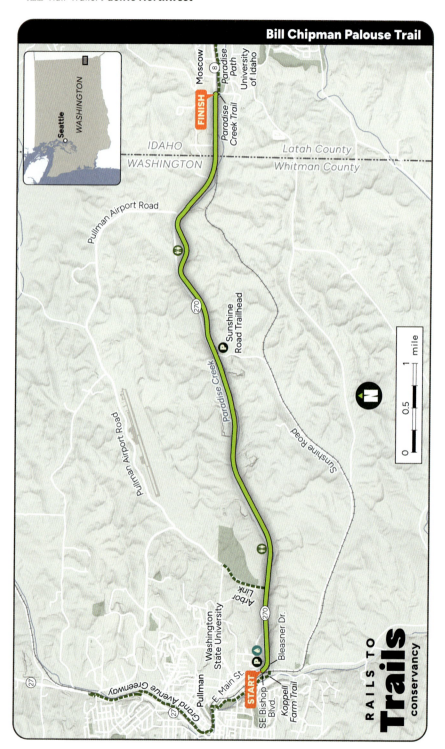

next to the trailhead at a lot shared with a motel. There are benches and an interpretive sign as you pass under an archway at the trailhead and begin a slight uphill grade east toward Moscow.

In about 300 feet you'll pass a pocket park with a drinking fountain; then in another 200 feet you'll make your first of 12 crossings of Paradise Creek. At a trail fork just past the bridge, a side trail heads right (south) for 300 feet to the Wil-Ru Trailhead on Bleasner Drive. Here you can connect with the Koppell Farm Trail, which heads west and north as part of the Pullman Loop Trail, or the "Loop." That trail and pathway system consists of nine trails that cover about 8 miles around the city.

The Bill Chipman Palouse Trail follows the creek and WA 270/ID 8 all the way to Moscow. The trail is buffered from the four-lane highway, although trail users will hear traffic noise. Also, there's not much shade in the central part of the trail.

Along the way, you might enjoy reading the frequent interpretive signs that describe the local history, plants, and animals. Benches are available for resting and bird-watching, and there are two restrooms and two emergency phones along the trail.

At 0.9 mile from the Washington trailhead, you'll pass a junction for the Arbor Link trail, which heads north and is another segment in the Loop trail system. At 3.8 miles, there's more parking at the Sunshine Road Trailhead.

Arriving in Moscow at Perimeter Drive/Farm Road, the trail meets the Paradise Creek Trail and Paradise Path and passes the north side of the college campus. It then connects to the Latah Trail (see page 251), which heads east into the countryside for another 16 miles on paved and gravel surfaces.

CONTACT: rtc.li/whitman-county

PARKING

Parking areas are located within Pullman and are listed from west to east. *Indicates that at least one accessible parking space is available.*

BILL CHIPMAN PALOUSE TRAILHEAD*: Parking lot shared with motel and office on SE Bishop Blvd., 0.2 mile south of E. Main St. (46.7213, -117.1639).

SUNSHINE TRAILHEAD*: Sunshine Road and WA 270/Moscow Pullman Road (46.7315, -117.0867).

124 Rail-Trails: Pacific Northwest

Burke-Gilman Trail

31

Seattle's Hall of Fame rail-trail is an active-transportation route with many different users vying for their piece of the 10- to 12-foot-wide trail as it passes through suburban and urban settings. The paved trail flows for about 20 miles, from the shady north shores of Lake Washington and through the University of Washington campus to busy commercial districts in the Fremont and Ballard neighborhoods to a sandy beach on Puget Sound.

Created in the 1970s, the Burke-Gilman Trail is one of the nation's oldest rail-trails and is part of several regional and nationwide trail networks. It's the westernmost segment of the 44-mile Locks to Lakes Corridor, which connects Puget Sound with the Cascade foothills via several paved trails. It is also part of the developing 900-mile Leafline Trail Network in the Central Puget Sound region and is a segment of the Great American Rail-Trail®, a 3,700-mile route connecting Washington, D.C., and Washington state.

The Burke-Gilman Trail follows the old corridor of the Seattle, Lake Shore and Eastern Railway, launched in the 1880s by prominent Seattle residents Thomas Burke and

County
King

Endpoints
Blyth Park, 16950 Riverside Dr. (Bothell); Shilshole Ave. NW and 17th Ave. NW; 24th Ave. NW and NW Market St.; Golden Gardens Park, Seaview Pl. NW and Seaview Ave. NW (Seattle)

Mileage
19.7

Type
Rail-Trail

Roughness Rating
1–2

Surface
Asphalt, Cement

In the Fremont neighborhood, the trail offers a spectacular view of Lake Union framed by the Aurora Bridge.

Daniel Gilman. The rail line was acquired by Northern Pacific Railroad in the 1890s and has become the basis for many regional rail-trails.

You can begin exploring the trail in the east at shady Blyth Park in Bothell, where the Burke-Gilman connects with the Sammamish River Trail (see page 225). It roughly follows WA 522 for 2.5 miles into Kenmore; there, it passes a seaplane base as well as picnic-friendly Log Boom Park on the north end of Lake Washington with views of perpetually snowcapped Mount Rainier.

The trail skirts the lake for 4.8 miles to Matthews Beach Park, a destination for sun worshippers in the summer and polar bear plungers on New Year's Day. This is one of the oldest trail sections, so watch for pavement lifted by tree roots. In 2 miles, you'll pass 350-acre Warren G. Magnuson Park, the second-largest park in Seattle and the site of a naval air base for much of the 20th century.

Veering inland, trail traffic increases in a mile at the U District, a busy commercial area and home to thousands of college students north of the University of Washington. Although a trail redesign through the campus makes a valiant attempt to separate walkers and bicyclists, there are several choke points where contact is unavoidable. On campus, you'll come to a pedestrian bridge above you. If you turn right off the trail onto the pathway just before this bridge, you'll reach the picturesque quad, with access to the light-rail station and Husky Stadium overlooking Lake Washington.

Back on the trail, you'll find a congested area of medical buildings, waterfront restaurants, marinas, and houseboats on the way to Gas Works Park, one of the most unique urban parks you can imagine. The 19-acre site features the rusting ruins of a coal gasification plant with arguably the best views of

The trail connects major destinations throughout Seattle, including the University of Washington.

downtown Seattle across Lake Union. Amenities include a large play barn and a hill for flying kites (access to the water is prohibited).

Leaving the park, the trail runs alongside the narrow Fremont Cut waterway, which connects Lake Union with Puget Sound. This is the Fremont neighborhood, home to a bizarre sculpture of a troll holding a Volkswagen Beetle under the Aurora Bridge, as well as many fine restaurants and quirky shops.

The infamous Burke-Gilman Missing Link trail gap emerges in the Ballard neighborhood, 2.7 miles past Gas Works Park. Finding a viable route through the next 0.7 mile that's agreeable to all stakeholders in this congested commercial zone has vexed politicians, city planners, bicycle advocates, and civic activists for years. Where the trail ends at 17th Avenue Northwest, users can take either Shilshole Avenue Northwest, Ballard Avenue Northwest, or Leary Avenue Northwest to the south side of Market Street at 24 Avenue Northwest, where the trail resumes as a cycle path.

Passing the National Nordic Museum in the Ballard retail and entertainment district, you'll arrive at the Hiram M. Chittenden Locks and Carl S. English Jr. Botanical Garden, where the U.S. Army Corps of Engineers raises and lowers boats navigating from the brackish Puget Sound to the inland freshwater lakes. Visitors can also watch annual salmon migrations in the summer months from an underwater viewing platform; see **ballardlocks.org/fish-salmon-ladder.html** for details.

The trail ends in 1.7 miles at Golden Gardens Park, where there is a wide sandy beach with views across Puget Sound to the Olympic Mountains. There's a playground, a bathhouse, and a couple of snack bars here as well.

CONTACT: rtc.li/burke-gilman and rtc.li/king-co-burke-gilman

PARKING

Parking areas are listed from east to west. *Indicates that at least one accessible parking space is available.*

BOTHELL*: Blyth Park, 16950 W. Riverside Dr. (47.7508, -122.2084).

BOTHELL: Wayne Park, 16721 96th Ave. NE (47.7497, -122.2135).

KENMORE*: Log Boom Park, 17415 61st Ave. NE (47.7576, -122.2634).

SEATTLE*: Matthews Beach Park, 5100 NE 93rd St. (47.6960, -122.2747).

SEATTLE*: Magnuson Park Frog Pond Park and Ride, 6520 NE 65th St. (47.6762, -122.2571).

SEATTLE*: Gas Works Park, 2101 N. Northlake Way (47.6467, -122.3347).

SEATTLE*: Ballard Locks (Hiram M. Chittenden Locks and Carl S. English Jr. Botanical Garden), 3015 NW 54th St. (47.6676, -122.3967).

SEATTLE*: Golden Gardens Park, 8498 Seaview Pl. NW (47.6887, -122.4029).

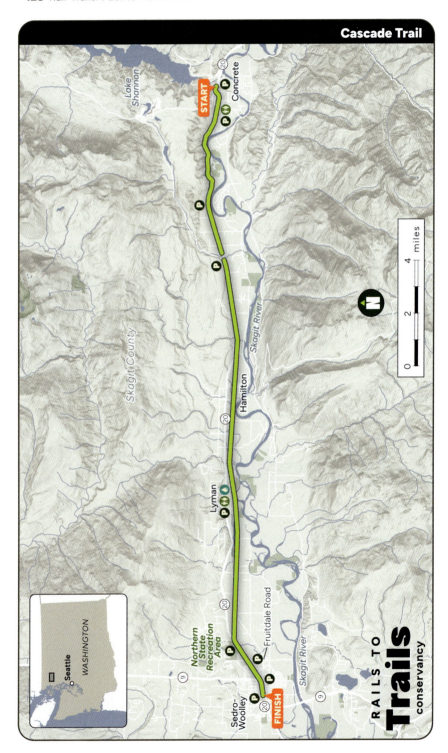

Cascade Trail

32

Northwest Washington's Cascade Trail connects the small town of Concrete with the larger Sedro-Woolley. Despite running parallel to WA 20, the trail follows the Skagit River through idyllic farmland and wilderness on a former Great Northern Railroad route that feels refreshingly remote.

Begin at the trail's eastern terminus in Concrete, located adjacent to the town's community center. There is ample accessible parking and a nearby historic district with restaurants and an ice-cream shop. As you undertake your nearly 23-mile journey, note that restrooms and water can be found near trailheads, but the so-called primitive multiuse trail is exactly that, with minimal wayfinding signage. While the scenery is stunning and views of Sauk Mountain and the Cascade Range are worth the trip, multiple barricades to prevent motorized vehicles from accessing the trail also make for tricky biking, requiring tight maneuvers through and around overgrown vegetation surrounding the barricades.

The trail is known to flood, and sections are currently washed out, with makeshift bridges keeping it usable. One section near Baker Lake Road detours around a blockage,

Although it parallels WA 20, the Cascade Trail offers a wilderness experience along the Skagit River.

County
Skagit

Endpoints
Dead end of Railroad Ave. (Concrete); Metcalf St. and Northern Ave. (Sedro-Woolley)

Mileage
22.9

Type
Rail-Trail

Roughness Rating
2

Surface
Concrete, Crushed Stone, Gravel

placing travelers onto the 12-inch-wide shoulder of a bridge on WA 20, adjacent to speeding traffic.

With several creek crossings, the Cascade Trail boasts a total of 23 trestles and two bridges made from repurposed railcars. Keep an eye out for elk, bison, red-winged blackbirds, and herons along the route.

At the western endpoint in Sedro-Woolley, you'll find a brief section of paved trail close to shops and eateries where you can refill your water and get something to eat.

CONTACT: rtc.li/skagit-county

PARKING

Parking areas are listed from east to west. Select parking areas for the trail are listed below; for a detailed list of parking areas and other waypoints, consult **TrailLink™**. *Indicates that at least one accessible parking space is available.*

CONCRETE*: Concrete Community Center, 45821 Railroad Ave. (48.5384, -121.7479).

CONCRETE: Baker Lake Road, 150 feet north of N. Cascades Hwy./WA 20 (48.5326, -121.8868).

LYMAN: Lyman City Park, W. Main St. and Cunningham Ave. (48.5270, -122.0686).

SEDRO-WOOLLEY: N. Cascades Hwy./WA 20, dead end of Helmick Road (48.5228, -122.1952).

SEDRO-WOOLLEY*: Moore St./N. Cascades Hwy./WA 20 and Fruitdale Road (48.5155, -122.2110).

SEDRO-WOOLLEY: Polte Road and Coffman Lane (48.5089, -122.2243).

SEDRO-WOOLLEY: Metcalf St. and Northern Ave. (48.5064, -122.2385).

Cedar River Trail

33

The Cedar River Trail follows the old Chicago, Milwaukee, St. Paul and Pacific Railroad corridor on a flat route from Lake Washington to the semirural countryside of Maple Valley. The first 12.3 miles are paved, and the remaining 5.1 miles consist of a packed-gravel surface.

Beginning on the trail's northern end at Cedar River Trail Park along the southern shore of Lake Washington, the trail rolls upstream along the fast-flowing Cedar River through the Seattle suburb of Renton. Bicyclists are not allowed on the first 0.6 mile of trail but may ride on paralleling Nishiwaki Lane. Be aware of the trail's 10 mph bicycle speed limit within Renton city limits, with steep fines for rule breakers. Additionally, trail users on foot and wheels must stay on their side of the yellow line. Although equestrian use is restricted within Renton, it's permitted on the rest of the trail.

Leaving downtown Renton, the trail passes under I-405 and enters an open field that housed brick and conduit maker Denny-Renton Clay & Coal Co. a century ago. All that remains today are scattered bricks in the blackberry thickets. After passing the Cedar River Dog Park, the trail winds along the river to Renton's 11-acre Riverview Park. Riverbank

Following the Cedar River, the pathway takes a southeastern course from Lake Washington to Maple Valley.

County
King

Endpoints
Cedar River Trail Park at Lake Washington (Renton); Landsburg Park at Landsburg Road SE and SE 252nd Pl. (Maple Valley)

Mileage
17.4

Type
Rail-Trail

Roughness Rating
1–2

Surface
Asphalt, Gravel

erosion has narrowed the trail to one lane, and bicyclists must yield to pedestrians. Roughly 3 miles from Cedar River Trail Park is the Cedar River Trestle Bridge, repaired in 2021 to maintain its long-term structural integrity, stabilize the riverbank, and ensure the continued safety of trail users.

After passing through Riverview Park, a golf course, Ron Regis Park, and Renton city limits, the trail becomes sandwiched between the scenic Cedar River and busy WA 169. (Those who prefer a shorter out-and-back journey may wish to start at the eastern endpoint and turn back before the trail crosses WA 18.) The river meanders through the valley and washes against high, sandy bluffs. In the fall, you'll witness a colorful spectacle as hundreds of salmon—sockeye, wild king (Chinook), and wild coho varieties—head up the river to spawn. The bright-red fish are easily seen from trestles or the scattered, county-owned natural areas that dot the river's edge. One such natural area, Cavanaugh Pond, is a year-round destination for spotting waterfowl.

The unpaved southern end of the Cedar River Trail winds through a forested corridor.

At Fred V. Habenicht Rotary Park, the trail intersects the northern endpoint of the 3.5-mile Green-to-Cedar Rivers Trail, which heads to Maple Valley's secluded Wilderness Lake and the 42-acre Lake Wilderness Arboretum. The park also marks the start of the soft-surface portion of the Cedar River Trail, which winds through groves of Douglas-fir, western red cedar, big-leaf maple, and alder to the trail's southeastern terminus at Landsburg Park.

The Cedar River Trail is part of the Leafline Trails Coalition network connecting trails across the central Puget Sound region. The northernmost portion of the trail is part of the developing Lake to Sound Trail, which will connect Lake Washington and the Puget Sound.

CONTACT: rtc.li/cedar-river and rtc.li/renton

PARKING

Parking areas are listed from north to south. *Indicates that at least one accessible parking space is available.*

RENTON*: Cedar River Trail Park, Nishiwaki Lane and Lake Washington (47.4996, -122.2147); parking spots here have a 4-hour limit.

RENTON*: Playground at Cedar River, 901 Nishiwaki Lane (47.4952, -122.2131).

RENTON: 405 Cedar River Trail Walk, south of Liberty Park (47.4803, -122.1996); gravel lot.

RENTON*: Riverview Park, 3201 Maple Valley Hwy. (47.4773, -122.1807).

RENTON: Maplewood Roadside Park, 3225 SE Seventh St. (47.4753, -122.1764).

RENTON*: Ron Regis Park, Renton–Maple Valley Road/WA 169 and 149th Ave. SE (47.4671, -122.1460).

MAPLE VALLEY: Cedar River Trailhead, Renton–Maple Valley Road/WA 169, between SE 214th St. and SE 216th Pl. (47.4094, -122.0385).

MAPLE VALLEY: Fred V. Habenicht Rotary Park, 22124 Witte Road SE (47.4044, -122.0403).

MAPLE VALLEY: Landsburg Park, 25188 Landsburg Road SE (47.3753, -121.9714).

Centennial Trail

34

Built upon the former Burlington Northern Railroad line, the Centennial Trail is a bright spot among Washington's exceptional trails. Construction began in 1989 during the state's centennial. From the northern endpoint near the border of Skagit County, where the trail weaves in and out of farms, pastures, and forested watersheds, to the bustle of small towns and the more urban experience of its southern endpoint in Snohomish, it offers a glimpse into the culture and heritage of the Puget Sound region. Two active volcanoes can also be spotted along the route: To the north is Mount Baker, which most recently erupted in 1843, and to the south is Glacier Peak, which last had a massive eruption more than 13,000 years ago. Note that black bears have also been spotted.

While there are many entry points to this popular trail that serves more than 500,000 people each year, it is recommended that an end-to-end trip begin at the trail's northernmost point, the Nakashima Heritage Barn North Trailhead, which offers plenty of parking for vehicles and horse trailers. The trailhead is anchored by the Nakashima Heritage Barn, built in 1908 and included in the Washington Heritage Barn Register. In 2012, the trailhead was dedicated to the Nakashima family, who worked the land for more

At Lake Cassidy, take a walk out onto the pier to look for wetland wildlife or to go fishing.

County
Snohomish

Endpoints
Nakashima Heritage Barn North Trailhead, 32325 WA 9 (Arlington); First St., between Maple Ave. and Willow Ave. (Snohomish)

Mileage
30.6

Type
Rail-Trail

Roughness Rating
1

Surface
Asphalt

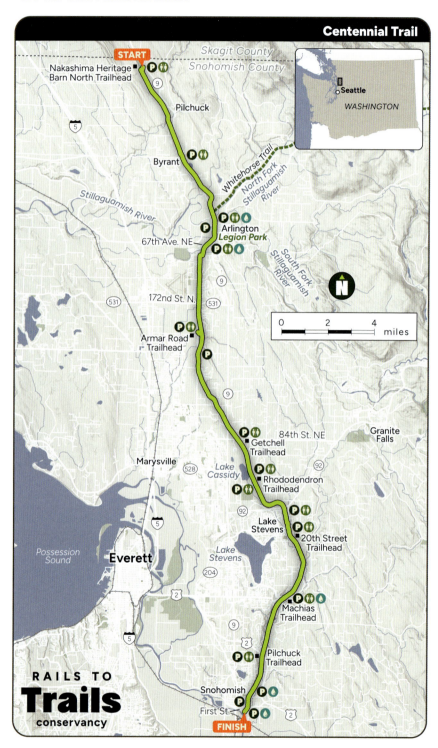

This trailside barn is dedicated to the Nakashima farming family, who were forced out during 1942's Japanese internment.

than 30 years before being forced out during the Japanese internment in 1942. The Nakashima Farm is the only dairy farm in Snohomish County to have been owned by Asian Pacific Americans and was among the earliest farms in Snohomish County.

Where the trail intersects with the Whitehorse Trail heading east to Darrington, a gleaming arch marks the junction—the perfect spot for a rest and a photo op before crossing the bridge that spans the churning confluence of the North and South Forks of the Stillaguamish River and that connects Arlington and former Haller City (which was absorbed by Arlington in the early 1900s). These two towns were rivals in pursuit of the depot that would serve the Seattle, Lake Shore and Eastern Railroad, which was being built to connect to Canada. Arlington was successful in its pursuit, and at the height of the town's railroad era it served local and international mail, freight, and passenger service trains multiple times a day. Passenger rail service ended in the 1940s, and the depot was closed in 1974. Now the town celebrates that heritage at Legion Park, through which the trail passes; the historic depot now houses restrooms. Heading out of Arlington and Legion Park, public art installations add to the experience.

On the outskirts of Arlington, the trail runs adjacent to busy 67th Avenue Northeast through a light industrial zone. At the intersection of 67th Avenue

Northeast and 172nd Street North/WA 531, trailside housing and retail developments illustrate the impact of this amenity on the community.

On the southern half of the trail, the terrain becomes more hilly, treating users to viewpoints of the Olympic Mountains to the west. The trail continues past Lake Cassidy into the former lumber mill town of Lake Stevens and, approximately 3 miles south of the 20th Street Trailhead in Lake Stevens, you'll reach the Machias Trailhead, which features a replica of the Machias Station railroad depot, built in the late 1890s. Between Machias Station and the endpoint in Snohomish, the Pilchuck Trailhead offers another access point to the trail approximately 3.6 miles south.

The trail's southern endpoint in Snohomish offers the perfect place for a relaxing lunch or an overnight stay where you can take in the antiques stores and other shopping along First Street.

CONTACT: rtc.li/centennial-trail

PARKING

Parking areas are listed from north to south. Select parking areas for the trail are listed below; for a detailed list of parking areas and other waypoints, consult **TrailLink™**. *Indicates that at least one accessible parking space is available.*

ARLINGTON*: Nakashima Heritage Barn North Trailhead, 32325 WA 9 (48.2911, -122.1973); horse trailer parking available.

ARLINGTON*: Bryant Trailhead, WA 9 and 53rd Ave. NE (48.2393, -122.1588).

ARLINGTON*: Armar Road Trailhead, 15333 67th Ave. NE (48.1350, -122.1405).

LAKE STEVENS*: Getchell Trailhead, 8318 Westlund Road (48.0717, -122.1008).

LAKE STEVENS: Rhododendron Trailhead, 10911 54th Pl. NE (48.0455, -122.0836).

LAKE STEVENS*: WA 92 Trailhead, 3651 127th Ave. NE (48.0309, -122.0588).

LAKE STEVENS: 20th St. Trailhead, 20th St. NE and N. Machias Road (48.01659, -122.05273).

SNOHOMISH*: Machias Trailhead, 1624 Virginia St. (47.9814, -122.0488); restroom available.

SNOHOMISH*: Pilchuck Trailhead, S. Machias Road, 0.1 mile northeast of Old Machias Road (47.9416, -122.0760).

SNOHOMISH*: Snohomish Skate Park, Second St. and Lincoln Ave. (47.9135, -122.0873).

Chehalis Western Trail

35

Beginning in the 1920s, the Weyerhaeuser Timber Co. harvested and shipped timber by rail from the vast forests south of Puget Sound to float along the waterway to mills in Everett. Today, you can log miles along the scenic Chehalis Western Trail, built along the same rail corridor.

From the north, the trail begins at the Woodard Bay Natural Resources Conservation Area, a wildlife sanctuary with a rich cultural history. It provides nesting habitat for hundreds of great blue herons and double-crested cormorants and protects forests, wetlands, and shoreline along Puget Sound. Its dense second-growth forest presents a shaded natural area for beginning your southward journey.

The tree-lined pathway makes its way through fields, farmland, and wetlands on its way to the community of South Bay. Be aware that the trail crosses many roadways, so be cautious as you approach these intersections. As the trail approaches the cities of Olympia and Lacey, trailside neighborhoods become more dense, with several new developments providing access points to the trail. Seemingly at once, the trees give way to an urban environment as the trail crosses over busy I-5.

County
Thurston

Endpoints
Woodard Bay Natural Resources Conservation Area (Olympia); Yelm–Rainier–Tenino Trail between Turner Road SE and Waddell Road SE (Rainier)

Mileage
21.2

Type
Rail-Trail/
Rail-with-Trail

Roughness Rating
1

Surface
Asphalt

A conservation area on the trail's northern end provides a nesting habitat for great blue herons and cormorants.

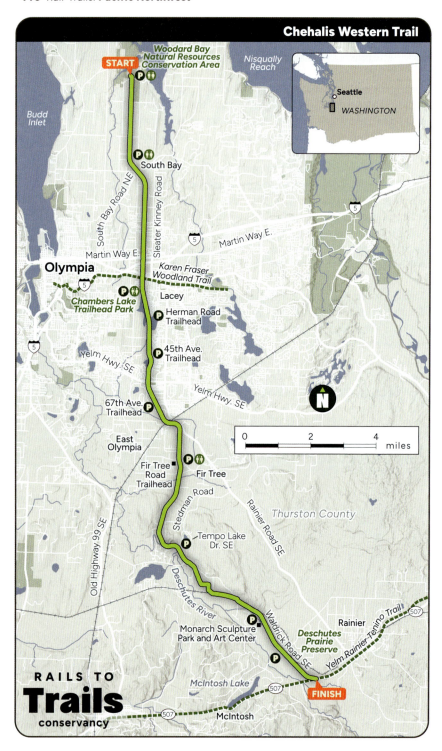

TRAIL 35 CHEHALIS WESTERN TRAIL

Just south of the interstate, you're greeted by a map and informational sign as the trail intersects the Karen Fraser Woodland Trail (see page 191), running east–west at the roundabout. From here, the trees return to line the trail as it continues south. Soon after the roundabout is Chambers Lake Trailhead Park, offering limited shoreline access and a boat launch for anyone interested in fishing for channel catfish, largemouth bass, and yellow perch.

After leaving the Olympia–Lacey area, the trail once again becomes rural and quiet, winding through forests and the occasional open field. The trail soon parallels the Deschutes River. Mile marker 15, at the corner of Stedman Road and Tempo Lake Drive Southeast, is an ideal spot for river access. At Waldrick Road SE, the trail veers left and parallels the active Rainer Rail line several miles.

Toward the end of the trail, you'll come across the Monarch Sculpture Park and Art Center and the Deschutes Prairie Preserve. Open from dawn to dusk, the sculpture park welcomes visitors with free walk-in and bike-in access to its gardens, which are lined with whimsical sculptures. The 142-acre Deschutes Prairie Preserve protects vital habitat and the wildlife that depends on it along the Deschutes River.

The trail comes to an end at the intersection of the Yelm–Rainier–Tenino Trail (see page 255), which provides a way to extend your journey to the east or

On its southern end, the trail shares the corridor with active railroad tracks.

west. Equestrian use is permitted for the first 2.9 miles of the Chehalis Western Trail—from its northern endpoint to the trail's intersection with South Bay Road Northeast—and for another 9.1 miles from the Fir Tree Road Trailhead to the southern terminus. Equestrians are encouraged to use side paths that parallel the main paved pathway.

CONTACT: rtc.li/thurston-county-trails

PARKING

Parking areas are listed from north to south. Select parking areas for the trail are listed below. For a detailed list of parking areas and other waypoints, consult **TrailLink.com™**. *Indicates that at least one accessible parking space is available.*

OLYMPIA*: Woodard Bay Natural Resources Conservation Area Parking Lot, Woodard Bay Road NE (47.1239,-122.8508).

OLYMPIA*: 3311 41st Ave. NE (47.0914, -122.8504).

OLYMPIA*: Chambers Lake Trailhead Park, 3725 14th Ave. SE (47.0336, -122.8397).

OLYMPIA: Chambers Lake Dr. Trailhead, 4103 Chambers Lake Dr. SE (47.0239, -122.8339).

OLYMPIA: Herman Road Trailhead, Herman Road SE, 0.2 mile west of Meadow Lake St. SE (47.0143, -122.8336); street parking.

LACEY*: 45th Ave. Trailhead, 45th Ave. SE, 0.1 mile west of Avonlea Dr. SE (47.0068, -122.8328).

OLYMPIA*: 67th Ave. Trailhead, 67th Ave. SE and Milano Court SE (46.9869, -122.8276).

OLYMPIA*: Fir Tree Road Trailhead, Fir Tree Road SE, 300 feet west of Summerwood Dr. SE (46.9640, -122.8129).

OLYMPIA: Stedman Road SE at Tempo Lake Dr. SE, 0.5 mile north of Waldrick Road SE (46.9275, -122.8116).

TENINO: Monarch Sculpture Park and Art Center, 8431 Waldrick Road SE (46.9016, -122.7602).

Cowiche Canyon Trail

36

Six miles from downtown Yakima, this wide gravel pathway runs along a former railroad bed as it follows Cowiche Creek (pronounced "cow-ee-chee") through the Cowiche Canyon. As you travel along the trail, keep an eye out for the numerous birds, mammals, and aquatic species that make the canyon their home, including beavers, yellow-bellied marmots, and Lucia's Blue butterflies.

Fourteen million years ago, flowing lava formed the canyon floor and south wall, while geological events 1 million years ago created the north wall, resulting in a stark contrast between the lush vegetation along the creek, the hillsides of sagebrush, and the towering basalt and rugged cliffs that make up the trail's surroundings. There are even some natural rock formations known as the Easter Island Faces because of their startling resemblance to the famous statues.

Winding along the canyon floor, the trail follows an old rail line built in 1913 by the North Yakima & Valley Railway to transport fruit between Yakima, Tieton, and Cowiche. Today, the trail offers a scenic adventure for hikers, runners, mountain bikers, cross-country skiers, and wildlife observers. Horseback riding is also permitted along the entire trail;

County
Yakima

Endpoints
Cowiche Canyon West Trailhead, 0.2 mile southeast of N. Weikel Road (Yakima); Cowiche Canyon Road, 2.2 miles west of W. Powerhouse Road (Yakima)

Mileage
2.9

Type
Rail-Trail

Roughness Rating
2

Surface
Boardwalk, Dirt, Gravel

You'll encounter nine boardwalk bridges that cross Cowiche Creek.

EILEEN SYMONS

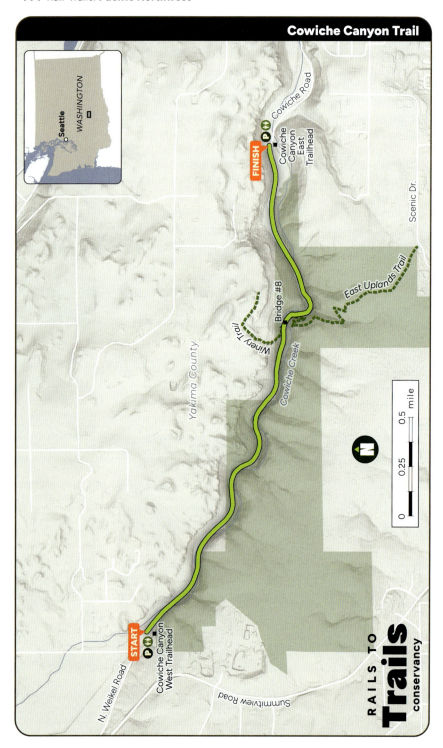

equestrians should use the western trailhead as its large gravel lot offers plentiful space for horse trailers.

Starting at the Cowiche Canyon West Trailhead off Weikel Road, the 2.9-mile rail-trail meanders through the canyon before ending at the Cowiche Canyon East Trailhead on Cowiche Road. The majority of the route is fairly flat and wide, with a few narrower portions where vegetation or the canyon walls more closely hug the trail. Along the way, you will encounter nine boardwalk bridges that cross over the creek. Be aware that most of the bridges do not have railings. Abundant trail signage includes informational panels about the area's geological history, flora, and fauna.

The Cowiche Canyon Trail is part of a larger trail system managed by the Cowiche Canyon Conservancy, which owns and maintains several recreational areas in the Yakima Valley region. From the rail-trail, you can connect to several steeper routes that explore more of the canyon. East of the eighth bridge, the East Uplands Trail heads up the south hillside and crosses the Cowiche Canyon Uplands. The 1.1-mile trail crosses the plateau and ends at another canyon access point with parking. Just west of the same bridge, the steep 0.8-mile Winery Trail leads to a dog-friendly winery and vineyard with splendid views of Mount Adams.

CONTACT: cowichecanyon.org

PARKING

Parking areas are located within Yakima and are listed from west to east.
Indicates that at least one accessible parking space is available.

COWICHE CANYON WEST TRAILHEAD: 0.2 mile southeast of N. Weikel Road (0.5 mile southeast of Summitview Road) (46.6315, -120.6658).

COWICHE CANYON EAST TRAILHEAD: Cowiche Canyon Road, 2.2 miles west of W. Powerhouse Road (46.6221, -120.6147).

Cross Kirkland Corridor

37

The Cross Kirkland Corridor is the bustling centerpiece of a former railbed that once carried freight and passengers through towns now in the eastern suburbs of Seattle. Just 5.8 miles long, the level, crushed-limestone trail links destinations in the lakeside city of Kirkland while connecting to other trails heading east and south for regionwide commuting or recreation. It's a segment of the Leafline Trail Network, which will eventually connect 900 trail miles in the central Puget Sound region.

The rail corridor started out as the Lake Washington Belt Line in the 1890s, hauling lumber and shingles. The line was acquired by the Northern Pacific Railroad in 1901 and completed operations as BNSF Railway in 2009, when the 42-mile line was sold.

Kirkland snatched up its share of the corridor, removed the rails, and spread a crushed-limestone surface. Most of the trail opened in 2015, although the final gap in a dense commercial district wasn't finished until 2023. Other sections of the BNSF Railway corridor to the north and south, known as Eastrail, are in various stages of completion.

County
King

Endpoints
Eastrail at 108th Ave. NE, 0.1 mile northeast of NE 37th Ct. (Bellevue); Eastrail at 132nd Ave. NE/Slater Ave. NE, 450 feet north of NE 124th St. (Kirkland)

Mileage
5.8

Type
Rail-Trail

Roughness Rating
1

Surface
Concrete, Crushed Stone

A shelter and railroad display created by Kirkland Rotary stand at a former depot site.

GENE BISBEE

To start, the nearby South Kirkland Park and Ride offers parking as well as service from bike rack–equipped buses. A 0.1-mile climb up 108th Ave. NE takes you to the Cross Kirkland Corridor on the left. You can catch close-by glimpses of Lake Washington (the ancestral home of several Coast Salish tribes), the Seattle skyline, and the Olympic Mountains far to the west, especially in the wintertime when the leaves have fallen.

In 1.6 miles, you'll pass Terrace Park, accessible down a stairway to your left. You'll probably notice that many neighborhoods connect to the trail. Homes and businesses are largely hidden by wildflowers, trees, and bushes; much of the vegetation is native and maintained by volunteers.

Feriton Spur Park emerges in 0.2 mile and continues alongside a paved section of trail for nearly a 0.5 mile through the Google campus. The park features basketball and pickleball courts, a sandy volleyball court, a zip line, a year-round garden, and a taproom and ice-cream parlor housed in a refurbished caboose. At the far end are an amphitheater, restrooms, and a drinking fountain.

About 0.4 mile past the park, a short section of rails and a vintage semaphore (signaling apparatus) mark the Kirkland Rotary's pavilion at the site of the former depot, which provided regular passenger service until 1922. This is also

A pedestrian overpass at Totem Lake allows for easy passage through this busy commercial center.

the location where, in 1942, Japanese Americans were ordered to gather for relocation by train to internment camps during World War II.

In a mile, you'll meet a sculpture of a frog clamoring over the fence. A trail on the left uses a stairway to climb a hill to Crestwoods Park, which has restrooms and a drinking fountain.

About 0.7 mile past the "frog crossing," you'll pass warehouses and businesses at the south end of the Totem Lake commercial area. Finding a way through here was difficult until the 2023 completion of the elevated Totem Lake pedestrian bridge that spans two major roads. The trail passes a lake and marsh that are home to birds and beavers and then ends in 0.3 mile at Slater Avenue.

From Slater Avenue, the former BNSF railbed heads east as Eastrail (**eastrail .org/trail-map**) for another 3 miles to Woodinville, or 4.4 miles southeast as the Redmond Central Connector. From the Cross Kirkland Corridor's southern endpoint, Eastrail heads south 2.3 miles, passing the Bellevue light-rail station and ending at Northeast Fourth Street. Plans are underway to extend Eastrail farther south, across the towering 1,000-foot-long Wilburton Trestle, to join the currently open 4.2-mile segment that runs from southern Bellevue to Renton along Lake Washington.

CONTACT: rtc.li/cross-kirkland-corridor

PARKING

Parking areas are located within Kirkland and are listed from south to north. *Indicates that at least one accessible parking space is available.*

SOUTH KIRKLAND PARK AND RIDE*: 3677 108th Ave. NE (47.6441, -122.1965).

TERRACE PARK: 10333 NE 67th St. (47.6656, -122.2011); trail accessible by stairway.

CENTRAL HOUGHTON*: 6711 106th Ave. NE (47.6661, -122.1994); behind Houghton Court Apartments.

FERITON SPUR PARK*: 604 Fifth Pl. S. (47.6713, -122.1977).

KIRKLAND ROTARY CENTRAL STATION: 1 Railroad Ave. (47.6753, -122.1922).

110TH AVE. NE*: 100 feet south of NE 96th St. (47.6861, -122.1934).

CRESTWOODS PARK*: 1818 Sixth St. (47.6900, -122.1972); parking lot contains accessible parking spaces; however, the trail is not wheelchair accessible due to a steep stairway.

TOTEM LAKE PARK*: 12031 Totem Lake Way (47.71161, -122.1782).

128TH LANE NE: 0.1 mile north of NE 124th St. (47.7121, -122.1697).

150 Rail-Trails: **Pacific Northwest**

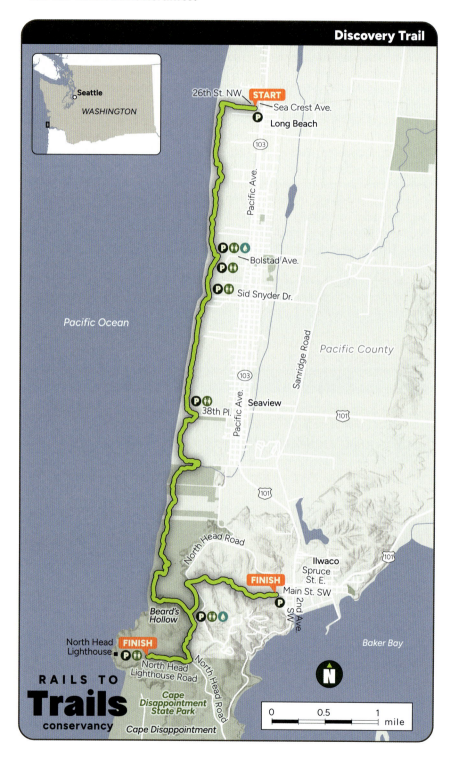

Discovery Trail

38

If you're seeking to explore the spectacular and varied landscapes of the coastal Pacific Northwest, look no further than Southwest Washington's Discovery Trail. It follows portions of the route traveled by the Lewis and Clark Corps of Discovery as they encountered the Pacific Ocean and set up camp before heading south across the Columbia River.

A north–south journey begins in Long Beach at a parking lot near the end of 26th Street Northwest. Just down the pathway, you'll come across a realistic-looking bronze replica of a 20-foot tree where William Clark carved his name and the date of his expedition's arrival in 1805.

As you head down the meandering trail, be on the lookout for additional sculptures and monuments dedicated to the area's wildlife and the Corps of Discovery, including a basalt monolith, a bronze sturgeon sculpture, and the remains of a gray whale skeleton.

The trail pleasantly winds through rolling coastal dunes, with several points along the way to access the beach just off to the west. Past a pavilion and parking lot on Bolstad

County
Pacific

Endpoints
26th St. NW, west of Sea Crest Ave. (Long Beach); North Head Lighthouse Road, 0.4 mile west of North Head Road (Ilwaco); Main St. SW and Second Ave. SW/WA 100 (Ilwaco)

Mileage
8.3

Type
Greenway/ Non-Rail-Trail

Roughness Rating
1–2

Surface
Asphalt, Gravel

JOE LACROIX

On its southern end, the trail becomes hillier and more forested as it heads into Cape Disappointment State Park.

Avenue, the trail parallels an impressive boardwalk. Watch your speed (and your head) as you pass under the boardwalk around its halfway point. The boardwalk ends at Sid Snyder Drive.

As you continue, the predominant grasses and dunes give way to coastal pines and a more shaded landscape as Cape Disappointment looms on the southern horizon. On the final stretch, the trail heads into a more densely forested area at Beard's Hollow in Cape Disappointment State Park. From here, a portion of the trail south of the Beard's Hollow parking lot will take you out to the North Head Lighthouse parking area, where the second of the three endpoints is located. This portion of the trail becomes quite hilly in some areas, with challenging grades. From the North Head Lighthouse parking lot, several hiking paths take you to the edge of the cape with stunning coastal views.

Heading back up to Beard's Hollow, the trail also branches off over a bridge to the northeast, leading to the third and final endpoint. The next quarter mile or so soon becomes more challenging, best suited for hikers and mountain bikers, as it winds through the forest on a gravelly singletrack. Crossing North Head Road, the trail becomes asphalt once again. The winding and hilly pathway can become slick with moss, so watch your speed and cornering on the steeper descents.

The trail comes to an end near the port of Ilwaco at the intersection of Main Street Southwest and Second Avenue Southwest/WA 100.

CONTACT: visitlongbeachpeninsula.com/things-to-do/recreation/discovery-trail

PARKING

Parking areas are listed counterclockwise, starting with the northernmost. *Indicates that at least one accessible parking space is available.*

LONG BEACH: 26th St. NW, west of Sea Crest Ave. (46.3710, -124.0552).

LONG BEACH*: Bolstad Pavilion, 205–203 Bolstad W. (46.3514, -124.0607).

LONG BEACH*: Sid Snyder Beach Approach, 410 Sid Snyder Dr. (46.3460, -124.0617).

SEAVIEW: Seaview Beach Approach, 38th Pl. (46.3305, -124.0635).

ILWACO*: North Head Lighthouse in Cape Disappointment State Park (46.2981, -124.0721); Discover Pass required (**discoverpass.wa.gov**).

ILWACO*: Beard's Hollow Trailhead on Beard's Hollow Road, Cape Disappointment State Park (46.3042, -124.0635); Discover Pass required (**discoverpass.wa.gov**).

ILWACO: Main St. SW and Second Ave. SW/WA 100 (46.3075, -124.0447); street parking.

East Lake Sammamish Trail

39

The East Lake Sammamish Trail skirts Lake Sammamish for 11 miles through the towns of Issaquah, Sammamish, and Redmond in the fast-growing eastern suburbs of Seattle. The paved trail is one link in the 44-mile Locks to Lakes Corridor of paved trails that connect Puget Sound with the Cascade foothills. It's also part of the developing 900-mile Leafline Trail Network and a segment of the Great American Rail-Trail®, a 3,700-mile route connecting Washington, D.C., and Washington state.

In the mornings and late afternoons, the trail carries bicycle commuters traveling between tech-centric employment centers. The rest of the time, it's used by recreational bicyclists, dog walkers, joggers, and even a few folks trying their hand with a rod and reel from the end of public piers.

Although hemmed in between expensive lakeside housing and the East Lake Sammamish Parkway, the trail offers expansive views of the lake and surrounding hillsides originally inhabited for thousands of years by members of the Snoqualmie and Sammamish tribes. The town of Issaquah and the lake's original name—Squak—were derived from their language.

GENE BISBEE

Open spaces alongside Lake Sammamish provide scenic views across the water.

County
King

Endpoints
NW Gilman Blvd. at NW Juniper St. (Issaquah); NE 70th St, 0.1 mile west of WA 202/ Redmond Way (Redmond)

Mileage
11

Type
Rail-Trail

Roughness Rating
1

Surface
Asphalt

154 Rail-Trails: Pacific Northwest

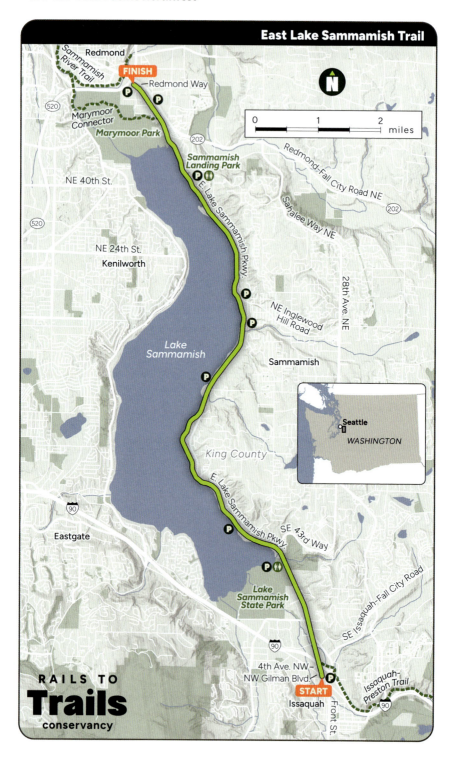

White settlers arrived in the mid-1800s, and by 1889 the tracks for the Seattle, Lakeshore and Eastern Railway ran alongside the waterfront. Trains hauled away timber harvested and milled locally, as well as coal mined in the Issaquah hills and hops grown at the end of the line in North Bend. The railbed was incorporated into the Northern Pacific Railroad in the 1890s, and King County bought the right-of-way in 1998.

Opened as a crushed-limestone track in 2006, the trail has been upgraded to a 12-foot-wide paved trail with 2-foot-wide gravel shoulders. Newly planted, noninvasive trailside landscaping has improved sightlines, and even drainage culverts under the trail have been improved to enable salmon to swim upstream to spawn.

Starting at Fourth Avenue and Gilman Boulevard in Issaquah's busy commercial district, the trail heads north 0.3 mile to a junction with the 5.5-mile Issaquah-Preston Trail (see page 187), on your right. In 2 miles, you'll arrive at a boat launch for Lake Sammamish State Park. A trail connects to the rest of the 500-acre park, which sweeps around the south end of the lake.

Continuing north, you'll be treated to perpetual views of the lake as you peer between and over multistory dwellings that line the waterfront. Stop signs are

The trailside Sammamish Landing Park offers a pier and picnic shelter.

posted for motorists at the frequent driveways that access these homes, but be aware of automobiles. Additionally, watch out for the many bollards posted in the middle of the trails at these crossings.

Benches stationed along the trail are good vantage points for watching bald eagles or ospreys flying overhead, as well as herons perched on private docks. You might enjoy reading the interpretive signs along the way, as well. There are many gates and stairways that lead to the waterfront, but these are private access only.

About 7 miles past the boat launch, you'll come to Sammamish Landing Park, which provides the only other public waterfront access, along with parking, restrooms, a picnic shelter, beaches, and a dock.

In 1 more mile, you'll pass the 1.5-mile Marymoor Connector to your left; it passes through the 640-acre Marymoor Park to the Sammamish River Trail (see page 225). The East Lake Sammamish Trail ends in another 0.5 mile, just before it gets to Northeast 70th Street in Redmond. Plans call for extending the trail another mile or so across Bear Creek to the Bear Creek Trail and the Redmond Central Connector once the Marymoor Village light-rail station is complete in 2025.

CONTACT: rtc.li/east-lake-sammamish

PARKING

Parking areas are listed from south to north. *Indicates that at least one accessible parking space is available.*

ISSAQUAH: Fourth Ave. NW Trailhead, Fourth Ave. and NW Gilman Blvd. (47.5403, -122.0393); 0.2 mile of street parking on Fourth Ave. adjacent to the trail.

ISSAQUAH: Lake Sammamish State Park boat launch, 4455 E. Lake Sammamish Pkwy. (47.5644, -122.0543); Discover Pass required (**discoverpass.wa.gov**).

SAMMAMISH: E. Lake Sammamish Pkwy. and SE 39th St. (47.5746, -122.07132); roadside parking, west side of E. Lake Sammamish Pkwy.

SAMMAMISH: Inglewood parking, E. Lake Sammamish Pkwy., 350 feet north of NE Inglewood Hill Road (47.6233, -122.0705).

SAMMAMISH*: 4607 E. Lake Sammamish Pkwy. NE (47.6492, -122.0883 and 47.6491, -122.0877); both sides of road, 0.6 mile north of NE 40th St.

REDMOND: 65th St. Parking, NE 65th St. and E. Lake Sammamish Pkwy. NE (47.6638, -122.1000).

REDMOND*: East Lake Sammamish Trailhead, NE 70th St., between 176th Ave. NE and WA 202/Redmond Way (47.6670, -122.1038).

Elliott Bay Trail

40

Elliott Bay offers trail users the opportunity to enjoy art, history, wildlife, and a wide variety of outdoor activities in a beautiful waterfront setting. In the Magnolia neighborhood, Elliott Bay Marina and Smith Cove Park boast beautiful mountain views, while the eastern half of the trail encompasses Myrtle Edwards Park, a public fishing pier, Olympic Sculpture Park, and more. Trail bridges facilitate access to city streets for recreation and commuting.

Elliott Bay Trail (sometimes referred to as the Terminal 91 Bike Trail) starts at the west end of the Elliott Bay Marina parking lot, which is a private lot. Public parking can be found 0.2 mile east of the marina at Smith Cove Park, where you'll enjoy bay views of the Great Wheel and Lumen Field, dwarfed by Mount Rainier. This is also the site of a once-active Northern Pacific Railway coal bunker pier, a 2,500-foot trestle that was later replaced by Great Northern Railroad piers 88 and 89. In 1921, the Port of Seattle built piers 40 and 41 (later renumbered 90 and 91), which, at 2,530 feet, were acknowledged to be the longest concrete piers in the world.

You'll have a view of the Pier 86 Grain Terminal, which is used to transfer inland-grown grains onto cargo ships.

CINDY BARKS

County
King

Endpoints
Elliott Bay Marina, dead end of W. Marina Pl. (Seattle); Olympic Sculpture Park, Broad St. and Alaskan Way (Seattle)

Mileage
3.9

Type
Rail-Trail

Roughness Rating
1

Surface
Asphalt

158 Rail-Trails: Pacific Northwest

Follow signs to a fenced pathway and past 20th Avenue West (which you'll reach in 0.9 mile) leading to the Ballard Locks. Rail enthusiasts will enjoy views of Balmer Yard, which often has a group of road engines set to pull a train or switcher pairs along 20th Avenue West. Beside the active BNSF Railway tracks, a steep overpass suggests walking your bike or sidestepping your skates down the very narrow descent before crossing a set of tracks.

Following the tracks, you'll pass under the Magnolia Bridge Ramp and then, in 0.3 mile, travel through the Expedia campus. Look out for the first of three bike/pedestrian bridges connecting the trail to Elliott Avenue West. Continuing another 0.2 mile to Elliott Bay Park, you'll pass the Pier 86 Grain Terminal right around the start of the second bike/pedestrian bridge. The Amgen Helix Pedestrian Bridge, including an elevator, heads over the railroad tracks to West Prospect Street and Elliott Avenue West.

Farther on is a fishing pier at Centennial Park, followed by Myrtle Edwards Park in another 0.3 mile, where a grassy area with benches and landscape art separates pedestrian and wheeled paths. Beginner skaters can expect a bit of buckled pavement and a few curves (the slope is gentler on the pedestrian

View from the trailside Rose Garden, located in Centennial Park

Centennial Park boasts great views of Elliott Bay, Mount Rainier, and the Seattle skyline.

path). To access a shopping and dining area, trail users can veer off the trail at Myrtle Edwards Park, taking a bike/pedestrian bridge over Elliott Avenue to reach West Thomas Street and Third Avenue West via ramp.

In a half mile, the bayside rocks, benches, and grassy areas of Olympic Sculpture Park offer a nice break at the trail's southeastern terminus. From trail's end, you could continue onto the 2-mile Seattle Waterfront Pathway to enjoy summer concerts, Pike Place Market, the Seattle Aquarium, the Great Wheel, Pioneer Square, and the ferries. The Elliott Bay Trail is also close to other Seattle trails, including the 1.9-mile Ship Canal Trail and the 3.6-mile Cheshiahud Lake Union Loop.

CONTACT: elliottbayconnections.org and rtc.li/elliott-bay-trail

PARKING

Parking areas are located within Seattle and are listed from northwest to southeast. *Indicates that at least one accessible parking space is available.*

SMITH COVE PARK: 1450 23rd Ave. W., south of Magnolia Bridge Ramp, across from pier 91 (47.6325, -122.3870).

PIER 86 GRAIN TERMINAL*: Dead end of Alaskan Way W., 400 feet south of Amgen Helix Pedestrian Bridge (47.6266, -122.3722); several spots designated for Elliott Bay Park users.

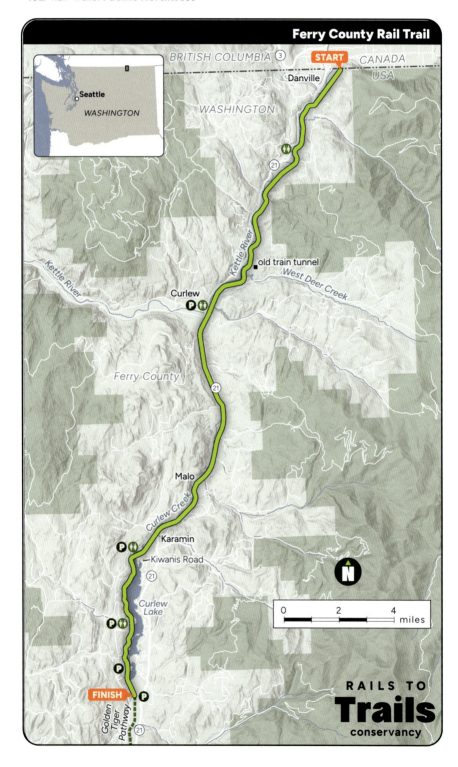

Ferry County Rail Trail

41

Running between the communities of Danville at the Canadian border and Republic in Northeast Washington, the Ferry County Rail Trail follows the former corridor of the Great Northern Railway. The rail-trail experience includes a short but beautiful tunnel cut into a rocky hillside, scenic views along the Kettle River and Curlew Lake, and two former railroad bridges. The trail's remote sections are home to wildlife including bald eagles, ospreys, ducks, geese, mule deer, white-tailed deer, and even brown bears.

Volunteers resurfaced two popular sections of the trail with well-compacted, finely crushed stone. These smooth sections provide an experience nearly indistinguishable from asphalt and are suitable for road bikes, in-line skates, and wheelchairs. Between these two improved sections, the trail is rough railroad ballast. The undeveloped portions are suitable for walking, horseback riding, and mountain biking. In winter, the trail is groomed for cross-country skiing and snowshoeing. There are limited amenities and no water fountains along the trail, so prepare accordingly.

Starting at the trail's northern endpoint at the US–Canada border in Danville, head south roughly 8 miles along

County
Ferry

Endpoints
US–Canada border, 0.2 mile east of Kettle River (Danville); Golden Tiger Pathway, northeastern endpoint, 300 feet south of W. Herron Creek Road (Republic)

Mileage
25

Type
Rail-Trail

Roughness Rating
1–3

Surface
Ballast, Crushed Stone

The rail-trail traverses rural Northeast Washington, brightened by aspen, western larch, and cottonwood trees in autumn.

J. FOSTER FANNING/ COURTESY FERRY COUNTY RAIL TRAIL PARTNERS

the Kettle River to an old train tunnel. The first resurfaced section heads south from the tunnel. In a half mile is a refurbished crossing of West Deer Creek, the work of volunteers to repair a washout in 2021. In another 1.5 miles is a trailhead in the community of Curlew. Continuing another 1.1 miles, you'll leave the Kettle River as you travel south.

The next (undeveloped) segment parallels and occasionally crosses WA 21. In 6.3 miles, the trail passes through the small community of Malo, followed by Karamin in another 2.8 miles as it crosses WA 21 one final time. A trailhead on Kiwanis Road comes up in 0.8 mile, just north of Curlew Lake. This is considered the main trailhead.

In less than 0.2 mile, the trail meets a 770-foot-long trestle. A trail highlight, the trestle takes users to the western shore of the lake. Following the trestle, the trail hugs the lake's western side another 4.6 (resurfaced) miles, leaving the lake for the final 0.5 mile. From the trail's terminus, the Golden Tiger Pathway heads 5.5 miles southwest into Republic and is open to ATVs in addition to nonmotorized uses.

CONTACT: ferrycountyrailtrail.com

PARKING

Parking areas are listed from north to south. All of the trail's designated parking lots are unpaved. *Indicates that at least one accessible parking space is available.*

CURLEW: Ferry St. and N. Main St. (48.8863, -118.5976).

REPUBLIC: Kiwanis Road, 800 feet northeast of Curlew Lake Trestle (48.7639, -118.6588).

REPUBLIC: Blacks Beach Road and Ruberts Road (48.7291, -118.6672).

REPUBLIC: Miyoko Point Road and Boat Ramp Road (48.7068, -118.6723).

REPUBLIC: W. Herron Creek Road and Capt. Daves Way (48.6930, -118.6673).

Fish Lake Trail

42

Starting in the suburbs of Spokane, the Fish Lake Trail offers a great escape into serene, nature-rich green spaces in the more rural vicinity of Cheney. Although it stops short of Fish Lake, a closer lake—Queen Lucas Lake—can be reached via the trail.

This 7.6-mile trail is perfect for anyone who wants to escape heavy vehicular traffic without venturing too far. The trail is ADA accessible, although there is a slight grade increase between Spokane and the trail's end about a mile north of Queen Lucas Lake. This scenic area was once home of the Spokane tribe, who were members of the Inland Salish Group.

The northern Fish Lake Trailhead is located at the intersection of West Ninth Avenue and South Lindeke Street and provides ample parking with access to restrooms and drinking fountains. A few hundred feet into your journey, you will cross I-90 via a pedestrian bridge as you travel on the Union Pacific Railroad's old railbed paralleling US 195.

Soon the surrounding suburbs are largely hidden from sight, and any trailside development fades away after you

The trail offers a natural escape in the suburbs southwest of Spokane.

County
Spokane

Endpoints
W. Ninth Ave. and S. Lindeke St. (Spokane); S. Scribner Road, between Summer Road and Cheney Spokane Road (Cheney)

Mileage
7.6

Type
Rail-with-Trail/Rail-Trail

Roughness Rating
1

Surface
Asphalt

cross West 16th Avenue on another bridge. Pockets of exposed rock are visible along the trail, which begins to veer away from US 195 at about mile 1.25.

At mile 2.15, there are stop signs and an at-grade crossing at South Marshall Road. You'll cross the road again in a mile on an overpass, and soon the trail begins to run parallel with Cheney Spokane Road through a 0.5-mile-wide rural valley carved by Marshall Creek. Expect to see a few horses grazing in pastures among the farm buildings.

This section of trail offers wide views of the surrounding countryside amid towering ponderosa pines, as well as your first look over active railroad corridors along the trail. In fact, beginning at mile 5.5, the trail passes between two railroads. You'll trace them for another 2 miles through the small community of Marshall to the official end of the trail at a trailhead on South Scribner Road.

Just past that trailhead, another mile of paved trail takes you to Queen Lucas Lake, which has plenty of benches and is a picturesque stop for lunch before you head back to the Scribner Road or Lindeke Street Trailhead.

There are hopes of creating an additional 2.5-mile segment from Queen Lucas Lake to Fish Lake, but it requires an expensive bridge over the rail corridor. Also, the City of Spokane and the state department of transportation are planning a new roadway that would require relocating more than a mile of the trail between Lindeke Street and Marshall Road. The relocated segment would become a separate pathway adjacent to the new roadway.

CONTACT: my.spokanecity.org/parks/trails

PARKING

Parking areas are listed from north to south. *Indicates that at least one accessible parking space is available.*

SPOKANE*: Fish Lake Trailhead, W. Ninth Ave. and S. Lindeke St. (47.6473, -117.4531).

CHENEY: Scribner Road Trailhead, S. Scribner Road, between Summer Road and Cheney Spokane Road (47.5553, -117.4998).

168 Rail-Trails: **Pacific Northwest**

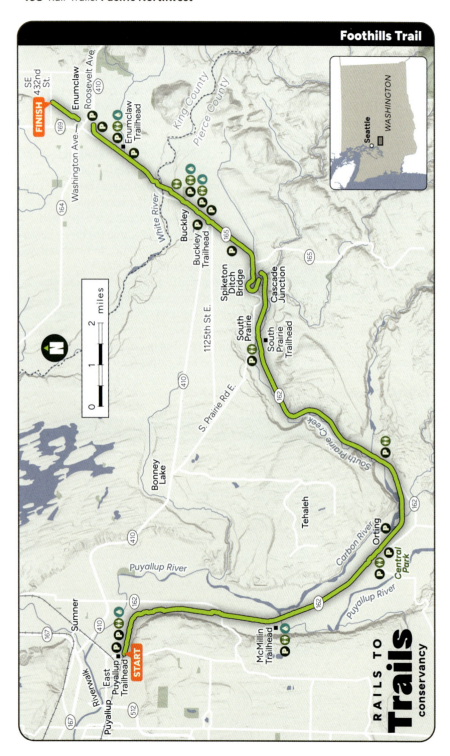

Foothills Trail

43

The Foothills Trail follows a mostly level, horseshoe-shaped course for 25 miles in western Washington under the watchful eye of Mount Rainier. The snowcapped peak is the most prominent in the state and considered an active volcano by geologists, although it hasn't erupted in 500 years. The trail passes through several small towns that once subsisted on coal mining, timber harvesting, and farming.

Completion of a long-sought pedestrian bridge across the fast-flowing White River in 2024 linked previously detached sections of the regional trail in King County and Pierce County, connecting the towns of Enumclaw and Buckley by trail. It also extended the reach of the Leafline Trail Network, which will eventually comprise 900 miles in the central Puget Sound region.

The emergency closure and removal of the dilapidated Spiketon Ditch Bridge between Buckley and South Prairie, however, created a new trail gap in 2024 with no available detour. The gap is located in Buckley between the bridge at Lower Burnett Road, 1.6 miles east of the South Prairie Trailhead, and 268th Ave. Ct. E., 1.3 miles west of the Linda

Counties
King, Pierce

Endpoints
Shaw Road E. and Pioneer Way E. (Puyallup); Lower Burnett Bridge W., 1.6 miles east of South Prairie Trailhead (Buckley); 268th Ave. Ct. E., 1.3 miles west of Linda Campbell Memorial Bench (Buckley); WA 410/Roosevelt Ave. and Garrett St. (Enumclaw); First St. and Washington Ave. (Enumclaw); SE 432nd St., 0.3 mile east of 268th Ave. SE (Enumclaw)

Mileage
24.7

Type
Rail-Trail

Roughness Rating
1

Surface
Asphalt

Mount Rainier looms over the Foothills Trail on the east side of Orting.

GENE BISBEE

Campbell Memorial Bench trail parking area. Pierce County Parks anticipates that a replacement will be in place by summer 2025.

The Northern Pacific Railway created the corridor used by the Foothills Trail in the 1870s and '80s when it laid track from its Tacoma terminus, across the Cascade Range at Stampede Pass, and into the Northern Plains. The railroad merged to become Burlington Northern in 1970, ending service in 1982. Residents soon formed the Foothills Rails-to-Trails Coalition, which launched construction of the Foothills Trail in 1998.

Starting at the western end of the trail at the East Puyallup Trailhead, you'll head east and south toward Alderton. Plans on the western side call for connections to Puyallup's Riverwalk heading toward Tacoma and the Sumner Link Trail, which connects to the Seattle-bound Interurban Trail. Members of the Puyallup and affiliated tribes originally populated villages along rivers in the area. White settlers arriving in the 1800s turned to agriculture, making this a center of daffodil production until recently. A bright-yellow daffodil bell tower still adorns downtown Orting about 7 miles ahead.

On the way to Orting, you'll cross the Puyallup River in 4.7 miles. Glacier melt makes this and other rivers run chalky white in the summer. Crossing numerous streets from subdivisions for the next 2.5 miles, you'll reach shady parks in downtown Orting, home to bakeries, cafés, and fast-food joints.

As you leave town, Mount Rainier appears to stand in the trail's path on this remote 12-mile run to Buckley. The trail skirts the Carbon River, which meanders through a wide channel filled with rock debris scoured off the mountain by the Carbon Glacier. The trail leaves the Carbon River behind in about 3 miles, then picks up South Prairie Creek. Although not fed by glaciers, the creek—like the other rivers the trail crosses—sees the return of spawning salmon every fall after they've fed and matured in the Pacific Ocean.

The trail reaches South Prairie in 4.4 miles at a convenient trailside coffee stand. In about 0.7 mile, you'll pass Cascade Junction, where a spur route carried trains south to coal camps in Carbonado and Fairfax. Opening a trail on this route is a long-term goal.

Pressing onward, the trail climbs about 250 feet in an overgrown canyon—a steep climb that railroad builders graded by creating a distinctive S-shaped switchback that is more obvious on maps than on the ground. About 5 miles past South Prairie, you'll reach Buckley, an old logging town that's home to the Buckley Log Show in June.

Crossing the rushing White River on the new pedestrian bridge, you've entered the town of Enumclaw, home of the King County Fair in July as well as bakeries, diners, and grocers. A small herd of steel-sculpted elk greets people arriving by trail from the south, and the developed trail comes to a gap in 0.8 mile. To continue, cross WA 410 to Garrett Street and go 0.2 mile. Turn left on Griffin Avenue and right on First Street. The trail resumes after crossing Washington Avenue. The final mile transitions from pavement to gravel and then dirt before ending at SE 432nd St.

CONTACT: piercecountywa.gov/1384/foothills-trail

PARKING

Parking areas are listed from west to east. *Indicates that at least one accessible parking space is available.*

PUYALLUP: Eighth Ave. SE and 33rd St. SE (47.1847, -122.2498).

PUYALLUP*: East Puyallup Trailhead, 80th St. E., between 33rd St. SE and 139th Ave. Ct. E. (47.1841, -122.2450).

ORTING*: McMillin Trailhead, 140th St. E. and WA 162 (47.1288, -122.2359).

ORTING*: Central Park, Van Scoyoc Ave. SW, between Calistoga St. W. and Train Ave. S. (47.0971, -122.2041).

ORTING*: Charter Park skate park, Washington Ave. SE and Olive St. SE (47.0944, -122.1991).

SOUTH PRAIRIE*: South Prairie Trailhead, WA 162/Pioneer Way E., between Emery Ave. S. and Rainier Ave. SE (47.1392, -122.0955).

BUCKLEY*: Buckley Trailhead, WA 410 and Wheeler Ave. (47.1599, -122.0333).

BUCKLEY*: Skate park, S. River Ave., 450 feet northeast of Wheeler Ave. (47.1605, -122.0319).

ENUMCLAW*: Enumclaw Trailhead, Warner Ave./SE 456th St. and WA 410/Enumclaw Buckley Road (47.1922, -121.9990).

ENUMCLAW*: Visitor Center parking at Stevenson Ave. and Railroad St. (47.2023, -121.9901).

172 Rail-Trails: **Pacific Northwest**

Green River Trail

Linking the southern Seattle suburbs of Kent and Tukwila, the Green River Trail offers a pleasant, paved route through several parks along the Green and Duwamish Rivers. Expanding its reach and utility, the nearly 20-mile trail connects to a handful of other trails and is part of the Leafline Trails Network across the central Puget Sound region.

As the trail experience feels more industrial and commercial on its northern end, you may wish to begin on its southern end in Kent. While the trail technically starts at a roadside pulloff along 94th Place South, a better place to kick off your journey is 2.3 miles from that endpoint at Foster Park, where you'll find the trail's southernmost parking lot, as well as a connection to the Interurban Trail South (see page 183). As the Green River Trail follows its namesake west and north from the park, you'll enjoy a tree-lined route through residential neighborhoods and along a golf course.

In 3.5 miles, the Neely-Soames Homestead appears trailside. Built in 1885, the two-story building is one of Kent's oldest homes and a designated National Historic Site. It once housed a store and post office, with a landing for

The trail traverses the lush Green River Valley between Tukwila and Kent.

County
King

Endpoints
94th Pl. S., 465 feet northwest of Green River Road (Kent); W. Marginal Pl. S., 0.2 mile northwest of S. 102nd St. (Tukwila)

Mileage
19.6

Type
Greenway/Non-Rail-Trail

Roughness Rating
1

Surface
Asphalt

riverboats nearby. Take a moment to read the informational signage and view the beautiful heritage garden behind the house.

In another 1.6 miles, you'll reach a highlight of the trail: Van Doren's Landing Park, where you'll find covered picnic tables and grills, restrooms, drinking water, plentiful parking, a large playground, and a tall viewing tower overlooking bird habitat.

At Three Friends Fishing Hole, 1.5 miles farther on, you'll be greeted by three tall carved cedar sculptures with motifs of boats and sea animals. Adjacent signage shares the story of the artistic memorial: In 2002, three good friends from the area had gone on a fly-fishing trip together in Alaska but died in a chartered plane crash. The 3-acre riverside park, which includes a wheelchair-accessible fishing platform, was created to honor them.

From there, you'll loop around Briscoe Park in 1.1 miles—a wide swath of open space dotted with covered picnic tables—and continue north past office parks, where the trail is beautified with wildflowers along each side. After exiting the park, you'll enter Tukwila and reach Bicentennial Park, with its bright playground, parking, and restrooms. Over the course of the next mile, you'll head under I-405 and reach another connection with the Interurban Trail as it crosses the Green River.

For most of the nearly 20-mile route, you will have views of the Green River.

On the final 4.5-mile stretch, you'll traverse sprawling Fort Dent Park, with its numerous sports fields, then parallel I-5 (separated from traffic by a tall concrete wall) before ducking under the interstate and reaching Cecil Moses Memorial Park. Offering restrooms and parking, the latter is a good place to end your journey. While the trail continues another 0.6 mile from the park, it closely parallels busy WA 99/Marginal Way before simply petering out next to the highway.

A northern extension of the Green River Trail, anticipated to begin construction in 2026, will continue the route northward to a connection with Seattle's Duwamish River Trail.

CONTACT: rtc.li/green-river

PARKING

Parking areas are listed from south to north. Select parking areas for the trail are listed below; for a detailed list of parking areas and other waypoints, consult **TrailLink™**. *Indicates that at least one accessible parking space is available.*

KENT: Foster Park, S. 259th St., 0.1 mile east of 74th Ave. S. (47.3697, -122.2403).

KENT: Green River Trailhead, 999 Hawley Road (47.3753, -122.2450).

KENT*: Neely-Soames Homestead, 5311 S. 237th Pl. (47.3889, -122.2675).

KENT*: Russell Woods Park, Russell Road, 385 feet northwest of Veterans Dr./S. 228th St. (47.3960, -122.2726).

KENT*: Van Doren's Landing Park, 21901 Russell Road (47.4037, -122.2716).

KENT*: Three Friends Fishing Hole, 19970 Russell Road (47.4225, -122.2642).

KENT*: Briscoe Park, 1901 62nd Ave. S. (47.4315, -122.2577); parking lot is 0.1 mile southeast of the park itself.

TUKWILA*: Bicentennial Park, 7200 Strander Blvd. (47.4565, -122.2474).

TUKWILA*: Fort Dent Park, Starfire Way, 0.1 mile west of Fort Dent Way (47.4679, -122.2497); multiple parking lots throughout the park.

TUKWILA: Cecil Moses Memorial Park, dead end of 27th Ave. S., 0.3 mile south of S. 102nd St. (47.5041, -122.2987); gravel lot.

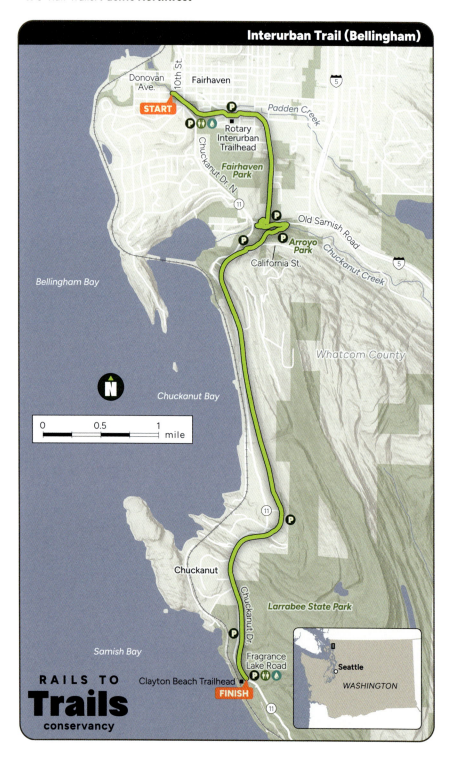

Interurban Trail (Bellingham)

45

Bellingham's Interurban Trail begins in the historic neighborhood of Fairhaven on the south end of the city and ends in Larrabee State Park. It follows portions of the former Bellingham & Skagit Interurban Railway and the Fairhaven & Southern Railroad. The largely wooded rail-trail offers stunning views of the San Juan Islands across Bellingham Bay when the forested canopy opens up enough to see them. In addition to pedestrian and cycling uses, horseback riding is also permitted along the entirety of the trail.

Begin at the northern trailhead at Donovan Avenue and 10th Street. As the trail heads southeast, it is relatively flat and crosses Padden Creek several times. In 0.2 mile, it reaches Fairhaven Park, where parking, a community building with restrooms, and a spray park are available. Continuing

The surface becomes crushed stone as the pathway gradually descends to the Clayton Beach Trailhead.

County
Whatcom

Endpoints
Donovan Ave. and 10th St. (Fairhaven); Larrabee State Park at Fragrance Lake Road and Chuckanut Dr. (Bellingham)

Mileage
6.7

Type
Rail-Trail

Roughness Rating
1–2

Surface
Asphalt, Crushed Stone, Dirt

through a residential area, the Rotary Trailhead—where you'll find informational panels about the creek—appears in 0.4 mile.

From the Rotary Trailhead, you'll approach a series of switchbacks in 1.1 miles that takes you down to Old Samish Road. Use caution when crossing this two-lane road to continue on the trail; there isn't a good sightline, and cars travel fairly rapidly there.

On the south side of Old Samish Road, the trail heads east to enter Arroyo Park. Within the park, the trail becomes a steep singletrack best suited for mountain bikes and would be difficult for those with mobility challenges due to rocks and exposed roots in the trail. The trail travels high above Chuckanut Creek, then descends to it and reaches a pedestrian bridge in 0.3 mile. As you leave the bridge, the trail climbs steeply back up.

Crossing California Street in 0.4 mile, the trail evens out and becomes quite smooth, heading past private residences and becoming an on-road route on a quiet, residential two-way street with a mix of lush tree canopy and spectacular wide-open views of Bellingham Bay.

Approaching the southern endpoint, the trail reverts to a crushed-stone surface and gradually descends to the Clayton Beach Trailhead in Larrabee State Park, which has parking and restrooms. The state park was the first in Washington, created with a donation of 20 acres by the Larrabee family in 1915.

CONTACT: cob.org/services/recreation/parks-trails/trail-guide

PARKING

Parking areas are located within Bellingham and are listed from north to south. Select parking areas for the trail are listed below; for a detailed list of parking areas and other waypoints, consult **TrailLink™**. *Indicates that at least one accessible parking space is available.*

FAIRHAVEN PARK: The parking lot is located 0.1 mile from the park entrance on Chuckanut Dr. N. (48.7144, -122.4976).

ROTARY TRAILHEAD*: 1999 Old Fairhaven Pkwy. (48.7156, -122.4935).

ARROYO PARK: Old Samish Road, 0.2 mile east of Chuckanut Dr. N. (48.7023, -122.4854).

NORTH CHUCKANUT MOUNTAIN TRAILHEAD: Chuckanut Dr. N. and California St. (48.7008, -122.4889).

FRAGRANCE LAKE TRAILHEAD: Larrabee State Park entrance on Chuckanut Dr. (48.6529, -122.4901); limited spaces.

CLAYTON BEACH TRAILHEAD*: Larrabee State Park at Fragrance Lake Road and Chuckanut Dr. (48.6482, -122.4869).

Interurban Trail (North)

46

In the early 20th century, electric railcars, called interurbans, were a common part of the transportation system across the United States. In Northwest Washington, the Everett-to-Seattle interurban provided an efficient way for residents to travel between the two cities. The Seattle-Everett Interurban rail line operated between 1910 and 1939, eventually being displaced by the automobile. Today, the route serves as an important multiuse, nonmotorized transportation corridor. The Snohomish County section even permits horses, except on the portions maintained and operated by the cities of Lynnwood and Everett.

The Interurban Trail (North) runs from Everett to downtown Seattle. Much of the route is utilitarian in nature, located in the right-of-way for I-5, a major north-south highway. The northern half of the 31-mile trail is incomplete and requires navigating several on-street sections and crossing at complicated multilane intersections. Nonetheless, there are sections that wind through pleasant suburban neighborhoods and small parks.

As there is no trailhead at the trail's northern endpoint at Colby Avenue and 41st Street in Everett, the beginning

Counties
King, Snohomish

Endpoints
Colby Ave. and 41st St. (Everett); Seventh Ave. and Westlake Ave. (Seattle)

Mileage
31.3

Type
Rail-Trail

Roughness Rating
1

Surface
Asphalt, Concrete

Along the way, you'll see art, rain gardens, and nods to the trail's railroad history.

KATE FOSTER

180 Rail-Trails: **Pacific Northwest**

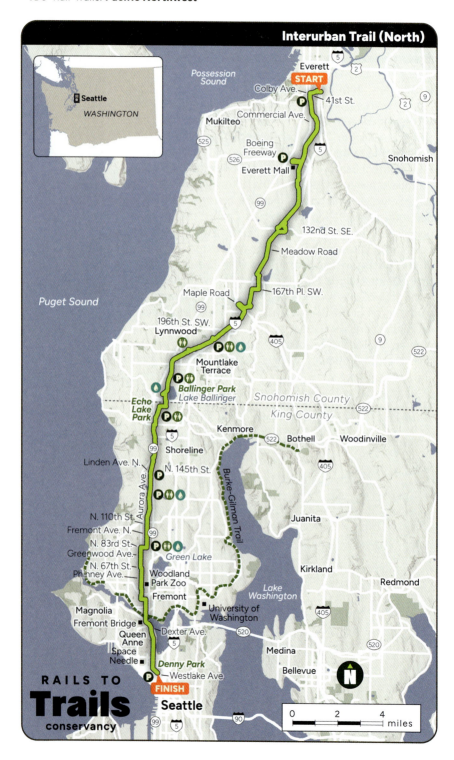

of the trail can be difficult to find. You may wish to start 0.3 mile farther south, where there is a small trail parking lot at Colby Avenue and 44th Street Southeast. Heading south, the trail has a suburban feel and is often buffered by trees.

In 1 mile, the trail will merge with Commercial Avenue, which you'll follow on-road for 0.9 mile, until it ends at Wetmore Avenue and the pathway picks up again. In 1.3 miles, you'll reach Casino Road and turn left under Boeing Freeway. On the other side of the freeway bridge, you'll turn left onto 84th Street Southeast, which you'll take east 0.5 mile until you reach the pathway again. The trail leads south and reaches Everett Mall in 0.7 mile.

Paralleling I-5, you'll travel south, crossing the interstate on a pedestrian bridge in 2 miles. Continuing south, now along the east side of the interstate, you'll have residential neighborhoods on one side and trees buffering I-5 on the other. In 2.9 miles, the trail comes to a T-intersection at Meadow Road; turn right and follow Meadow Road south on-road or on the paralleling sidewalk. The road becomes 13th Avenue and, when it intersects 167th Place Southwest, in 0.6 mile, you'll be able to hop back on the pathway.

In 1.2 miles, you'll cross I-5 once again—this time on Maple Road—and begin paralleling the interstate on its west side through Lynnwood and then Mountlake Terrace and Shoreline. As you continue south, the busy commercial corridor gives way to residential neighborhoods. In 5.6 miles, you can catch glimpses of Lake Ballinger off to your left and stop in Ballinger Park if you need to reach a restroom. In 1.4 miles, you'll reach another lake and have access to the amenities at Echo Lake Park.

You'll cross WA 99/Aurora Avenue on a pedestrian bridge in 2.3 miles and then have your choice of eateries as you head through Shoreline's busy commercial area. A trailhead on North 145th Street, which offers benches and a limited number of parking spaces, will pop up in 0.6 mile. After crossing North 145th Street, you'll have a 0.8-mile stretch of protected cycle path (or sidewalk) along Linden Avenue North until you reach North 128th Street and pick up the dedicated pathway again.

This pathway portion of the trail ends at the intersection of North 110th Street and Fremont Avenue North. From there, the remainder of the route—just over 7 miles—is an on-road experience, providing access to downtown Seattle, a zoo, museums, and other attractions. To continue your trip on-road, turn left on Fremont Avenue and follow the green INTERURBAN NORTH signs, as well as the painted bicycle markings on the pavement to navigate the route.

You'll continue south on Fremont Avenue 1.6 miles to North 83rd Street, where you'll turn right and continue two blocks to Greenwood Avenue. Take a left on Greenwood and continue south 0.8 mile to an intersection with North 67th Street; veer left here onto Phinney Avenue. Follow Phinney Avenue 2 miles, passing Woodland Park Zoo on your left, to North 43rd Street, where you will take a left as you continue to follow the green signs. You'll be reunited with Fremont Avenue in four blocks, at which point you'll turn right.

You'll take Fremont Avenue 0.7 mile to the bright-blue Fremont Bridge; although you'll share the bridge with vehicle traffic, you'll have a separated lane. After crossing the waterway, continue south on Dexter Avenue. Along the way, you'll have a view of Seattle's famed Space Needle and be just blocks away from a handful of museums.

In 2 miles, you'll pass Denny Park on your left and cross Denny Way, where Dexter becomes Seventh Avenue. As you continue down Seventh, the trail becomes a protected pathway, separated from traffic by a narrow median. The route ends at Westlake Avenue in another 0.3 mile, just after passing The Spheres, a unique greenhouse dome.

CONTACT: snohomishcountywa.gov/1182/trails

PARKING

Parking areas are listed from north to south. Select parking areas for the trail are listed below; for a detailed list of parking areas and other waypoints, consult **TrailLink™**. *Indicates that at least one accessible parking space is available.*

EVERETT: Colby Ave. and 44th St. SE (47.9593, -122.2074); limited parking available on the south side of 44th St. SE.

MOUNTLAKE TERRACE*: Ballinger Park, 23000 Lakeview Dr. (47.7892, -122.3295).

SHORELINE*: Echo Lake Park, N. 200th St. and Ashworth Ave. N. (47.7737, -122.3407).

SHORELINE*: Trailhead at N. 145th St. and Linden Ave. N. (47.7345, -122.3479); limited parking spaces.

SEATTLE*: Metered on-street parking on Seventh Ave. between Westlake Ave. and Lenora St. (47.6154, -122.3379).

Interurban Trail (South)

47

The main segment of the **Interurban Trail (South)** follows a former trolley line 16.1 miles on a mostly straight and flat trajectory through several towns south of Seattle, providing a route for commuting and recreation east of the I-5 corridor. In addition, two shorter trail segments that total 3.7 miles allow space for outdoor pursuits on a ridge near Tacoma.

The Interurban Trail South follows the route of the Puget Sound Electric Railway, which ran between Seattle and Tacoma from 1902 until 1928, when it was shut down due to competition from cars and trucks. With links to several trails in King and Pierce Counties, the trail plays a role in the Leafline Trail Network, which will connect more than 900 miles of trail in the central Puget Sound region. Public restrooms and drinking fountains are scarce along the route, and shade is mostly nonexistent under the power lines.

SEGMENT 1

Starting in the north, plenty of parking is available at a soccer facility next to Fort Dent Park in Tukwila, an area inhabited for centuries by the Duwamish Tribe, Indigenous people related to the Coast Salish of the Pacific Northwest.

At the south end of the parking lot, follow a sign marked RIVER TRAIL to cross a small bridge; then find the Interurban Trail beginning at a junction with the Green River Trail

Counties
King, Pierce

Endpoints
Segment 1: Green River Trail, Fort Dent Way and Interurban Ave. S. (Tukwila); Stewart Road SE, between WA 167 Frontage Road and Thornton Ave. SW (Pacific) *Segment 2:* 114th Ave. E., 400 feet north of Jovita Blvd. E. (Edgewood); Military Road S., between 31st Ave. and S. 382nd St. (Milton) *Segment 3:* S. 380th St., 400 feet west of 26th Dr. S. (Milton); 20th St. E., 0.1 mile east of Wapato Way E. (Fife)

Mileage
19.8

Type
Rail-Trail/Rail-with-Trail

Roughness Rating
1

Surface
Asphalt

Boxcars parked in a rail yard flank the trail in Auburn.

GENE BISBEE

184 Rail-Trails: **Pacific Northwest**

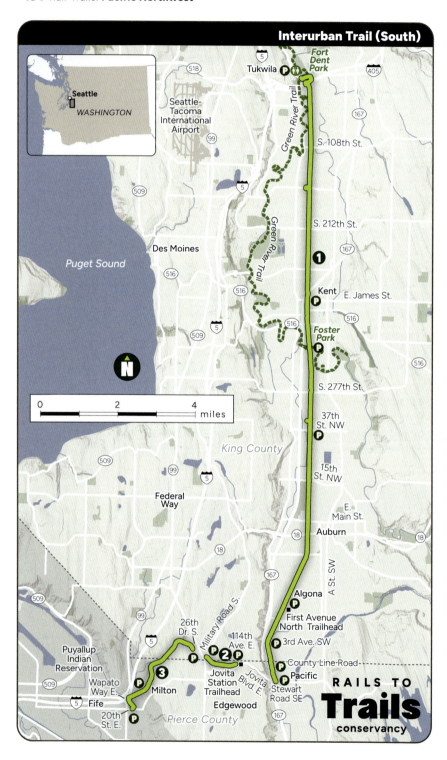

(see page 173) in less than a mile. Take a left, follow the trail around an amusement park, pass under I-405, and then begin an 11-mile stretch of straight trail marked by a line of tall utility towers marching south to the horizon.

While the first few miles pass through congested commercial and light industrial areas, the trail is screened from surrounding warehouses by ditches where wildflowers, bushes, and grasses proliferate. Songbirds are drawn to these marshy areas, and you'll hear their calls and see them flitting across the trail.

In 7.2 miles, you'll cross the southern end of the Green River Trail at Foster Park in Kent. You can use it to make a tidy 20-mile loop back to the soccer complex, if you like. Continuing south, the Interurban passes through a sprawling rail yard where trains are staged for passage to the Seattle and Tacoma harbors. The trail intersects a couple of rail crossings, which can be blocked by trains. The surroundings then take on a more agricultural nature for a few miles. Three miles past Foster Park, the Emerald Downs thoroughbred racetrack comes into view.

Commercial and residential development borders the trail in another mile. You can find a giant outlet mall with fast-food restaurants on the right as you head south through Auburn, and there are two cafés and a small grocer at the First Avenue North Trailhead in Algona. This trail segment ends in 2.2 miles on Stewart Road Southeast in Pacific, after you pass three parks with war memorials.

A short segment of the trail runs through Edgewood.

SEGMENTS 2 AND 3

Two separate Interurban Trail segments follow the old corridor over the ridge toward Tacoma in the west. The Jovita Station Trailhead in Edgewood features a historic railway display, followed by a 0.8-mile segment of trail. Farther west, a 2.9-mile section lying partly in the Puyallup Indian Reservation runs through a forested canyon. Planning is under way to connect these two segments.

Long-range plans call for connecting the Interurban Trail to the Foothills Trail (see page 169) in Pierce County via the Sumner Link Trail and the Puyallup Riverwalk Trail. Another trail project will connect the Interurban to the Tacoma waterfront by 2029.

CONTACT: rtc.li/king-co-interurban-south, rtc.li/milton-interurban-trail, and rtc.li/edgewood-interurban-trail

PARKING

Parking areas are listed from north to south, and east to west. *Indicates that at least one accessible parking space is available.*

TUKWILA*: Starfire Sports, 14800 Starfire Way (47.4686, -122.2490).

KENT*: Kent/James St. Park and Ride, 902 W. James St. (47.3864, -122.2426).

ALGONA*: First Ave. N., between Main St. and Stanley Ave. (47.2792, -122.2501).

PACIFIC*: Third Ave. SW, between Frontage Road S. and Seattle Blvd. S. (47.2651, -122.2598).

PACIFIC: Roy Road SW, 0.4 mile west of Valentine Ave. SE (47.2552, -122.2578).

EDGEWOOD*: 20 114th Ave. E. (47.2562, -122.2775).

MILTON: S. 380th St. (47.2611, -122.3008); on-street parking 200 feet west of 26th Dr. S.

FIFE*: 7203 20th St. E. (47.2393, -122.3342).

Issaquah-Preston Trail

48

Visitors to the Issaquah-Preston Trail will find themselves on a visually appealing 5.5-mile route through an evergreen forest at the foot of the Cascade foothills. Although you'll hear the noise of the surrounding urban environment, including traffic on nearby I-90, you can still enjoy this much-needed natural oasis tucked into the city. Mountain bikers also frequent this trail to access the singletrack in Grand Ridge Park.

The Issaquah-Preston Trail connects the East Lake Sammamish Trail (see page 153) in the lakeside community of Issaquah to the Preston-Snoqualmie Trail (see page 219), beginning in Preston. *Issaquah* translates to "sound of the water birds" in the language of the Sammamish people, who have inhabited the region for thousands of years.

The trail is part of the Leafline Trail Network, which will eventually comprise more than 900 miles of trail in the central Puget Sound region, and is a segment of the Great American Rail-Trail®, a 3,700-mile route connecting Washington, D.C., and Washington state.

The trail follows the route of the Seattle, Lakeshore and Eastern Railway, which got its start in the 1880s and is today

The trail journeys through an evergreen forest at the base of the Cascade foothills.

County
King

Endpoints
East Lake Sammamish Trail at Fourth Ave. NW, 0.1 mile northeast of NW Gilman Blvd. (Issaquah); Preston-Snoqualmie Trail, SE High Point Way and 300th Ave. SE (Preston)

Mileage
5.5

Type
Rail-Trail

Roughness Rating
1–2

Surface
Asphalt, Gravel

188 Rail-Trails: **Pacific Northwest**

responsible for more than 100 rail-trail miles locally. Originally conceived to connect Seattle with farmland of Eastern Washington and north to Canada, the eastern branch didn't get much farther east than the hop fields in Snoqualmie before it was acquired by the Northern Pacific Railroad in the 1890s.

Parking for the trail is shared with the East Lake Sammamish Trail along Fourth Avenue Northwest in northern Issaquah's shopping district. The trail begins as asphalt beneath the I-90 overpass, crosses busy Front Street/East Lake Sammamish Parkway at a signalized intersection, and then begins an uphill grade in about 0.5 mile. About 1 mile into the climb, take the left fork and pass through a tunnel under Highlands Drive Northeast. Turn left at the following T-intersection to stay on course; a right goes downhill via the Rainier Trail to the East Sunset Way Trailhead at the base of Tiger Mountain.

Soon after the Highlands Drive junction, the trail surface transitions to packed limestone gravel, and the second-growth forest of Douglas-fir, red cedar, and hemlock closes in. About 1 mile past the tunnel, a singletrack for mountain bikes takes off to the left up into Grand Ridge Park; a map posted at the junction shows the site of an old coal mine where cement foundations can be seen in the undergrowth. Another mountain bike trail takes off uphill in 0.4 mile. This forested section ends in 0.7 mile at the High Point Way Trailhead.

The trail follows a wooded strip along I-90 for 1.3 miles until it ends at Southeast High Point Way. If you wish to continue to Preston, there's a wide, two-way cycle track on the south side of the road for 0.7 mile to the junction with the Preston-Snoqualmie Trail in an industrial park at 300th Avenue Southeast. There are no services along the Issaquah-Preston Trail.

CONTACT: issaquahwa.gov/742/trails

PARKING

Parking areas are within Issaquah and are listed west to east. The trail is wheelchair accessible, but there are no dedicated accessible parking spots.

FOURTH AVE. TRAILHEAD: Fourth Ave. NW beginning at NW Gilman Blvd. (47.5432, -122.0405); 0.2 mile of street parking by the trailhead.

E. SUNSET WAY TRAILHEAD: E. Sunset Way at Sixth Ave. SE (47.5297, -122.0255).

HIGH POINT WAY TRAILHEAD: SE High Point Way at I-90 (47.5320, -121.9802).

190 Rail-Trails: **Pacific Northwest**

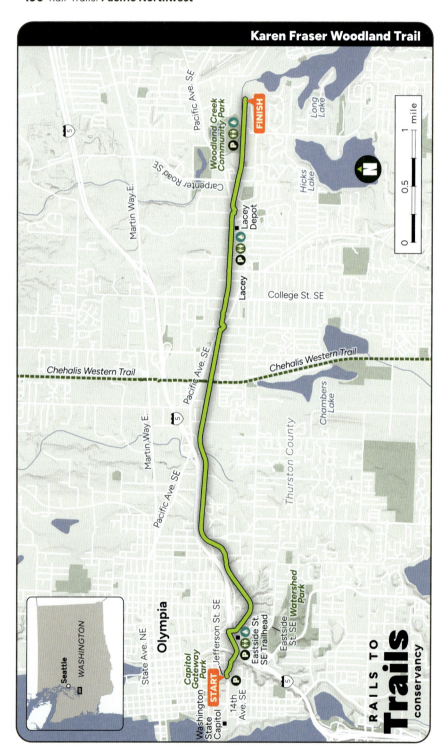

Karen Fraser Woodland Trail

The Karen Fraser Woodland Trail is a scenic and peaceful multiuse trail that connects Washington's capital, Olympia, with the neighboring town of Lacey. Just over 5 miles long, this well-maintained, paved trail serves as a mostly off-road thoroughfare offering a vital and safe active-transportation option for local residents, as well as a peaceful recreational outlet of green space in the heart of a residentially urban corridor. Formerly known as the Woodland Trail Greenway, it was renamed in honor of Karen Fraser, a longtime state legislator and local leader who has been a champion of environmental preservation and public service. The path is part of a larger network of trails in Thurston County and serves as a valuable corridor for pedestrians, cyclists, and even wildlife.

On the western end is a small trailhead at Capitol Gateway Park, which offers fantastic views and access to the capitol building. After a short jog along the East Bay Drive Trail, the route heads south onto the I-5 bike trail, which includes a small on-road section along Eastside Street Southeast and a road crossing before arriving at a larger trailhead facility with restrooms, water, and ample parking. It continues under wooded canopy along the eastern edge of Olympia, connecting neighborhoods, parks, and natural areas.

JOE LACROIX

The rail-trail offers serene green space in the heart of the residentially dense corridor between Olympia and Lacey.

County
Thurston

Endpoints
Capitol Gateway Park, 14th Ave. SE and Jefferson St. SE (Olympia); east end of Woodland Creek Community Park (Lacey)

Mileage
5.2

Type
Rail-Trail

Roughness Rating
1

Surface
Asphalt

At the dividing line between Olympia and Lacey, the Karen Fraser Woodland Trail crosses paths with the Chehalis Western Trail (see page 139) at a well-manicured roundabout. This intersection includes permanent installations highlighting both trails' railroad origins and the region's efforts to use rail-trails to connect local communities.

After crossing into Lacey, the trail exits the tree-lined canopy and parallels Pacific Avenue Southeast through town. There are a few roundabout road crossings, but the trail is easy to find, with trail crosswalks featuring warning lights that make them more visible to traffic. Lacey Depot offers another charming nod to the trail's railroad history. The recently restored train depot was converted into a community space, complete with restrooms, water, sheltered picnic tables, historical markers, and even a train-themed playground for children. The adjacent gravel lot is a frequent meeting point for local food trucks, should you need a snack during your time on the trail.

The trail reenters a densely wooded patch of stunning Pacific Northwest pine trees along the southern edge of Woodland Creek Community Park, where it reaches its eastern terminus. (Keen travelers will note that the former rail corridor continues east, with a FUTURE TRAIL CONNECTION sign hinting at a possible extension.) Woodland Creek Community Park offers a plethora of community facilities, including restrooms, water, playgrounds, sports fields, disc golf, and ample parking.

The Karen Fraser Woodland Trail is an undeniable community asset, blending urban convenience with restorative access to nature. Its dedication to accessibility and environmental preservation makes it a beloved destination for both locals and tourists looking to experience the natural beauty of Washington.

CONTACT: rtc.li/olympia-parks and
laceyparks.org/parks_trails/karen-fraser-woodland-trail

PARKING

Parking areas are listed from west to east. *Indicates that at least one accessible parking space is available.*

OLYMPIA: Capitol Gateway Park, 14th Ave. SE and Jefferson St. SE (47.0360, -122.8952).

OLYMPIA*: Eastside St. SE Trailhead, Eastside St. SE and Wheeler Ave. SE (47.0346, -122.8865).

LACEY*: Across from Lacey Depot, Lebanon St. SE and Pacific Ave. SE (47.0367, -122.8111).

LACEY*: Woodland Creek Community Park, 6729 Pacific Ave. SE (47.0387, -122.7939).

Klickitat Trail

50

Spanning 31 miles, the remote Klickitat Trail provides varied scenery along its rugged landscape. Visitors can bike or walk beside the designated Wild and Scenic Klickitat River as they pass through grassy fields, forests, and wildflower-filled canyons populated by flitting butterflies. Prepare to unplug, as cell service is nonexistent along most of the trail.

The multiuse trail follows the first 31 miles of the former Columbia River & Northern Railway, built between Lyle and Goldendale in the early 1900s. Later owned by the Spokane, Portland & Seattle Railway and then the Burlington Northern Railroad, the corridor was acquired for trail use in the 1990s.

The Klickitat Trail Conservancy, which oversees the trail along with Washington State Parks and the U.S. Forest Service, invites equestrians to use the western 13 miles of trail but recommends against the remainder of the trail for horseback riding. Also, the nearly 12-mile Swale Canyon segment, between the Wahkiacus and Harms Road Trailheads, is closed from mid-June to mid-October due to wildfire hazards.

The trail begins at the Klickitat Trailhead in Lyle, a small town on the Columbia River. There's plenty of parking, restrooms, and a drinking fountain here, but these are the last services for 13.3 miles, until the town of Klickitat, named for the Klickitat tribe that the Lewis and Clark Expedition encountered here in 1805.

County
Klickitat

Endpoints
WA 142 and WA 14/Lewis and Clark Hwy. (Lyle); Durkee Road and WA 142 (Klickitat); Klickitat River, 2.5 miles west of Swale Canyon Trailhead on Schilling Road (Wahkiacus); Uecker Road and Centerville Hwy. (Warwick)

Mileage
31

Type
Rail-Trail

Roughness Rating
2–3

Surface
Asphalt, Ballast, Crushed Stone, Dirt, Gravel

EDUARDO COYOTZI ZARATE

Travel beside the designated Wild and Scenic Klickitat River through grassy fields, forests, and wildflower-filled canyons.

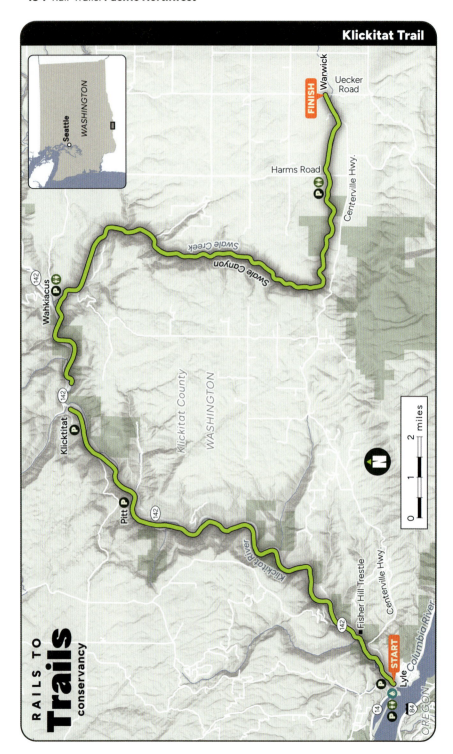

Starting as a paved trail, it transitions to gravel and dirt before reaching the Fisher Hill Trestle, which provides a breathtaking view above the Klickitat River in 1.6 miles. Once across the wooden span, the trail again is gravel and dirt (surface change is common on the Klickitat Trail). Moving toward the community of Pitt, the trail provides plenty of tree cover and stunning views of the rushing Klickitat River, which is only feet from the trail at times.

You will pass near private property and are expected to stay on the trail and keep your distance from any poultry and livestock you may spot. Rattlesnakes, ticks, and poison oak are also common along most of the trail.

You will arrive in the town of Klickitat in 13 miles. The town provides opportunities to recharge and refuel with a coffee shop, a gas station, a restaurant, and an ice-cream shop nearby.

There's a 0.5-mile gap between Klickitat and where the next section of trail begins to the east. However, that segment starts at a dead-end on the banks of the Klickitat River at the site of a bridge that's been removed. A better place to pick up the trail again is 2.5 miles farther east at the Wahkiacus Trailhead, which has parking and restrooms. Here, you will enter the 12-mile-long Swale Canyon. Although it is fairly dry most of the year, wildflowers fill it in the spring. Tree cover and shade are scarce, but wildlife is plentiful.

On this remote segment, you'll travel over a rocky, uneven railbed and cross trestles with original decking. There's no exit from the canyon until the Harms Road Trailhead, and there's no food or water. Visitors are advised to remain on the trail while on this section. Gates that appear along the trail must be closed after passing through them.

The trail concludes in 2.2 miles at Uecker Road, near Centerville Highway.

CONTACT: klickitat-trail.org

PARKING

Parking areas are listed from west to east. *Indicates that at least one accessible parking space is available.*

LYLE*: Lyle Trailhead, WA 142 and Spokane Ave. (45.6967, -121.2901).

PITT: Upper Pitt Boat Ramp, WA 142, 0.1 mile east of Fishon Road (45.7947, -121.1977).

KLICKITAT: Klickitat Community Center, WA 142 and Durkee Road (45.8182, -121.1505).

WAHKIACUS: Swale Canyon Trailhead, Horseshoe Bend Road and Schilling Road (45.8232, -121.0986).

CENTERVILLE: Harms Road Trail Access, Harms Road, 0.5 mile north of Centerville Hwy. (45.7236, -121.0308).

Lower Yakima Valley Pathway

The Lower Yakima Valley Pathway is a journey through the agricultural heart and wine country of the Lower Yakima River Valley in south-central Washington. You will see agricultural equipment along the route, some of which is used in the annual Lighted Farm Implement Parade in downtown Sunnyside, which takes place in December and celebrates the area's agricultural heritage with decorated tractors, combines, and antique farm equipment.

Begin your trip on the northwest end of the trail in Sunnyside, where the first 6 miles follow a clearly delineated, paved path that parallels the Gibbon-Granger Shortline Railroad. Trail markers will let you know how many miles you have traveled, as well as the distance to the next park or city. While on the Sunnyside portion of the pathway, keep an eye out for the painted rock collection that includes inspirational messages, like "Believe in Yourself," "Life is Tough, So Are You," and "Keep Your Sunnyside Up." Along the route, there are several covered park benches; however, the only restrooms and water sources are located midtrail in Grandview.

After those first 6 miles, the experience changes beginning at the intersection of Wine Country Road and North

On its northwest end in Sunnyside, the first 6 miles of the trail parallel the Gibbon-Granger Shortline Railroad.

Counties
Benton, Yakima

Endpoints
Southeast end of the parking lot at Yakima Valley Hwy. and Morgan Road (Sunnyside); Wine Country Road and Grant Ave. (Prosser)

Mileage
14

Type
Rail-Trail/Rail-with-Trail

Roughness Rating
1

Surface
Asphalt

Euclid Street, where the asphalt pathway becomes a mixture of sidewalks and bike lanes within the city of Grandview. Continue on Wine Country Road, which then becomes East Wine Country Road, until you reach the intersection of East Wine Country Road and Fir Street in 1.5 miles. You can then use the pedestrian crossing to enter Legion Park; here you will find Palacios Parkway, which doubles as a United Way Born Learning Trail for children, and the Grandview Rose Garden, with a gazebo, a restroom facility, and shaded grassy areas perfect for picnics.

The remainder of the pathway (the last 6.5 miles) is a direct route to the city of Prosser. Be cautious at road crossings, as some do not have designated crosswalks. You will end your journey in the city of Prosser, where you can enjoy a meal or some popular Northwest cherries.

There are long-range plans to connect the Lower Yakima Valley Pathway with the existing Yakima Greenway (see page 251) in the upper valley around the city of Yakima. This connection will cement the route as a recreational resource and a crucial transportation corridor.

CONTACT: yakimacounty.us/759/parks-trails

PARKING

Parking areas are listed from northwest to southeast. *Indicates that at least one accessible parking space is available.*

SUNNYSIDE: Yakima Valley Hwy. and Morgan Road (46.3265, -119.9972).

GRANDVIEW*: Wine Country Road, 175 feet northwest of N. Euclid Road (46.2628, -119.9172).

GRANDVIEW*: Grandview Public Parking, 106 Ave. A, 200 feet south of Wine Country Road (46.2554, -119.9033).

GRANDVIEW*: Grandview Rose Garden, Wine Country Road, 200 feet east of Vista Grande Way (46.2550, -119.8839).

PROSSER*: Wine Country Road and S. Wamba Road/Nunn Road (46.2112, -119.7795).

Old Railroad Grade

52

The Old Railroad Grade trail begins about a mile outside of Gold Bar, the closest town, in Wallace Falls State Park, about 45 miles northeast of Seattle. The name *Wallace* is derived from the surname of the land's original homesteaders, Joe and Sarah Kwayaylsh, members of the Skykomish tribe.

The trail offers a rugged out-and-back experience with a view of waterfalls at its eastern end. The only trailhead, located on the trail's western end, has a large parking lot and restrooms. Be sure to download a map of the trail before venturing out, as signage can be confusing and there are multiple trail options within the park. Due to its challenging terrain, the trail is best suited for hiking or mountain biking.

The trail begins along a utility right-of-way but splits in two after 0.3 mile. If you are traveling by bike, you'll have to take the route to the left, following a former railbed, originally a logging route used between 1921 and 1941 by the Wallace Falls Timber Company. Those wishing to hike can take the Woody Trail, which splits off to the right and offers a more direct route to the waterfalls.

Along the rail-trail, you'll follow a gentle uphill grade through a lovely evergreen forest that is still recovering

The rail-trail follows a former logging route used by the Wallace Falls Timber Company.

County
Snohomish

Endpoint
Wallace Falls State Park, 14503 Wallace Lake Road (Gold Bar) (out-and-back trail)

Mileage
3.6

Type
Rail-Trail

Roughness Rating
2

Surface
Gravel

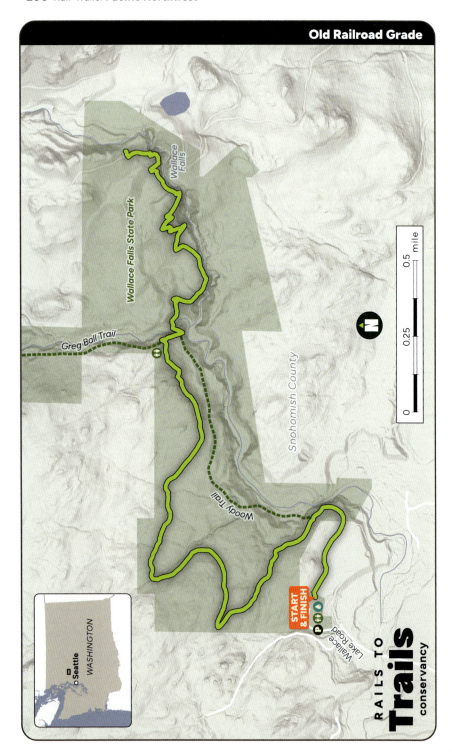

from early-20th-century clear-cutting. Moss-coated tree limbs frame much of the trail, creating a fantastical, old-world feeling as you make your way up toward the waterfalls.

The trail divides again in about 1.1 miles, where it meets a short trail for hiking or mountain biking that branches off to the left. (*Caution:* A large sign with a bicycle symbol can mislead casual cyclists into taking this trail, but it is suitable only for hiking or serious mountain biking.) This connecting trail cuts over to an unsigned road that is used largely by the Department of Natural Resources and logging trucks but can also be used to reach Wallace Lake, about 5 miles along the road.

For those who choose to follow the railroad grade, continue another 0.8 mile to the end of the rail-trail, where there is a restroom. From there, you can continue on foot along a 1.1-mile hiking trail that leads to the beautiful Wallace Falls, plus another 0.2 mile to trail's end at a dirt road. Those who make the trek will be rewarded with breathtaking views of the tallest waterfall in the Cascade Mountains, at 265 feet.

CONTACT: parks.wa.gov/find-parks/state-parks/wallace-falls-state-park

PARKING

Only one parking lot is available for this out-and-back trail. It's located in Gold Bar on the west end of the trail. *Indicates that at least one accessible parking space is available.*

WALLACE FALLS STATE PARK*: 14503 Wallace Lake Road (47.8671, -121.6783); Discover Pass required (**discoverpass.wa.gov**).

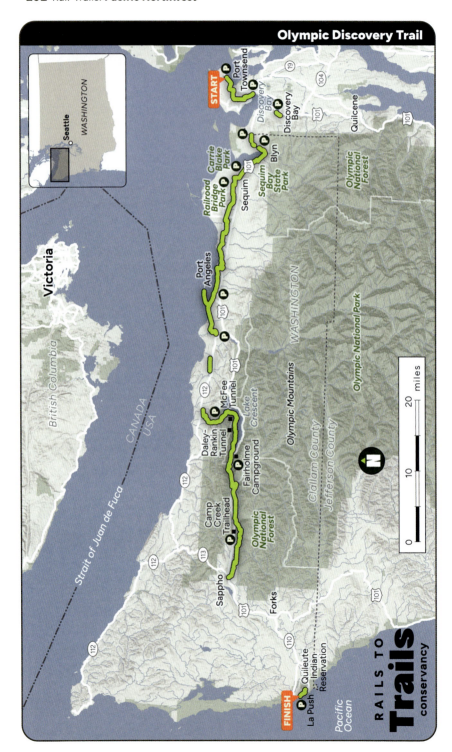

Olympic Discovery Trail

Sandwiched between the Olympic Mountains and the Strait of Juan de Fuca, the Olympic Discovery Trail traverses a spectacular route across the Olympic Peninsula. The 123-mile trail connects Puget Sound with the Pacific Ocean, with some 65 miles of trail completed as of early 2025, most of which are paved. The remainder of the route is either on low-traffic roads or highways with shoulders.

The trail hosts the westernmost segment of the Great American Rail Trail®, a 3,700-mile cross-country route that connects Washington state and Washington, D.C. The trail visits well-stocked towns, including Port Townsend, Sequim (pronounced "skwim"), Port Angeles, and Forks, on its route through dense Pacific Northwest forests and farmland. It also travels over the ancestral lands of the Coast Salish, S'Klallam, and Quileute peoples.

The rail-trail sections follow the corridor of the Chicago, Milwaukee, St. Paul and Pacific Railroad, which had completed its transcontinental route to the eastern shore of Puget Sound in 1909. It acquired a local railway in 1918 and began hauling timber and passengers across Puget Sound via railcar and barge. Passenger service ended in 1931 with the opening of US 101/Olympic Highway, and rail service on the peninsula ended altogether in 1987, followed soon

The Elwha River Bridge in Port Angeles has two decks: one for vehicles and one for pedestrians and bicyclists.

Counties
Clallam, Jefferson

Endpoints
Boat St. and Washington St. (Port Townsend); Quileute Oceanside Resort, 330 Ocean Dr. (La Push). See a full list of segments and their endpoints on the next page.

Mileage
64.5

Type
Rail-Trail

Roughness Rating
1–2

Surface
Asphalt, Crushed Stone

thereafter by the formation of the Peninsula Trails Coalition. Another section of rail-trail, the Spruce Railroad Trail, skirts the north shore of Crescent Lake in Olympic National Park. Horseback riding is permitted, except for the section in Sequim.

Check the Jefferson County Transit (**jeffersontransit.com**) and Clallam Transit (**clallamtransit.com**) schedules for their bicycle-rack-equipped bus fleets to avoid the higher-traffic parts of the route.

Note that the map accompanying this description shows trail segments, as well as all low-stress routes that comprise the trail. As of early 2025, the endpoints for the completed sections of off-road, developed trail are as follows, from east to west:

- Boat St. and Washington St. (Port Townsend); S. Discovery Road and Milo Curry Road (Port Townsend)
- US 101/Olympic Hwy., 0.5 mile north of WA 20 (Port Townsend); Old Gardiner Road and US 101/Olympic Hwy. (Sequim)
- Old Gardiner Road and US 101/Olympic Hwy. (Sequim); Michigan School Road E., 0.3 mile west of Knapp Road (Sequim)
- Michigan School Road W. and Pierce Road (Sequim); Old Blyn Hwy. and US 101/Olympic Hwy., 260 feet north of Neal Lane (Sequim)
- US 101/Olympic Hwy. and Blyn Road (Sequim); Old Blyn Hwy. and Blyn Crossing/Woods Road (Blyn)
- West end of Old Blyn Hwy., 0.7 mile southwest of E. Sequim Bay Road (Blyn); south end of Dawley Road, 0.9 mile southeast of Schoolhouse Point Lane (Sequim)
- Ramblewood Retreat Center, Sequim Bay State Park, 269035 US 101, north end of Dawley Road (Sequim); Albert Haller Playfields/Carrie Blake Park, E. Fir St. and N. Blake Ave. (Sequim)
- W. Hendrickson Road and N. Sequim Ave. (Sequim); N. Lincoln St. and E. Railroad Ave. (Port Angeles)
- Pebble Beach Park, N. Oak St. and Railroad Ave. (Port Angeles); Valley Creek Estuary Park, Marine Dr. and W. First St. (Port Angeles)
- Marine Dr. and W. Boathaven Dr. (Port Angeles); Marine Dr. and W. Hill St. (Port Angeles)
- 10th St. and S. Milwaukee Dr. (Port Angeles); Milwaukee Dr., 0.2 mile west of W. 14th St. (Port Angeles)
- W. 18th St. and S. Milwaukee Dr. (Port Angeles); Elwha Bridge, Elwha River Road, 0.1 mile south of Sisson Road (Port Angeles)
- Freshwater Bay Road, 0.2 mile north of Everett Road (Port Angeles); Onella Road and Thompson Road (Port Angeles)

➤ Gossett Road, 0.3 mile south of WA 112/Strait of Juan de Fuca Hwy. (Port Angeles); unnamed gravel road, 1.3 miles south of WA 112/Strait of Juan de Fuca Hwy. and Reynold Road (Port Angeles)
➤ Spruce Railroad Trail, 4189 E. Beach Road (Port Angeles); Cooper Ranch Road, 0.2 mile south of US 101/Olympic Hwy. (Port Angeles)
➤ WA 110/La Push Road, 0.2 mile southeast of By-Yak-Way (La Push); Ocean Dr. and Quileute Oceanside Resort (La Push)

PORT TOWNSEND TO BLYN

Port Townsend, which sits on a harbor at the north end of Puget Sound, underwent a building boom in the Victorian era and still looks the part today. Although it didn't fulfill the dreams of early boosters, it is a regional commercial and cultural center with an emphasis on wooden watercraft.

A 7-mile section of packed-limestone trail begins at a busy waterfront boatyard. The trail, named the Larry Scott Trail after a coalition founder, steadily climbs a slope with commanding views of the harbor for a mile, then turns inland, running adjacent to WA 20 until it crosses on an underpass at mile 2.6. The trail

The trail begins in Port Townsend on the north end of Puget Sound.

heads due west from here and crosses under South Discovery Road before arriving at Cape George Trailhead Park. Passing through the park, you'll cross South Discovery Road again in 2 miles before arriving at the Milo Curry Trailhead at Four Corners after a 0.3-mile stretch of low-traffic road with no shoulder.

The route beyond to Discovery Bay takes you on WA 20, which has heavy truck traffic. The Peninsula Trails Coalition suggests using Jefferson County Transit's Sequim route from here to Discovery Bay, Blyn, or Sequim.

Discovery Bay is a small community that sits on the shores of the eponymous bay off the Strait of Juan de Fuca. It was named by English explorer George Vancouver after the ship that carried his crew here in 1792.

The paved trail runs north for less than a mile, then uses a combination of Gardiner Road, Old Blyn Highway, the wide shoulder of US 101/Olympic Highway, and trail for the next 11 miles to Blyn, center of the Jamestown S'Klallam Reservation, which sits at the base of Sequim Bay.

BLYN TO PORT ANGELES

The paved trail in Blyn begins in the woods about 0.5 mile north of the Jamestown S'Klallam Tribal Library, which is located in Sequim at 1070 Old Blyn Hwy. and serves as an official trail parking area. The trail route is paved for 24.1 of the next 26.1 miles to the waterfront in Port Angeles.

Although about 70% of the trail follows the graded railbed, there are a couple of climbs in this section. The longest starts in Sequim Bay State Park, 2 miles north of Blyn, and climbs about 3 miles away from the shoreline to the prairie

The Spruce Railroad Trail section passes through two tunnels next to Lake Crescent.

surrounding Sequim. Along the way, you'll cross the curved and banked Johnson Creek Trestle; at 410 feet long and 86 feet high, it's the largest on the route.

In 2.5 miles, you'll arrive at Carrie Blake Park in Sequim, another commercial and residential center on the peninsula that's also known for its dry weather. The area sits in the rain shadow created by peaks in nearby Olympic National Park and gets only 16 inches of rain annually, compared to about 26 inches in nearby Port Angeles and more than 100 inches in the rainforests to the west. The summer warmth and dryness make this area ideal for growing lavender, and purple and violet fields draw tourists to the Annual Sequim Lavender Festival in July (**lavenderfestival.com**).

Three miles west of the park, you'll cross the Dungeness River—one of nine river crossings between Sequim and Port Angeles—at Railroad Bridge Park. The adjacent Dungeness River Audubon Center displays local flora and fauna. The Dungeness River trestle bridge was restored in 2022 during a larger floodplain and habitat restoration effort. Another 4 miles brings you to shady Robin Hill Farm County Park, where you can explore the woods and marshes on narrow bike, jogging, and equestrian paths.

You'll cross two unique bridges after leaving the park: In 0.3 mile, the trail crosses McDonald Creek on a 93-foot-long railroad flatcar bed, and in 6.4 miles, you'll cross Bagley Creek on a ramp formerly used at the Bainbridge Island ferry terminal. This second bridge is in a steep ravine and comes after a sharp turn that's dicey in wet weather.

Emerging from the ravine to US 101/Olympic Highway, you can enjoy spectacular sights of the Olympic Mountains to the south, weather permitting. In another 1.6 miles, the trail arrives at another scenic section—a 4-mile stretch of shoreline trail to Port Angeles with stunning vistas across the Strait of Juan de Fuca to Canada.

PORT ANGELES TO LAKE CRESCENT

After exploring the parks, restaurants, museums, and shops in the vicinity of the City Pier in Port Angeles, you can admire more views of the harbor and strait as you make a gentle but steady 6-mile climb to a bridge overlooking the Elwha River gorge. Dammed upstream in the early 1900s to supply hydroelectric power, the river was restored to its previous pristine state as a salmon-spawning river after Congress voted to remove the upstream dams. The last one was removed in 2014. You can see spectacular views of the river from a 589-foot pedestrian bridge suspended directly below the Elwha River Road bridge.

Once across the bridge, a mostly on-road section of the Olympic Discovery Trail route heads 20 miles to Lake Crescent, the next destination. Much of the 11-mile section between the bridge and Gossett Road is along busy, two-lane WA 112/Strait of Juan de Fuca Highway. An alternative is Clallam Transit's No. 10 Joyce bus route.

In either case, turn left off WA 112 onto Gossett Road, then turn right onto the paved trail in 0.3 mile. Follow the winding path through 1.6 miles of forest to a gravel road heading south. The trail coalition warns that people on the trail may encounter heavy trucks here during logging season. You'll arrive at the Spruce Railroad Trailhead on East Beach Road in 3.4 miles.

LAKE CRESCENT TO LA PUSH

Although it sports its own name, the Spruce Railroad Trail is a 4-mile segment of the Olympic Discovery Trail that lies within Olympic National Park. The paved trail runs along the northern part of the gleaming blue, clear waters of glacially carved Lake Crescent, with many unobstructed views of forested mountains ending at the water's edge.

The trail is named for the Sitka spruce, a large Pacific Northwest evergreen whose wood was used to build World War I airplanes. The U.S. Army built the railroad to haul the lumber out of the forest, but the war ended around the same time as the completion of the line. Private operators used it until the 1950s.

Heading south from the trailhead, the paved trail has been graded and improved to accommodate wheelchair access. In a mile, you'll arrive at the 450-foot McFee Tunnel; a flashlight might be needed, as the tunnel is curved and the opposite end is not visible. As you approach, a dirt trail to the left goes out to a bridge across a small cove called Devil's Punchbowl. In 1.8 miles, you'll come to the Daley-Rankin Tunnel, which is shorter. Both of these tunnels were dynamited after the tracks were pulled up in the 1950s. They were cleared and reopened in 2017 and 2020, respectively.

In 4.6 miles, you'll arrive at the Ovington Trailhead; here, you can join Camp David Junior Road, which goes 2.9 miles to the national park's Fairholme Campground and camp store on the lake's west shore. Otherwise, remain on the trail through cedars, Douglas-firs, red alders, and madrones for 4.5 miles to a junction. A left turn leads to parking on US 101, and a right fork takes the trail across US 101 and through a grove of spruce trees into dense forest surrounding the Sol Duc River heading west.

In 8.3 miles, past US 101, the trail ends at Camp Creek Trailhead on Cooper Ranch Road. From here, the route follows lightly traveled Cooper Ranch Road and Mary Clark Road 9.6 miles (follow the signs) to Sappho on US 101. You'll take the wide shoulder of US 101 for 10.4 miles to Forks, the setting for the *Twilight* books and movies.

The next 12 miles follow a narrow shoulder on WA 110/La Push Road; an alternative is Clallam Transit's No. 15 La Push route.

The final 1.3 miles of the Olympic Discovery Trail to the Pacific Ocean were completed through the Quileute Indian Reservation with the assistance of tribe members.

CONTACT: olympicdiscoverytrail.org

PARKING

Parking areas are listed from east to west. Select parking areas for the trail are listed below; for a full list of parking areas and other waypoints, consult **TrailLink™**. *Indicates that at least one accessible parking space is available.*

PORT TOWNSEND: Haven Boatworks, Haines Pl. and Eighth St. (48.1055, -122.7809).

PORT TOWNSEND: Milo Curry Trailhead, Milo Curry Road, 0.1 mile northwest of S. Discovery Road (48.0505, -122.8275).

DISCOVERY BAY: Trailhead, US 101/Olympic Hwy., 0.3 mile north of W. Uncas Road (47.9935, -122.8882); roadside parking along Olympic Hwy.

WASHINGTON: Diamond Point Trailhead, US 101/Olympic Hwy. and Diamond Point Road (48.0508, -122.9511).

BLYN*: Blyn Trailhead, Old Blyn Hwy., 0.4 mile north of Woods Road/Blyn Crossing and US 101/Olympic Hwy. (48.0267, -122.9950).

SEQUIM*: Carrie Blake Park, N. Blake Ave. and E. Fir St. (48.0831, -123.0853).

SEQUIM*: Railroad Bridge Park, 2151 W. Hendrickson Road (48.0853, -123.1468).

PORT ANGELES*: Waterfront Trailhead, N. Lincoln St. and E. Railroad Ave. (48.1200, -123.4295).

PORT ANGELES: Elwha River Bridge, Crown Z Water Road, 0.7 mile northwest of Forsberg Road (48.1138, -123.5532); underneath Elwha River Road overpass.

CRESCENT*: Spruce Railroad Trailhead, E. Beach Road, 4.1 miles west of US 101/Olympic Hwy. (48.0932, -123.8019).

FAIRHOLME: US 101/Olympic Hwy. and Sol Duc–Hot Springs Road (48.0752, -123.9541); roadside parking.

BEAVER: Camp Creek Trailhead, Cooper Ranch Road, 0.2 mile south of US 101/Olympic Hwy. (48.0611, -124.1092).

LA PUSH: Second Beach Trailhead, WA 110/Ocean Dr., 0.1 mile west of Quileute Heights (47.8981, -124.6237).

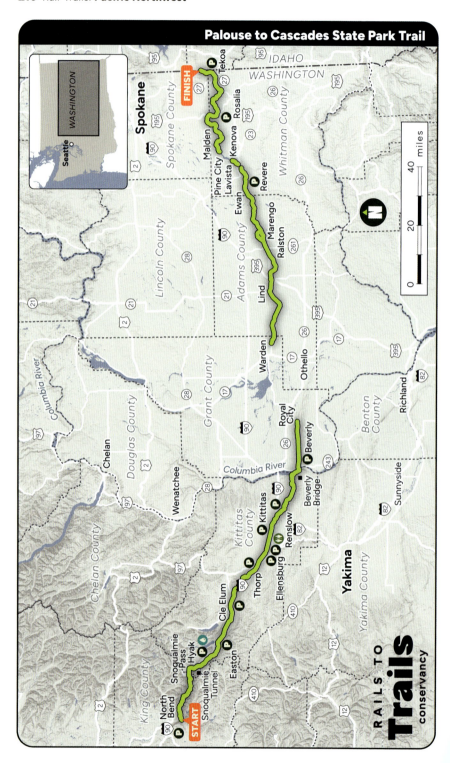

Palouse to Cascades State Park Trail

54

GREAT AMERICAN RAIL-TRAIL

One of the longest rail-to-trail conversions in the nation, the Palouse to Cascades State Park Trail offers users an adventure across many landscapes. The unpaved corridor runs for 286 miles (about 245 miles are passable), from the forested slopes of the Cascade foothills east of Seattle to the Palouse hills and the Idaho border.

For detours, visit the Palouse to Cascades Trail Coalition website, **palousetocascadestrail.org.**

Along the way, you'll encounter numerous tunnels (the longest is 2.3 miles), trestles across scenic canyons in the Cascades, a U.S. Army training base, the Columbia River basin, arid open country scoured clean by Ice Age floods, and the fertile wheat fields of the Palouse hills. What you won't see are lots of traffic signals and frequent minimarts to resupply your provisions. Carry plenty of food and water, especially east of the Columbia River.

The trail follows the route of the Chicago, Milwaukee, St. Paul & Pacific Railroad, also known as the Milwaukee Road.

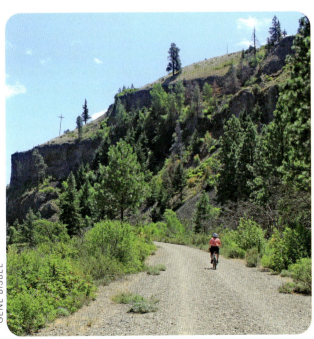

GENE BISBEE

The rail-trail features a varied landscape shaped by ancient volcanoes and Ice Age floods.

Counties
Adams, Grant, King, Kittitas, Spokane, Whitman

Endpoints
See next page.

Mileage
245.6

Type
Rail-Trail

Roughness Rating
2–3

Surface
Ballast, Crushed Stone, Dirt, Gravel

> **Endpoints**
> *Western section (includes a gap in Ellensburg):* **Rattlesnake Lake Recreation Area at Cedar Falls Road, 1 mile south of SE 177th St. (North Bend); Lower Crab Creek Road SW at Road E. SW (Royal City)** *Eastern sections (includes several gaps):* **Fir Ave. and E. First St. (Warden); Washington–Idaho state line, 5.3 miles past Tekoa Trestle at Tekoa Idaho Road and S. Idaho Road (Tekoa)**
>
> For an interactive map of all the completed trail segments and current gaps in the trail, go to rtc.li/palouse-to-cascades.

It blazed a corridor across the state by 1909, in many cases following millennia-old trading routes established by Indigenous peoples.

Railroad operations ceased, and the Washington State Department of Natural Resources acquired much of the right-of-way in 1980 under the name John Wayne Pioneer Trail. When Washington State Parks took ownership of the entire trail in 2018, it renamed it Palouse to Cascades State Park Trail to recognize the regions it connects. The trail is a segment of the Great American Rail Trail®, a 3,700-mile route connecting Washington, D.C., and Washington state.

An old railroad trestle crosses a side canyon overlooking Rock Lake in Eastern Washington.

The trail surface west of the Columbia River is mostly packed limestone, except through the U.S. Army Yakima Training Center, where it's dirt and sand. On the western side of the trail, you'll find informative trailheads, trailside campsites, and more restrooms and parking areas. Washington State Parks classifies the longer, eastern segment as mostly unimproved, with some areas still surfaced with original railroad ballast.

Visitors will experience breathtaking scenery all along the trail. For bicycling, many recommend wider tires treated with a sealant to repel punctures from goat's head, a type of thorn. Some segments east of the Columbia River require detours around rockslides, trestles destroyed by wildfires, flooded railroad cuts, and an active railroad.

Keep your eyes open for black-tailed deer and Douglas squirrels in the western forests. After crossing into Eastern Washington, mule deer and coyotes can be seen.

CEDAR FALLS TO SNOQUALMIE TUNNEL

The westernmost segment is the busiest. Starting in North Bend at the Cedar Falls Trailhead, the uphill grade (no more than 2%) passes through heavily forested slopes on the "wet" side of the Cascades to the 2.3-mile Snoqualmie Tunnel at the summit. Some bicycling groups shuttle between the Cedar Falls and Snoqualmie Pass (Hyak) Trailheads via I-90 for a 22-mile downhill run on the packed-limestone trail.

Cedar Falls is where the Milwaukee Road originally split: A spur heading northwest toward Everett is now the Snoqualmie Valley Trail (see page 233); a railbed heading southwest toward Tacoma later became the Cedar River Trail (see page 131), which begins in the Landsburg area of Washington.

The 1,500-foot grade to the tunnel boasts three high trestles that span rocky drainages and afford views of nearby granite peaks and I-90 winding through the canyon hundreds of feet below. Depot stops are still marked, and occasional mile markers show the distance from Chicago (Cedar Falls is milepost 2136). There are two primitive trailside campsites, at Alice Creek and Carter Creek (three to four campsites each; first come, first served), with vault toilets and tent pads. Note that most backcountry campsites are closed from November 1 to April 30.

The Snoqualmie Tunnel, built between 1912 and 1914, is cold, damp, and pitch-dark; take a jacket and a flashlight. It is closed in November and usually reopens in May. Check the Washington State Parks website (**rtc.li/palouse-to-cascades-state-park-trail**) for estimated opening dates in spring.

HYAK TO COLUMBIA RIVER

This 90-mile section descends from Snoqualmie Pass to the Columbia River. The tunnel's East Portal opens up at the Hyak Trailhead, which has water and parking. Snowmobiling is allowed in the winter between Stampede Pass Road and Cabin Creek only. To participate in winter sports at Sno-Parks located along the trail, you will need a seasonal or day permit between December 1 and March 31. Hyak, Crystal Springs, and Lake Easton Sno-Parks also require a groomed-trail permit sticker with the seasonal permit. Daily permits do not require a sticker.

The trail travels east along the shoreline of Keechelus Lake, the source of the Yakima River, for about 4 miles, passing primitive campsites at Cold Creek and Roaring Creek. Eight miles past the lake, you'll arrive at Lake Easton State Park, passing through two short tunnels along the way. The park has hiker-biker campsites. Another 12 miles brings you to the South Cle Elum Depot and Rail Yard (**milwelectric.org/visit**), where a circa 1909 depot has been restored as part of an old rail yard walking tour. An electrical substation that powered the trains still stands here.

Leaving this rail yard, you'll probably notice a steady tailwind whistling eastward; wind turbines dot the hills to take advantage of it. The trail enters the tight Upper Yakima River Canyon in about 5 miles, where you'll pass through two more tunnels, one long enough to require a flashlight, and the Ponderosa Campground, which is open year-round.

In 25 miles, the trail breaks at North Waters Street in downtown Ellensburg for the Central Washington University campus. You'll find plenty of diners and groceries in this town, the largest on the trail. The trail resumes on North Alder Street, just south of East 10th Avenue.

Another 6 miles leads to Kittitas, which also has a circa 1909 railroad depot. Winding through farmland for 6 miles, the trail crosses I-90 on the recently reopened Renslow Trestle and enters the U.S. Army's Yakima Training Center. The base is open to trail users, who must register at either entrance (Renslow in the west or Doris in the east). The trail through this arid landscape is gravelly and sandy. The tunnel at Boylston is closed, but there is a detour. Passing through the final rocky railroad cuts on the Army base, you'll enjoy a grand view of the Columbia River.

COLUMBIA RIVER TO IDAHO BORDER
The 3,000-foot Beverly Bridge across the Columbia River was refurbished and reopened to non-motorized users in 2022, rejoining the east and west segments after a 42-year gap.

You must preregister online (**rtc.li/palouse-cascades-registration**) before entering any portions of the trail east of Beverly. You will receive combinations for the 50 locked gates that cross private property over the next 150 miles, as well as updates on trail closures and detours.

The trail is open, although the surface is described as "unimproved" for 16 miles, from Beverly to Royal City Junction. A short line railroad uses the Milwaukee Road railbed to Warden, requiring trail users to detour for about 40 miles on low-traffic roads. Both Othello and Warden are towns with ample opportunities to replenish supplies.

The trail resumes on the east side of Warden and travels another 22 miles east through irrigated farmland to Lind (you'll have to detour around a closed trestle west of town), another town with services. Heading east, you'll notice the farmland transitions to an arid landscape of bare bedrock, and rocky formations emerge. This is known as the channeled scablands, created when tumultuous Ice Age floods swept away soil to the bedrock, leaving behind coulees, buttes, and other scenic landforms.

Pushing ahead 15 miles to Ralston, you'll find water at the cinder-block Grange Hall, just off the trail (head south on WA 261 for 0.1 mile), and tent space at Keppler Memorial Park, just across the street from the Grange Hall. The trail is blocked about 3 miles ahead at Cow Creek by the missing 1,400-foot trestle across the canyon, which still contains the foundations of the bridge supports. An on-road northern detour avoids the gap, as does a more direct southern bypass that's open March 1–October 31 across a landowner's field.

Milwaukee Road relics, like the Seabury Bridge on the trail's eastern end, frequently appear along the route.

Farther east on the Palouse to Cascades trail, you'll intersect the north–south Columbia Plateau State Park Trail between Marengo and Revere, although fencing and steep hillsides prevent access to the other trail.

The next 40 trail miles to Malden are interrupted by detours and bypasses due to property ownership, rockslides, and lingering damage to trestles from the 2020 Babb Road wildfire. Those three fire-damaged bridges around Pine City are slated for reopening in 2028. Areas like scenic Rock Lake between Ewan and Pine City can be reached by out-and-back travel, but the trail does not go through.

Many homes in Malden were destroyed by the 2020 fire, but the town is rebuilding and welcomes visitors. Camping is allowed between the newly rebuilt city hall and a playground, and showers are available at the fire station.

The next 32 miles into the rolling Palouse farmland to Tekoa (pronounced "tee-ko") have been improved, although they're still rough. There are several trestles at road crossings that have been removed, so the trail descends and crosses the road, then climbs up on the other side. The picturesque Seabury Trestle is intact but does not have side rails. The towns of Rosalia and Tekoa in this section have groceries and diners. Arriving in Tekoa, you'll cross the 977-foot-long Tekoa Trestle—reopened in 2022—which crosses Hangman Creek 125 feet below and commands a view of the valley.

The trail surface for the final 5 miles to the Idaho border can be slippery in wet weather. The trail continues into Idaho on private property, but the owners allow bicyclists for the 3.25 miles to Mowry Road. After that, take surface roads to the Trail of the Coeur d'Alenes.

CONTACT: rtc.li/palouse-to-cascades-state-park-trail and palousetocascadestrail.org

TRAIL 54 PALOUSE TO CASCADES STATE PARK TRAIL

PARKING

Parking areas are listed from west to east. Select parking areas for the trail are listed below; for a full list of parking areas and other waypoints, consult **TrailLink™**. *Indicates that at least one accessible parking space is available.*

A Discover Pass (**discoverpass.wa.gov**) is required to park in trailheads operated by Washington State Parks, the Washington State Department of Natural Resources, or the Washington Department of Fish & Wildlife. Sno-Park passes may be required in the wintertime.

CEDAR FALLS*: Cedar Falls Trailhead, Cedar Falls Road SE, 0.3 mile south of SE 177th St. (47.4325, -121.7663).

HYAK*: Hyak Trailhead, NF 906, 0.5 mile east of I-90 Exit 54 (47.3920, -121.3922).

EASTON: 0.3 mile southeast of fire station on Cabin Creek Road (47.2311, -121.1720); you'll drive along the trail to reach the parking lot in 0.3 mile, on your right.

SOUTH CLE ELUM*: South Cle Elum Trailhead, 801 N. Milwaukee Ave. (47.1833, -120.9560).

THORP: Thorp Trailhead, Thorp Depot Road, 0.4 mile west of Thorp Hwy. S (47.0594, -120.6736).

ELLENSBURG: Water St. Trailhead, at 1501–1503 N. Water St., 100 feet north of W. 15th Ave. (47.0071, -120.5505).

ELLENSBURG: Fairgrounds Trailhead, N. Alder St., 450 feet south of E. 10th Ave. (47.0007, -120.5316).

KITTITAS: Kittitas Trailhead, Main St., 200 feet south of Railroad Ave. (46.9820, -120.4178).

RENSLOW: Army West Trailhead, Stevens Road, 0.1 mile south of Boylston Road (46.9542, -120.2977).

BEVERLY: Nunnally Lake Trailhead, Lower Crab Creek Road SW, 1.9 miles east of WA 243 (46.8340, -119.8970).

REVERE: Washington Department of Fish & Wildlife, Revere Wildlife Area, Davis Road, 9.9 miles west of WA 23 (47.0859, -117.9191).

ROSALIA: Rosalia City Park, W. Ninth St. and S. Park Ave. (47.2316, -117.3726).

TEKOA: Washington State Parks, Tekoa Trailhead, Washington St. and Spring St. (47.2291, -117.0750).

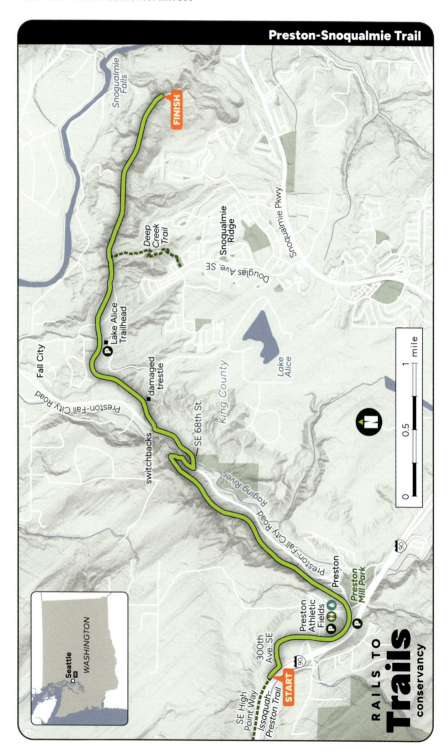

Preston-Snoqualmie Trail

55

GREAT AMERICAN RAIL-TRAIL

The Preston-Snoqualmie Trail follows a graded route through steep, wooded terrain into the Cascade foothills. The 6.5-mile trail is enjoyable year-round, as the asphalt provides a good surface for day-trippers to enjoy the forest habitat and maybe catch a glimpse of far-off Snoqualmie Falls at the end. (Note that a demolished trestle and another damaged one interrupt a smooth passage.)

The trail is part of the Leafline Trail Network, which will connect 900 miles of trail in the central Puget Sound region. It's also a segment of the Great American Rail-Trail®, a 3,700-mile route connecting Washington, D.C., and Washington state.

The trail uses the former Seattle, Lake Shore and Eastern Railway corridor, which hosts other rail-trails in King and Snohomish Counties. Dating to the 1880s, the eastern branch ran between Seattle and Snoqualmie before owners ran out of money and sold it to the Northern Pacific Railway. Discontinued in 1974, a segment of the railroad survives as a tourist train operated by the Northwest Railway Museum (**trainmuseum.org**) out of a vintage passenger station in nearby

You'll cross a vintage concrete arch bridge spanning the Raging River.

County
King

Endpoints
Issaquah-Preston Trail, 300th Ave. SE and SE High Point Way (Preston); dead end 1.9 miles east of Lake Alice Road SE (Snoqualmie)

Mileage
6.5

Type
Rail-Trail

Roughness Rating
1

Surface
Asphalt

Snoqualmie. Deer, elk, coyotes, and bears inhabit the area, and thick stands of red cedar, Douglas-fir, big-leaf maple, and Sitka spruce shade the trail.

The trail begins at a light industrial park on the outskirts of Preston, an old logging community. In 0.9 mile, you'll arrive at parking and a trailhead next to Preston Athletic Fields, which has drinking fountains and restrooms. You'll start your journey with an easy downhill grade. In 0.3 mile, a stairway on the right descends to the rustic Preston Community Center, built in 1939 by the Depression-era Works Progress Administration. Across Preston-Fall City Road via an underground walkway, a dilapidated 1890s shingle mill has been transformed into Preston Mill Park.

The trail follows a slight downhill grade for 1.7 miles to an overlook where a railroad trestle once crossed the Raging River. The Northern Pacific replaced the trestle after a tragic 1900 collapse, then removed it permanently after rail service ended. To cross the river, follow the steep, paved descent to busy Preston-Fall City Road, use the crosswalk, and then head right behind the concrete traffic barriers. Turn left on Southeast 68th Street in 0.1 mile, then cross the vintage concrete arch bridge spanning Raging River. In another 0.1 mile, a series of seven tight switchbacks climbs out of the ravine to the railroad grade. In 0.2 mile, you'll encounter a timber trestle that was closed in 2022 after a large tree fell into it, damaging the support pilings. As of 2024, no timeline exists for a replacement.

To see the rest of the trail, you must return to the Preston Trailhead and drive about 4 miles to the site of a former depot at the Lake Alice Trailhead in Fall City (see GPS coordinates below). The damaged bridge is about 0.8 mile west of there. Continuing east, the trail meets Deep Creek Trail, a soft-surface singletrack leading to Snoqualmie suburbs. The Preston-Snoqualmie Trail ends at a chain-link fence marked **NO TRESPASSING** 1.9 miles from the Lake Alice Trailhead. Three benches here provide views of the 268-foot-high Snoqualmie Falls in the distance. Obscured in the spring and summer, the scene comes into better view in the fall when trees drop their leaves.

CONTACT: rtc.li/king-county-preston-snoqualmie-trail

PARKING

Parking areas are listed from west to east. *Indicates that at least one accessible parking space is available.*

PRESTON*: Preston Athletic Fields, 30634 SE 87th Pl. (47.5232, -121.9350).

PRESTON*: Trailhead, SE 87th Pl., 200 feet east of Preston–Fall City Road (47.5225, -121.9337).

FALL CITY: Lake Alice Trailhead, Lake Alice Road SE and SE 56th Pl. (47.5507, -121.8877).

Richland Riverfront Trail

56

The **Richland Riverfront Trail** is part of the larger 23-mile Sacagawea Heritage Trail, which runs through the Tri-Cities (Richland, Kennewick, and Pasco). Both trails follow the beautiful Columbia River, which you can learn more about through a collection of educational signs along the route called Pompy's Lessons, named after Sacagawea's son.

If you choose to travel south to north, you'll start your journey at Columbia Point Marina Park, where you will find accessible restrooms, water fountains, a beautiful waterside park, and a few restaurants. In 1 mile, you'll reach the Bradley Boulevard Trailhead, which offers parking and is located adjacent to Bradley Park.

Follow the trail another 0.6 mile to reach Howard Amon Park, which features a playground, tennis courts, beaches along the river, and the annual two-day Art in the Park festival in the summer. There are two accessible parking lots within the park and accessible restrooms and water fountains near the Richland Rotary Centennial Plaza. Please note that to avoid congestion and unsafe conditions in the parks it travels through, the Richland Riverfront Trail splits into two median-separated paths, with biking permitted on the path closest to the main road and walking and mobility devices

County
Benton

Endpoints
Columbia Point Marina Park, Columbia Point Dr., adjacent to I-182/US 12 (Richland); dead end of Ferry Road, 300 feet east of Harris Ave. (Richland); dead end of Sprout Road, 300 feet east of Harris Ave. (Richland); USS Triton Sail Park at Port of Benton Blvd. and Richardson Road (Richland)

Mileage
7

Type
Greenway/Non-Rail-Trail

Roughness Rating
1

Surface
Asphalt

You'll journey through a handful of parks flanking the Columbia River.

ISABELLE LORD

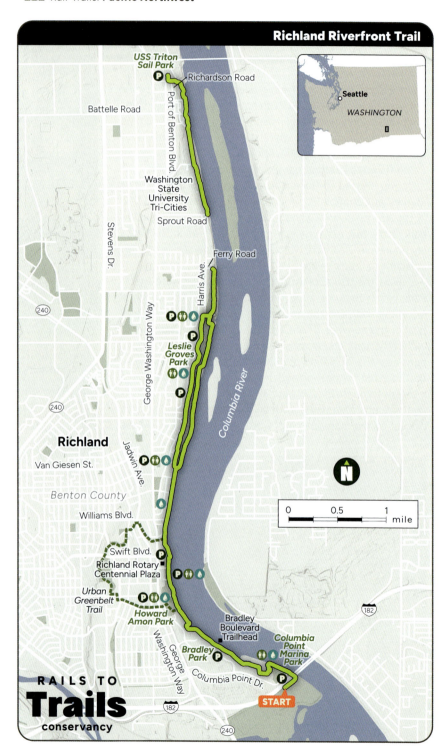

permitted on the other path closest to the river. Markings on the ground will direct you to the appropriate path to follow through the parks.

Just north of Richland Rotary Centennial Plaza (in 0.1 mile), the trail connects to the 3.25-mile Urban Greenbelt Trail, which makes a loop. If you stay on the Riverfront Trail, you will reach Leslie Groves Park in 1.7 miles; there you can find several accessible parking lots, restrooms, and water fountains in addition to barbecue areas, volleyball and tennis courts, and riverfront beaches. Here, you will again use different trails depending on your mode of transportation.

In another mile, you'll reach Ferry Road, where this segment of the trail ends. After a 0.5-mile gap, another section of trail spans 1.5 miles to the north. To reach it, at the end of Ferry Road (in about 250 feet), turn right (north) onto Harris Avenue and follow this street until you reach Sprout Road; turn right onto Sprout Road and pick up the trail where the road ends, in 0.5 mile. The remainder of the trail runs between the riverfront and Washington State University Tri-Cities. Toward the end of the trail, you can enjoy the wide-open views before you end your journey at the historic USS Triton Sail Park, a national park showcasing the first submarine to circumnavigate the earth underwater.

Whether you're an avid biker, a volleyball star, a history buff, or all of the above, the Richland Riverfront Trail has something for everyone!

CONTACT: richlandparksandrec.com/parks

The trail connects the riverside communities of Richland, Kennewick, and Pasco.

PARKING

Parking areas are located within Richland and are listed from south to north. Select parking areas for the trail are listed below; for a detailed list of parking areas and other waypoints, consult **TrailLink™**. *Indicates that at least one accessible parking space is available.*

COLUMBIA POINT MARINA PARK*: Dead end of Columbia Point Dr., adjacent to I-182/US 12 (46.2636, -119.2461).

BRADLEY BOULEVARD TRAILHEAD: Bradley Blvd., 0.3 mile northwest of Columbia Point Dr. (46.2671, -119.2608).

HOWARD AMON PARK*: Amon Park Dr. and Lee Blvd. (46.2748, -119.2712).

RICHLAND ROTARY CENTENNIAL PLAZA*: 652 Amon Park Dr. (46.2808, -119.2716).

LESLIE GROVES PARK*: River Road, 350 feet from Hains Ave. (46.2941, -119.2685); follow the sign to Leslie Groves Park to reach the parking lot.

LESLIE GROVES PARK*: Dead end of Newcomer St., 250 feet east of Harris Ave. (46.3035, -119.2657).

LESLIE GROVES PARK*: Dead end of Park St., 300 feet east of Harris Ave. (46.3072, -119.2644).

LESLIE GROVES PARK*: Harris Ave. and Saint St. (46.3114, -119.2623).

SNYDER BOAT LAUNCH PARKING LOT*: 34 Snyder St. (46.3148, -119.2613).

USS TRITON SAIL PARK*: Port of Benton Blvd. and Richardson Road (46.3485, -119.2695).

Sammamish River Trail

Wine enthusiasts can find a lot to like on the Sammamish River Trail, which passes through the Woodinville Wine Country, home to some 60 tasting rooms and restaurants.

The trail spans a 10.3-mile stretch of the 44-mile Locks to Lakes Corridor, which connects Puget Sound with the Cascade foothills. The trail is also part of the region's developing 900-mile Leafline Trail Network and the Great American Rail-Trail®, a 3,700-mile route that will eventually connect Washington, D.C., and Washington state.

At one time, flat-bottomed steamboats carried trade on the Sammamish River, which meanders between Lake Washington and Lake Sammamish. In the 1960s, the U.S. Army Corps of Engineers completed a flood-control project that left behind a mostly level, paved trail atop a levee. It opened to the public in 1979.

Today the trail serves the towns of Redmond, Woodinville, and Bothell in Seattle's eastern suburbs. The trail is one of the busiest in the area. Despite this traffic, it's not unusual to see bald eagles, herons, or beavers along the river, as well as deer and small mammals in the adjacent fields.

Starting the Sammamish River Trail in Marymoor Park in Redmond, home of tech giant Microsoft, you'll find plenty of

County
King

Endpoints
Marymoor Connector Trail in Marymoor Park, 300 feet northwest of NE Marymoor Way and W. Lake Sammamish Pkwy. NE (Redmond); Burke-Gilman Trail, 400 feet east of tunnel beneath 96th Ave. NE near Blyth Park (Bothell)

Mileage
10.3

Type
Greenway/Non-Rail-Trail

Roughness Rating
1

Surface
Asphalt

The Sammamish River is the trail's constant companion as it winds through Seattle's eastern suburbs.

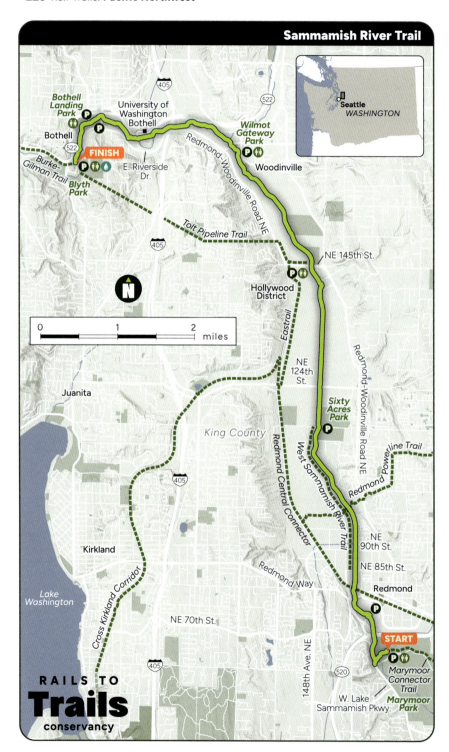

parking. The trail begins at the junction with the Marymoor Connector, which heads east 1.6 miles to its junction with the East Lake Sammamish Trail (see page 153). Note that equestrians are allowed on a side path adjacent to the trail that runs north to Wilmot Gateway Park in Woodinville (this path is different from the West Sammamish River Trail, shown on the map).

In 1.1 miles, you'll pass under the Redmond Central Connector, a segment of the Eastrail network that's scheduled to link Redmond and Kirkland by spring of 2025.

The next mile or so can be the most congested, especially during lunch hour, given the nearby offices. Across the river, via Northeast 85th Street, a companion trail—the West Sammamish River Trail—runs for 2 miles north on a soft surface. It's open to all users, although wheelchairs are not recommended.

The gravel-surfaced Redmond Powerline Trail crosses the Sammamish River Trail in 1.1 miles. By now, the trail corridor has widened and is buffered by a row of tall poplar trees.

You'll pass acres of athletic fields over the next 3.2 miles to the Northeast 145th Street intersection. This is the Hollywood District of Woodinville Wine Country, home to a cluster of wineries and tasting rooms. Crossing the river on a NE 145th Street side path takes you to the swank, French-style estate of Chateau Ste. Michelle Winery. The oldest winery in the state, it's also home to a popular summer concert series. (Check **ste-michelle.com,** as the property has been sold and redevelopment plans are in the works.)

Serving as an important community connector, the popular trail links Redmond, Woodinville, and Bothell.

Back on the trail, you'll pass the dirt Tolt Pipeline Trail junction in 0.3 mile. Wilmot Gateway Park, with its shady pergola, expansive lawn, and playground, awaits in 1.5 miles. Beyond, the trail traces the curvy river route through Bothell. On the right as you pass beneath the elevated I-405 interchange in 1.1 miles, you'll see the North Creek Trail, which connects to the University of Washington Bothell campus.

The Sammamish River Trail next enters a wooded area and passes a pedestrian bridge that crosses the river to Bothell Landing Park, which contains a history museum and houses several historic buildings from the late 1800s. Before white settlers arrived in the area, the Sammamish people had populated this area for some 10,000 years.

The trail ends at the Burke-Gilman Trail (see page 125) in 0.7 mile. A left turn will take you to facilities at Blyth Park, while a right turn takes you 20 miles to Golden Gardens Park on Puget Sound.

CONTACT: rtc.li/king-co-sammamish-river-trail

PARKING

Parking areas are listed from south to north. *Indicates that at least one accessible parking space is available.*

REDMOND*: Marymoor Park, NE Marymoor Way, 0.3 mile east of W. Lake Sammamish Pkwy. NE (47.6648, -122.1209); Lot K; nominal fee.

REDMOND*: Sixty Acres South, York Road/NE 116th St., 0.6 mile east of Willows Road NE (47.7038, -122.1415).

REDMOND*: Sixty Acres Park, York Road/NE 116th St., 0.6 mile east of Willows Road NE (47.7043, -122.1420).

WOODINVILLE*: Northshore Athletic Fields, NE 145th St./WA 202 and Village Road (47.7331, -122.1447).

WOODINVILLE*: Woodin Creek Park, 13201 NE 171st St. (47.7509, -122.1638).

WOODINVILLE*: Wilmot Gateway Park, 17301 131st Ave. NE (47.7530, -122.1657).

BOTHELL*: Sammamish River Park, 17995 102nd Ave. (47.7583, -122.2042).

BOTHELL*: The Park at Bothell Landing, NE 180th St., 220 feet south of Woodinville Dr./WA 522 (47.7590, -122.2062); cross the river to reach the trail.

BOTHELL*: Blyth Park, 16950 W. Riverside Dr. (47.7506, -122.2081); take the Burke-Gilman Trail north 0.1 mile, then turn left to Sammamish River Trail.

Similkameen Trail

58

Beginning on the west side of Oroville and ending just shy of the Canadian border, the Similkameen Trail follows a river by the same name. The dirt-and-gravel rail-trail crosses a scenic high bridge over the Similkameen River to enter a dramatic river gorge leading to a waterfall.

Despite the nearby Okanogan Highlands and Cascade Range, the trail has an easy grade. High temperatures here can soar to 100°F in the summer and drop to 30°F in the winter, with snow cover possible between November and March. The Similkameen Trail forms a section of the developing 1,200-mile Pacific Northwest Trail, which will travel from Glacier National Park in Montana to Washington's Olympic Peninsula.

Wildlife enthusiasts, photographers, and history buffs will not be disappointed by this trail. As one of the most biologically diverse watersheds in western North America, the cross-border valley is home to grizzly bears, wolves, lynx, fishers, wolverines, elk, snowshoe hares, mule deer, and a great diversity of birds, including owls, woodpeckers, eagles, and falcons. In a setting of shrub steppe and occasional evergreens, the trail passes benches, views of the

You'll have a view of the historic Enloe Dam Powerhouse near the northwestern end of the trail.

County
Okanogan

Endpoints
Dead end of Kernan Road (Oroville); 1.5 miles northwest of Enloe Dam, west of the Similkameen River (Oroville)

Mileage
4.9

Type
Rail-Trail

Roughness Rating
2

Surface
Dirt and Gravel

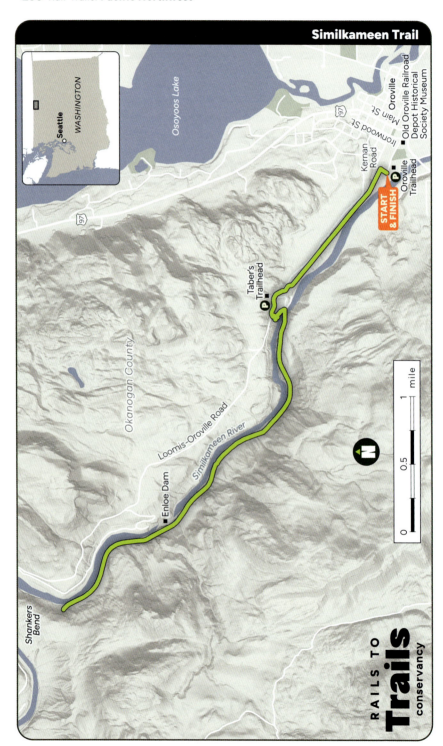

river, and interpretive signage telling the history of the Okanogan and Similkameen Valleys.

Built in 1907 by the Washington & Great Northern Railroad (which would merge with other rail lines to become the Burlington Northern Railroad in 1970), the original tracks fell into disuse in 1972 when a record flood caused bridge damage on the line. You can learn more about the area's history and culture at the Old Oroville Railroad Depot Historical Society Museum and Log House on Ironwood Street, just up the road from the Oroville Trailhead.

About 1.5 miles from the Oroville Trailhead, the trail passes Taber's Trailhead and crosses the Similkameen River gorge on a 400-foot-long girder bridge. In season, salmon and steelhead runs can be seen 90 feet below in the river.

The route formerly ended at a gate with a vista of the nearly 100-year-old Enloe Dam and waterfalls variously known as Coyote, Similkameen, or Enloe Falls. The trail now extends 1.5 miles farther, ending before the east end of a 1,761-foot-long timber-lined tunnel that cuts off a bend in the river known as Shankers Bend. The huge timbers supporting the tunnel's entrances speak of another era, when the rail system was created to haul ore to market. Dredging tools used to look for the elusive flecks of gold still can be seen in the shallows of the river.

There is no trail parking at the northwestern endpoint. Out-and-back visitors will experience a noticeable incline from that endpoint back down to the girder bridge. Equestrian use is allowed on the entire trail, though riders must dismount and walk their horses across the girder bridge. There is sufficient parking for horse trailers at both parking areas.

CONTACT: rtc.li/similkameen

PARKING

Parking areas are located within Oroville and are listed from southeast to northwest. *Indicates that at least one accessible parking space is available.*

KERNAN ROAD: Dead end of Kernan Road, 0.3 mile west of Ironwood St. (48.9384, -119.4441).

TABER'S TRAILHEAD: 3521 Loomis-Oroville Road (48.9514, -119.4643); gravel lot across the road from the trailhead.

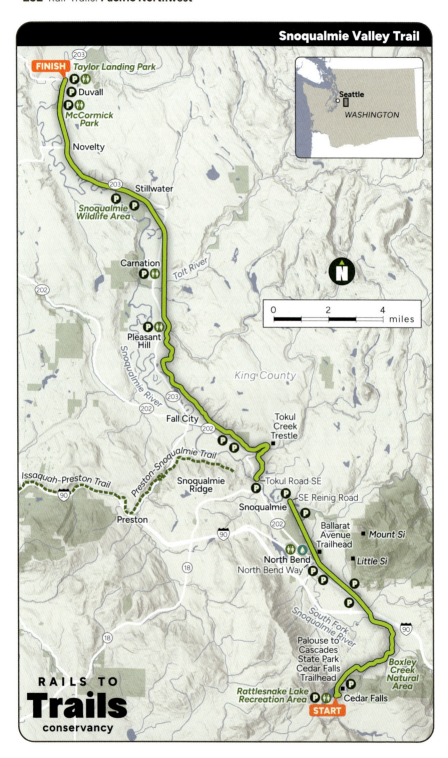

Snoqualmie Valley Trail

59

The 30-mile **Snoqualmie Valley Trail** plunges out of the Cascade Range to enter an enchanting mix of forests and farmland, protected natural areas, and bustling small towns. Be aware that this trail goes through some remote areas where cougars and bears may be present.

The trail is part of both the Leafline Trail Network, which will connect more than 900 miles of trails in the central Puget Sound region, and the Great American Rail-Trail®, which will eventually span 3,700 miles between Washington, D.C., and Washington state. It follows the railbed of the Everett Branch of the Chicago, Milwaukee, St. Paul and Pacific Railroad. Known as the Milwaukee Road, the corridor opened locally in 1909 and crosses much of Washington as the Palouse to Cascades State Park Trail (see page 211) in the east and the Cedar River Trail (see page 131) and Olympic Discovery Trail (see page 203) in the west. The state acquired the right-of-way in the 1980s.

In fact, the Snoqualmie Valley Trail starts at a junction with the Palouse to Cascades State Park Trail at Rattlesnake Lake near Cedar Falls. Parking can be scarce in the summer

County
King

Endpoints
Rattlesnake Lake Recreation Area, Iron Horse Trail and NF 50 (Cedar Falls); SE Reinig Road, 330 feet west of 396th Dr. (Snoqualmie); Tokul Road SE, just southwest of SE 60th St. (Snoqualmie); Taylor Landing Park, Main St. NE and NE Woodinville Duvall Road (Duvall)

Mileage
29.5

Type
Rail-Trail

Roughness Rating
1

Surface
Crushed Stone

Following a Milwaukee Road route, the rail-trail connects a handful of bustling small towns from Cedar Falls to Duvall.

at the 111-acre lake, which is operated by Seattle Public Utilities. There's also parking at the adjacent Palouse to Cascades Trailhead, where a Discover Pass is required. Plan ahead, as there is no drinking water or food available at the lake.

The crushed-limestone trail starts with a 600-foot descent through a second-growth evergreen forest in the first 5.5 miles, within earshot of rippling creeks in the Boxley Creek Natural Area. At the base, you'll cross the rushing South Fork Snoqualmie River and pass into the wide Snoqualmie Valley virtually in the shadow of the steep slopes of Mount Si and Little Si in the east.

Restrooms and water fountains are available in parks on the outskirts of North Bend, and the Ballarat Avenue trailhead is two blocks from the town's main drag on North Bend Way, where you can fill up on burgers, milkshakes, or pie at several cafés. Over the next 2.5 miles, you'll cross several trestles and the Mount Si Golf Course en route to Snoqualmie.

A trail gap begins 0.8 mile past the golf course's main entrance, at a stairway at the end of a trestle in Snoqualmie. If you're uncomfortable descending a dozen steps with your bike, you can take a detour: At the golf course entrance, exit left to low-traffic Park Street and turn right to follow the road 0.7 mile northwest to Meadowbrook Way Southeast, where a right turn takes you across the Snoqualmie River on the Meadowbrook Way Bridge. Either way, you'll end up on the Reinig Road/Southeast Mill Pond Road "on road connector" (if you are coming from the detour, take a sharp left (west) onto Mill Pond Road to continue on the route). Look for signs pointing to the Snoqualmie Valley Trail in 1.8 miles, taking the first exit from a traffic circle at WA 202. A 0.7-mile climb on Tokul Road here leads to the developed trail, on the left. You'll have to descend a short path with loose footing to reach the trail.

Note: The second exit off the traffic circle goes about 0.2 mile west to observation decks for Snoqualmie Falls (**snoqualmiefalls.com**), a breathtaking 270-foot waterfall. You might recognize some scenes from David Lynch's *Twin Peaks* television series circa 1990, which was filmed here. The third exit takes you back south on the other side of the river into downtown Snoqualmie past dozens of old locomotives and railcars to the Northwest Railway Museum (**trainmuseum.org**) at a restored 1890 Northern Pacific Railway depot.

For the next 8 miles, the trail travels along a forested ridge. After about 1 mile along this section, you'll cross the spectacular 400-foot-long curved Tokul Creek Trestle, which soars 100 feet above the forest floor. A popular mountain biking area is accessible from side paths; a permit from the logging company owner is required for entry (**cgrecreationpermit.com**).

The trail emerges from the forest in Carnation at Remlinger Farms (open to the public) and crosses the rocky Tolt River. A half mile beyond is the trailhead for the town of Carnation. Located at the confluence of the Tolt and Snoqualmie Rivers, this area was inhabited for thousands of years by the Indigenous Snoqualmie people.

TRAIL 59 SNOQUALMIE VALLEY TRAIL

The influence of a former Carnation Evaporated Milk Co. research facility is seen in the town name, as well as the many hay barns that dot the pastures over the next 9 miles to Duvall. This shady, flat section passes through the Stillwater Unit of the Snoqualmie Wildlife Area, where you'll often find birders scanning the ponds and treelines for waterfowl and migratory songbirds on the Pacific Flyway.

The trail ends in Duvall on the banks of the Snoqualmie River. A restored and relocated railroad depot near McCormick Park marks one of many upgrades in the town, which has been rejuvenated in recent years by growth in the suburbs east of Seattle.

CONTACT: rtc.li/king-co-snoqualmie-valley-trail

PARKING

Parking areas are listed from south to north. *Indicates that at least one accessible parking space is available.*

NORTH BEND*: Palouse to Cascades State Park, Cedar Falls Trailhead (47.4323, -121.7663); Discover Pass required (**discoverpass.wa.gov**).

NORTH BEND*: Rattlesnake Lake Recreation Area, Cedar Falls Road SE, 0.4 mile south of SE 177th St. (47.4326, -121.7681).

NORTH BEND*: Ballarat Ave. N. and NE Fourth St. (47.4966, -121.7814).

SNOQUALMIE*: Centennial Fields Park, 39903 SE Park St. (47.5228, -121.8088); go 0.5 mile south on Meadowbrook Trail, which runs alongside SE Park St., to Snoqualmie Valley Trail access at Mount Si Golf Course.

FALL CITY: 4261 356th Dr. SE (47.5677, -121.8652).

CARNATION: Nick Loutsis Park, 32401 Entwistle St. (47.6475, -121.9078).

CARNATION: Snoqualmie Wildlife Area, Stillwater Unit South Parking, Carnation-Duvall Road NE, 0.1 mile northwest of NE Stillwater Hill Road (47.6831, -121.9238); Discover Pass required (**discoverpass.wa.gov**).

DUVALL*: Depot Park, 26227 NE Stephens St. (47.7399, -121.9878).

DUVALL*: Park and Ride, 16011 Main St. NE (47.7436, -121.9864).

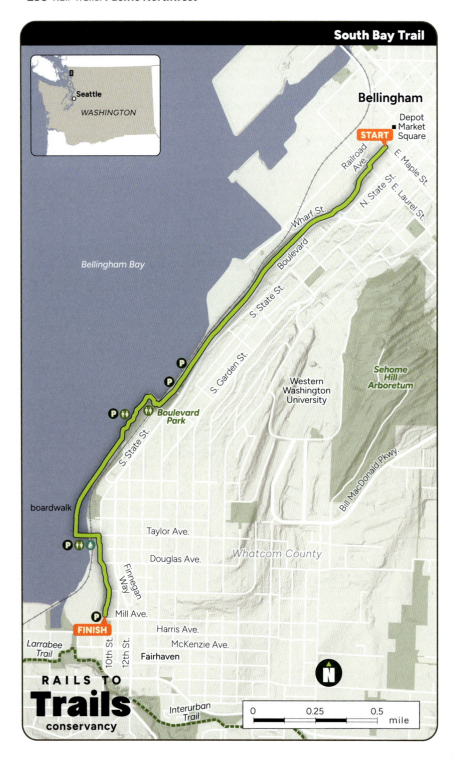

South Bay Trail

Following the route of the former Bellingham and Skagit Interurban Railway, the South Bay Trail connects Bellingham and Fairhaven in Northwest Washington. Beginning from its northern end in downtown Bellingham, you'll experience a gradual descent as you head southwest to a spectacular boardwalk over Bellingham Bay. Along the way, you can view unique art installations and native wildflowers while enjoying a lush tree canopy for most of the trail.

Begin at East Maple Street and Railroad Avenue, across from Depot Market Square. Although the trail is unsigned, look for the yellow bollards that restrict vehicle access to the pathway. After one block, you'll reach East Laurel Street and see an entrance to the trail. Following the trail southwest, you'll pass condominiums, community gardens, and beautiful murals celebrating biking. Small shops and a pocket park also pop up along the tree-lined trail.

In 0.3 mile, you'll reach Wharf Street; use caution when crossing here, as the intersection doesn't have a signal. In 0.2 mile, a stairway offers access to the main thoroughfare, Boulevard, which the trail parallels. Another access point appears in 0.5 mile that will take you to Boulevard and South State Street.

County
Whatcom

Endpoints
E. Maple St. and Railroad Ave. (Bellingham); Mill Ave. and 10th St. (Fairhaven)

Mileage
2.5

Type
Rail-Trail

Roughness Rating
1

Surface
Asphalt, Boardwalk, Concrete, Crushed Stone

You'll enjoy a spectacular boardwalk over Bellingham Bay near the end of the trail.

Access to Boulevard Park is available in another 0.3 mile via an at-grade railroad crossing. Restrooms, parking, a fishing dock, and a coffee shop are located within the park. From here, the trail transitions to a route along Bellingham Bay. A highlight is the wooden boardwalk over the bay, where you can watch for shorebirds. (Note that bikes are to yield to pedestrians on the boardwalk.) A yoga sculpture depicting *natarajasana* (dancer's pose) also adorns a rock outcropping on the bay.

As the boardwalk trail heads up to 10th Street (which you'll reach in 0.8 mile) and off the water, there are several benches on which to rest and take in the views. Follow 10th Street to Mill Avenue and the end of the trail in 0.4 mile. From here, you'll be within easy reach of Fairhaven's shops and restaurants.

CONTACT: cob.org/services/recreation/parks-trails

PARKING

Parking areas are located within Bellingham and are listed from north to south.
Indicates that at least one accessible parking space is available.

S. STATE STREET LOT: S. State St., 0.2 mile north of 14th St. (48.7347, -122.4974); limited spaces.

S. STATE STREET LOT: S. State St., 0.1 mile north of 14th St. (48.7337, -122.4981); limited spaces.

BOULEVARD PARK*: 470 Bayview Dr. (48.7310, -122.5027).

10TH ST. PARKING*: 10th St. and Taylor Ave. (48.7255, -122.5051).

MILL AVE. PARKING*: 10th St. and Mill Ave. (48.7209, -122.5043); metered parking.

Spokane River Centennial State Park Trail

61

The beauty of the Spokane River Centennial State Park Trail (Centennial Trail) comes alive in stands of ponderosa pines and Douglas-firs, blooms of elderberry and sumac, exposed basalt in the deep river canyon, and the bridges and waterfalls of downtown Spokane. A day on the 40-mile trail offers many activities, such as swimming at beaches, exploring the site of the 1974 World's Fair, or touring Gonzaga University. While the Centennial Trail features mild grades, there is a slight decline heading west, ending at a Spokane River beach at Nine Mile Recreation Area.

Starting at the trailhead on East Appleway Avenue and Spokane Bridge Road in Liberty Lake, take the Liberty Lake Stateline Trail east to a junction in 0.2 mile. The right fork is the North Idaho Centennial Trail (see page 29), which heads east 23 miles to the shores of Lake Coeur d'Alene. The left fork begins the Spokane River Centennial State Park Trail. It crosses under I-90 to Gateway Regional Park and runs west along the south bank of the Spokane River, passing Spokane Valley Mall and Mirabeau Point Park before crossing to the north shore at Denny Ashlock Memorial Bridge after 13 miles.

County
Spokane

Endpoints
North Idaho Centennial Trail at Washington–Idaho state line, off I-90 Exit 299 (Liberty Lake); Riverside State Park/Nine Mile Recreation Area, 0.5 mile north of W. Charles Road (Nine Mile Falls)

Mileage
40

Type
Greenway/Rail-Trail

Roughness Rating
1

Surface
Asphalt

One of the trail's most iconic bridges crosses Deep Creek, which flows into the Spokane River.

JESSE VOREMBERG

Shortly thereafter you'll reach your first on-street segment of the trail, at Donkey Island Trailhead (mile 14). Take either the shoulder of North Farr Road or the low-traffic alternative of North Maringo Drive to East Upriver Drive. Turn left and continue on the shoulder or sidewalk 0.6 mile, where the multiuse path restarts at Boulder Beach (mile 16).

In another mile, you can watch climbers at the Minnehaha Climbing Rocks. Soon you'll be routed back onto East Upriver Drive, where you can ride in the striped bike lane 1.7 miles to North Greene Street (mile 19.5) and back onto the trail in downtown Spokane. Take the trail to Mission Avenue (mile 21); turn right, cross the train tracks, and use the crosswalk to cross Mission Avenue at Mission Park. The trail follows the railroad south before veering west through Gonzaga University's campus and back across the Spokane River (mile 22).

Continue west and use any of the next three bridges to turn right and cross onto Riverfront Park. Explore the site of the Expo '74 World's Fair before crossing the Post Street Bridge (mile 23) with views of Spokane Falls and the gondolas traversing the river. Leaving town, back on the north side of the river, the Kendall Yards residential/commercial area is your last chance for food and water as you head into a more remote area.

At mile 24.5, there's an opportunity to head south and cross the Sandifur Memorial Bridge to connect to the Fish Lake Trail (see page 165) via an on-street route (take West Riverside Avenue west to South Government Way).

Continuing on the Centennial Trail, vistas of the Spokane River canyon open up as the trail heads north. You'll follow the trail alongside North Pettet Drive, cross the road before the bridge, and use the barrier-protected sidewalk to cross TJ Meenach Bridge (mile 27). Follow the trail markings on the pavement and loop under the bridge to continue west on the trail. You'll remain on the south bank of the river for the remainder of your trip.

The final 10 miles of the Centennial Trail are within Riverside State Park. There are many opportunities to take a mountain bike onto unpaved side trails. Consult the Washington State Parks website, below. Weaving through pine forests, you'll pass a military cemetery before descending to the Equestrian Area parking (mile 30). You'll share the Riverside Park roadway with minimal vehicular traffic 0.7 mile, until you reach the Morin Trailhead. The trail continues north to the Wilbur Trailhead (mile 34), where you'll again share the roadway with parkgoers in cars. Proceed 0.7 mile and cross West 7 Mile Road to continue along the Riverside Park roadway to the McLellan Trailhead.

The remainder of the trail is off-street, as the Spokane River widens and the forest grows thicker. The trail crosses Carlson Road, then West Charles Road as it enters the Sontag Day Use Area (mile 38). The final 2 miles wind through Riverside State Park before a steep descent to the Nine Mile Recreation Area (mile 40), where you're greeted by an inviting beach at a calm and wide section of the Spokane River.

CONTACT: rtc.li/spokane-river

PARKING

Parking areas are listed from east to west. *Indicates that at least one accessible parking space is available.

Spokane Transit Authority (**spokanetransit.com**) provides weekday and weekend bus service that can be used to access the Centennial Trail. All buses have bike racks to transport up to three bikes.

LIBERTY LAKE*: Liberty Lake Trailhead, E. Appleway Ave. and Spokane Bridge Road (47.6939, -117.0487).

LIBERTY LAKE: Harvard Road Trailhead, E. Wellington Pkwy. and N. Harvard Road (47.6813, -117.1115).

SPOKANE VALLEY*: Mirabeau Trailhead, 13500 E. Mirabeau Pkwy. (47.6848, -117.2245).

SPOKANE VALLEY*: Islands Trailhead, E. Upriver Dr., 0.2 mile east of N. Pierce Road (47.6945, -117.2496).

SPOKANE: Boulder Beach, E. Upriver Dr., 0.4 mile west of E. Hodin Dr. (47.6949, -117.3075).

SPOKANE*: Logan Neighborhood, 1208 E. Mission Ave. (47.6713, -117.3904).

SPOKANE: Riverside State Park Equestrian Parking Area, 0.3 mile north of W. Trails Road/Government Way (47.6885, -117.4903); horse trailer parking available; Discover Pass required (**discoverpass.wa.gov**).

NINE MILE FALLS*: Riverside State Park at McLellan Trailhead, approximately 0.7 mile north of Riverside Park and W. 7 Mile Road (47.7484, -117.5297); Discover Pass required (**discoverpass.wa.gov**).

NINE MILE FALLS*: Sontag Day Use Area, 10000 W. Charles Road (47.7783, -117.5496).

NINE MILE FALLS*: Riverside State Park–Nine Mile Recreation Area (47.7927, -117.5675); Discover Pass required (**discoverpass.wa.gov**).

Tommy Thompson Parkway

62

Following a former Seattle and Northern Company rail line, the Tommy Thompson Parkway—named after a local railroad enthusiast—journeys across Fidalgo Bay in Northwest Washington on a former railroad trestle connecting the bay's western and eastern shores. Along the way, you'll have stunning views of Mount Baker, Fidalgo Bay, local art installations, and plenty of wildlife, including sea lions who know how to ham it up for adoring audiences.

Starting at 11th Avenue and Q Street in Anacortes, the paved trail heads south, passing marinas and boatyards. In 0.7 mile, you'll reach Ben Root Skatepark (at R Avenue and 22nd Street), where parking, restrooms, and drinking water are available. Heading along the western shore of Fidalgo Bay, you'll enjoy clear views of Mount Baker on the eastern horizon if the weather is cooperating.

Continuing southeast, after traveling 1.6 miles from the skatepark, you'll reach Weaverling Road, where parking and portable toilets are available. After crossing the road, you'll come to the boardwalk trestle crossing Fidalgo Bay. As a great spot for bird-watchers, families, and sea lion fans, the trestle can get crowded at peak hours but provides

CAS MARBURGER

The trail traces the Fidalgo Bay shoreline in the ferry port of Anacortes.

County
Skagit

Endpoints
11th St. and Q Ave. (Anacortes); March's Point Road, 0.1 mile south of N. Texas Road (Anacortes)

Mileage
3.3

Type
Rail-Trail

Roughness Rating
1

Surface
Asphalt, Boardwalk

TRAIL 62 TOMMY THOMPSON PARKWAY

You'll cross Fidalgo Bay on a causeway and boardwalk connecting Weaverling Spit and March's Point.

unmatched views. Interpretive signs describing the local history, environment, and wildlife also dot the way.

The trail ends in 1 mile at March's Point Road on the east shore of Fidalgo Bay.

CONTACT: anacorteswa.gov/1061/tommy-thompson-parkway

PARKING

Parking areas are located within Anacortes and are listed from north to south.
*Indicates that at least one accessible parking space is available.

BEN ROOT SKATEPARK*: 2313 R Ave. (48.5037, -122.6093).

34TH ST. STATION: Street parking along 34th St., one block east of V Ave. (48.4947, -122.6025).

WEAVERLING ROAD LOT: Dead end of Weaverling Road (adjacent to the Fidalgo Bay boat ramp), 0.1 mile northeast of Fidalgo Bay Road (48.4834, -122.5918).

246 Rail-Trails: **Pacific Northwest**

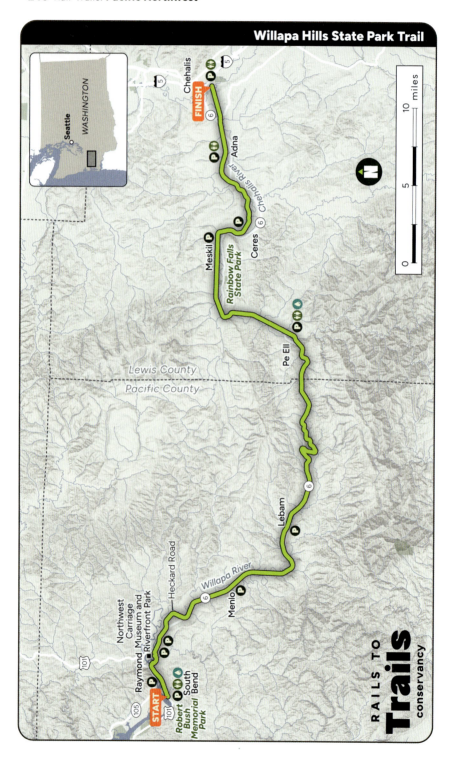

Willapa Hills State Park Trail

63

How many trails can boast that they start near the world's largest oyster? Only one: the Willapa Hills State Park Trail. Robert Bush Memorial Park in South Bend is near the western end of the 56-mile trail, and it's worth a quick visit to check out the park's oyster sculpture before or after enjoying a ride or walk on one of Washington's longest trails. Even if you miss it, you won't be able to miss the piles of oyster shells all around town. South Bend markets itself as the Oyster Capital of the World, claiming that one in every six oysters consumed in the United States is harvested right out of nearby Willapa Bay.

The westernmost trailhead is located along US 101 at Summit Avenue (0.2 mile east of the western endpoint). The trail is nicely paved for its first few miles, from South Bend through Raymond. Once you cross the Willapa River at Raymond, a quick detour to the northwest will bring you to the Northwest Carriage Museum and Riverfront Park, offering interpretation of the local history. Along the trail in and around Raymond, you'll find whimsical metal statues of various outdoor activities, including a waving cyclist and a fisherman. See how many you can spot!

KEVIN BELLE

The trail winds along—and frequently crosses—the Willapa and Chehalis Rivers, as well as several smaller creeks.

Counties
Lewis, Pacific

Endpoints
Monroe St. N. and US 101 (South Bend); dead end of SW Hillburger Road, 0.4 mile south of SW Sylvenus St. (Chehalis)

Mileage
56

Type
Rail-Trail

Roughness Rating
1–2

Surface
Asphalt, Ballast, Crushed Stone, Grass, Gravel

About 3 miles east of Raymond, where it crosses Heckard Road, the trail becomes unimproved and is largely impassable for the next 27 miles. Washington State Parks is undertaking major improvements to several bridges and has plans to upgrade the entire surface of the Willapa Hills State Park Trail. When those efforts are completed in the next several years, the entire trail will be a gem.

In the meantime, it is recommended to complete this trail in segments, bypassing the middle section, between Heckard Road and the Pe Ell Trailhead. There is trail access in the towns of Menlo and Lebam, and surfacing improvements with crushed stone between Menlo and Pluvius are planned for 2025. Although two bridges remain out in this middle section, the trestles between Lebam and Pe Ell are passable. Before exploring this section, be sure to check the website, opposite, for construction updates and temporary-closure notices.

Once back on the trail in Pe Ell, the surface is unpaved but in good condition for about 17 miles, into Adna. Along this stretch, make sure to stop at Rainbow Falls State Park, which is directly accessible by the trail. The park contains some of the last old-growth tree stands along the Chehalis River. The trail largely parallels the river in this section, which provides beautiful views and welcome shade in the summer months.

You'll cross several century-old trestles along the rail-trail.

TRAIL 63 WILLAPA HILLS STATE PARK TRAIL **249**

From Adna, the trail continues another 4 miles along farmlands to its eastern terminus, just outside of Chehalis and with easy access to I-5. Horseback riding is allowed all along the route.

CONTACT: parks.wa.gov/find-parks/state-parks/willapa-hills-state-park-trail

PARKING

Parking areas are listed from west to east. Select parking areas for the trail are listed below; for a detailed list of parking areas and other waypoints, consult **TrailLink™**. *Indicates that at least one accessible parking space is available.*

SOUTH BEND: Summit Ave. and US 101 (46.6696, -123.7848).

RAYMOND*: Northwest Carriage Museum, 314 Alder St. (46.6832, -123.7313).

RAYMOND: Henkle St. and Cherry St. (46.6799, -123.7221).

RAYMOND*: Kelsey St. and Garden St. (46.6760, -123.7051).

MENLO: Bullard Ave. and WA 6 (46.6239, -123.6487).

LEBAM: WA 6 and Water St. (46.5604, -123.5534).

PE ELL*: Front St. and E. Fourth Ave. (46.5698, -123.2970).

CERES: Ceres Hill Road and Aust Road (46.6084, -123.1539).

ADNA*: Dieckman Road, 0.2 mile north of Bunker Creek Road (46.6326, -123.0622).

CHEHALIS*: Dead end of SW Hillburger Road, 0.4 mile south of SW Sylvenus St. (46.6472, -122.9738).

250 Rail-Trails: **Pacific Northwest**

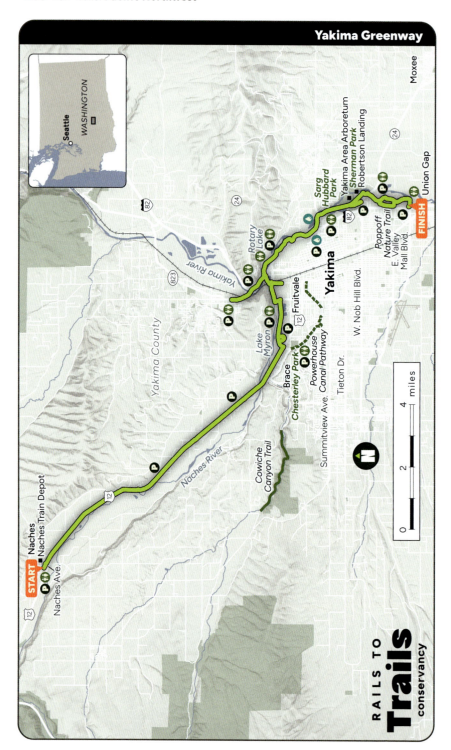

Yakima Greenway

64

Spanning nearly 23 miles, the Yakima Greenway is a network of trails and recreational areas in Yakima County. It connects charming parks, bustling fishing lakes, access points to the Yakima River, and an array of protected natural areas. The greenway serves as a natural habitat for birds, fish, and other animals, making it a great spot for nature enthusiasts. While parts of the trail have been washed out by the river, most of it remains accessible and well maintained.

Your journey begins northwest of Yakima, in the town of Naches. After crossing Naches Avenue, you can't miss an eight-sided Art Deco building with a tall spire. The small white structure, once part of a gas station, is now a distinctive town landmark. Immediately after is the charming historic Naches Train Depot, which also serves as a visitor center. Built in 1906, the depot was used for both freight and passenger service until the early 1950s.

Heading southeast out of Naches, the northern section of the trail loosely parallels US 12 through the eastern foothills of the Cascades. Roughly 9 miles from the northern endpoint, enjoy views from a refurbished railroad bridge over the Naches River. Next up is Lake Myron, a tranquil spot

The greenway provides access to the Yakima River in the eastern foothills of the Cascades.

County
Yakima

Endpoints
Second St., 440 feet west of Naches Ave. (Naches); E. Valley Mall Blvd. and I-82 (Union Gap)

Mileage
22.9

Type
Rail-Trail

Roughness Rating
1

Surface
Asphalt

at the heart of the trail known for bird-watching, fishing, and picnicking. Encircled by natural habitats between the neighborhoods of Brace and Fruitvale, this section of the trail provides a peaceful and immersive nature experience.

The trail heads east, crossing US 12 at North 16th Avenue before heading beneath I-82, where the Naches and Yakima Rivers meet. Just south of this convergence is Rotary Lake, a popular fishing and recreational spot for locals. Enjoy beautiful views of the Yakima River, surrounded by lush terrain and diverse wildlife.

Next, the trail leads to Sarg Hubbard Park, a central location and community gathering spot for Yakima residents and tourists. The park also serves as the most common access point for the Yakima Greenway in Yakima. South of the park is the Yakima Area Arboretum, which features walking paths through beautifully landscaped gardens and showcases the region's diverse plant life. Farther south is Sherman Park, another popular spot among locals.

Approaching the southern endpoint, the trail extends into Union Gap, where you can find more amenities and parking options. Soon after Sherman Park, you'll pass Robertson Landing, a boat ramp in the community of Moxee, followed by the Poppoff Nature Trail in 1.6 miles. The Yakima Greenway ends between the nature trail and I-82/US 12/US 97, just across the interstate from downtown Union Gap.

Nearby trails include the 3-mile Cowiche Canyon Trail (see page 143), featuring the region's wilder, desertlike terrain, and the 2.7-mile Powerhouse Canal Pathway, located just 0.2 mile south of the Yakima Greenway. To reach the canal trail: After crossing US 12—but before turning left at a traffic light to continue on the Yakima Greenway toward Lake Myron—head south on North 40th Avenue to Chesterley Park in Fruitvale, where the Powerhouse Canal Pathway begins.

CONTACT: yakimagreenway.org

TRAIL 64 YAKIMA GREENWAY **253**

PARKING

Parking areas are listed from northwest to southeast. Select parking areas for the trail are listed below. For a detailed list of parking areas and other waypoints, consult **TrailLink™**. *Indicates that at least one accessible parking space is available.*

NACHES: Second St., 440 feet west of Naches Ave. (46.7306, -120.7025).

YAKIMA: Naches Pathway Suntides Trailhead, Old Naches Hwy./Powerhouse Road and US 12 (46.6399, -120.5948).

YAKIMA*: Lake Myron Parking, Fruitvale Blvd., 0.2 mile southeast of US 12 (46.6212, -120.5566).

YAKIMA*: N. 16th Ave., between the Naches River and US 12 (46.6250, -120.5321).

YAKIMA*: Harlan Landing, Rovetto Road, southwest of I-82 (46.6323, -120.5216).

YAKIMA*: Rotary Lake Park & Ride, E. Freeway Lake Road (46.6240, -120.5002).

YAKIMA*: Yakima Valley Visitor Center, 101 N. Fair Ave. (46.6075, -120.4886).

YAKIMA*: Sarg Hubbard Park, 111 S. 18th St. (46.6020, -120.4750).

YAKIMA*: Sherman Park, 2441 W. Birchfield Road (46.5854, -120.4686).

UNION GAP*: E. Valley Mall Blvd. and I-82 (46.5639, -120.4710).

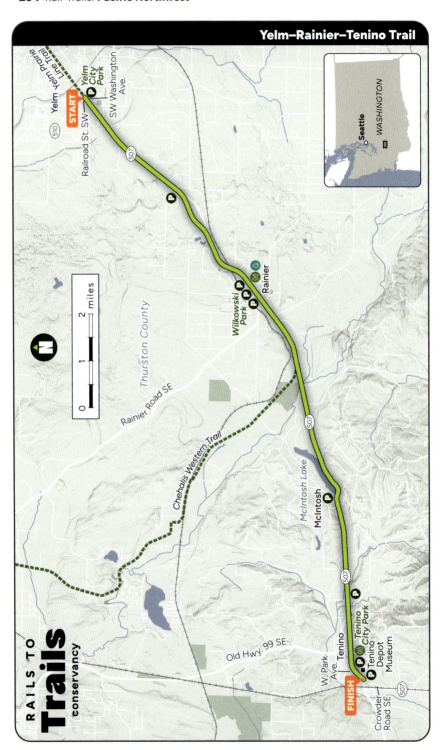

Yelm-Rainier-Tenino Trail

65

The Yelm–Rainier–Tenino Trail is a well-used, wonderfully maintained trail that stretches across Thurston County, traversing relatively gentle terrain through roughly 14 miles of the former Burlington Northern Railroad line. Connecting its three namesake towns, the trail offers recreational opportunities and vital off-road connectivity to its host communities, alternating between secluded rural landscapes, access to the towns, and community amenities such as parks and historical sites. Horseback riding and cross-country skiing are allowed along the entire length of the trail.

On the eastern end, the trail begins in Yelm, a quaint town known for its stunning views of Mount Rainier. It offers a decent offering of boutique shops and food options just feet from the trailhead at Yelm City Park, adjacent to the city hall. As the trail extends southwest out of Yelm, it has many neighborhood access points for travelers, families, and residents.

On either side of the midway town of Rainier, which is less urbanized than the endpoint towns, the path cuts through picturesque farmland and shaded forests. The trail serves as the backbone of Wilkowski Park and parallels Rainier's main

The Tenino Depot Museum's sandstone building, built in 1914, once served trains running between Seattle and Portland.

JOE LACROIX

County
Thurston

Endpoints
Railroad St. SW and SW Washington Ave. (Yelm); Crowder Road SE and W. Park Ave. (Tenino)

Mileage
14.5

Type
Rail-Trail

Roughness Rating
1

Surface
Asphalt

thoroughfare, making it a viable transportation alternative through town. West of Rainier, the trail intersects the southern terminus of the Chehalis Western Trail (see page 139), presenting a north–south connection to Olympia all the way to the southern tip of Puget Sound.

Before entering the historic town of Tenino, the trail passes through a densely wooded corridor with some notable but gentle slopes. Next is a stretch of trail contouring the south bank of McIntosh Lake, which is open year-round and offers stocked rainbow trout in addition to yellow perch, largemouth bass, and brown bullhead catfish. Following this lakeside section is a major road crossing on a curve across WA 507. The road is not heavily trafficked, but vehicles move quickly.

Entering Tenino, the trail sits against the southern edge of town and runs along the length of Tenino City Park, complete with restrooms, Little League fields, playgrounds, and picnic areas, as well as historical markers that dive into Tenino's history as a quarry town and railroad hub. Here, the trail again provides easy access to the amenities and offerings of a quaint town, including lodging, restaurants, and shops. Near the western terminus of the trail, visitors will find a preserved railroad car and historical trailside schoolhouse at the restored Tenino Depot Museum.

CONTACT: rtc.li/thurston-county-trails

PARKING

Parking areas are listed from east to west. *Indicates that at least one accessible parking space is available.*

YELM*: Railroad St. SW and Washington St. SW (46.9419, -122.6081).

YELM: Manke Road SE and WA 507 (46.9126, -122.6478).

RAINIER*: Wilkowski Park, Rochester St. E. (46.8913, -122.6852).

RAINIER: Rainier City Hall, Centre St. N. and Rochester St. W. (46.8887, -122.6896).

RAINIER: Minnesota St. N. and Rochester St. W. (46.8878, -122.6910).

TENINO: Military Road SE and Heidi Lane SE (46.8614, -122.7814); roadside pullout.

TENINO: Churchill Road SE and WA 507 (46.8574, -122.8232); roadside pullout.

TENINO*: Tenino City Park, W. Park Ave. and S. Olympia St. (46.8555, -122.8517).

TENINO: W. Park Ave. at Crowder Road SE (46.8518, -122.8581); roadside parking.

Index

Adna (WA), 248–249
Algona (WA), 185
Alton Baker Park (OR), 96
Anacortes (WA), 243
Anderson Park (OR), 53
Apple Capital Loop Trail (WA), 112, 114–117
Appleway Trail (WA), 112, 118–120
arboretums, 44, 46, 134, 236, 250, 252
Arlington (WA), 136
Arroyo Park (WA), 178
Art Museum of Eastern Idaho, 22, 24
Ashton-Tetonia Trail (ID), 8, 9 (photo), 10–13
Astoria & Columbia River Railroad (OR), 51
Astoria-Megler Bridge (OR), 52
Astoria Nordic Heritage Park, 51
Astoria Riverfront Trolley (OR), 151
Astoria Riverwalk (Astoria River Trail) (OR), 48, 50–52
Aubrey Reach (OR), 65–66
Avery (ID), 33, 35

Bagley Creek, 206
Baker Lake (WA), 130
Baker Lake Road (WA), 130
Ballinger, Lake (WA), 180–182
Banks-Vernonia State Trail (OR), 48, 53–56
Bariscoe Park (WA), 174
Bear Creek Canyon (ID), 26, 27
Bear Creek Greenway (OR), 48, 57–59
Beatty (OR), 84–87
Beaverton (OR), 72–73, 75
Beggars Tick Wildlife Refuge (OR), 99
Bellevue (ID), 44–47
Bellevue (WA), 149
Bellingham (WA), 176–178, 236–238
Bellingham & Skagit Interurban Railway (WA), 177
Ben Root Skatepark (WA), 143
Bernadine Quinn Riverside Park (ID), 16
Beverly Bridge (WA), 214
Big Wood River (ID), 46
bikes. *See* cycling
Bill Chipman Palouse Trail (WA), 27, 121–123
bird-watching, 87, 95, 99, 123, 235, 243, 252
Bitterroot Mountains, 34, 39

Blaine County Recreation District (ID), 45, 47
Bly (OR), 84–87
Blyth Park (WA), 126–127, 225, 228
Boise (ID), 14–17
Boise River Greenbelt (ID), 8, 14–17
Boring (OR), 97–100
botanical gardens, 99, 127, 198
Bothell (WA), 125–127, 225–228
Bothell Landing Park (WA), 228
Boulder Beach (WA), 241
Boulevard Park (WA), 236, 238
Bridge of the Gods (OR), 49 (photo)
Buckley (WA), 169–171
Burke-Gilman Trail (WA), 124–127
Burlington Northern Railroad (WA), 135, 170, 193, 231, 255

Cambridge (ID), 40, 43
Canyon Rim Trail (ID), 8, 18–20
canyons
    Bear Creek, 26, 27
    Canyon Rim Trail, 8, 18–20
    Cowiche Canyon Trail, 143–145, 143 (photo)
    Deschutes River Trail, 64–71
    Hells, 42–43
    Klickitat Trail, 193–195
    Spokane River Centennial State Park Trail, 28, 112, 239–242
    Swale, 193, 195
    Upper Yakima, 214, 215
    Weiser River National Recreation Trail, 40–43
Capitol Gateway Park (WA), 191
Carbon River (WA), 170
Carbonado (WA), 170
Carl C. English Jr. Botanical Garden (WA), 127
Carnation (WA), 232, 234–235
Carrie Blake Park (WA), 207
Cascade Junction (WA), 170
Cascade Locks (OR), 49 (photo), 76–79
Cascade Mountains (WA), 201
Cascade Trail (WA), 128–130
Cassidy, Lake (WA), 135 (photo), 138
Cataldo (ID), 36, 38
Cavanaugh Pond (WA), 133
Cedar Falls (WA), 232, 233
Cedar River Trail (WA), 131–134

257

Celebration Park (WA), 159–160
Centennial Trail (WA), 135–138
Central Washington University, 214
Chatcolet Bridge (ID), 36, 37–38
Chehalis/Chehalis River (WA), 247, 248–249
Chehalis Western Trail (WA), 139–142, 192, 254, 256
Cheney (WA), 265
Chicago, Milwaukee, St. Paul and Pacific Railroad, 34, 131, 203, 211, 232–235
Chuckanut Creek (WA), 178
Civitan Park, Idaho Falls (ID), 22, 23
Clackamas (OR), 83
Clark, William, 151
Cle Elum (WA), 59–62
Coast Salish people, 203
Coeur d'Alene (ID), 28–31
Coeur d'Alene, Lake (ID), 28–30, 37, 239
Columbia County Museum Association, 61
Columbia & Palouse Railroad, 121
Columbia Plateau State Park Trail (WA), 217
Columbia River, 49 (photo)
    Astoria Riverwalk, 50–52
    I-205 Multi-Use Path, 80–83
    John Wayne Pioneer Trail, 212. *See also* Palouse to Cascades State Park Trail (WA)
    Klickitat Trail, 193–195
    Maritime Museum, 52
Columbia River & Northern Railroad (WA), 193
Conant Creek (ID), 11, 12
Concrete (WA), 129
Corbin Park (ID), 28, 30
Cornwall (ID), 26, 27
Cottage Grove (OR), 91–93
Cottage Grove Manufacturing Company (OR), 93
Council (ID), 40–43
Cowiche Canyon Conservancy (WA), 145
Cowiche Canyon Trail (WA), 143–145
Crescent Lake (WA), 204
cross-country skiing, trail use icon for, 7
Cross Kirkland Corridor (WA), 146–149
Crown Zellerbach Trail (OR), 48, 53, 60–63
Culp Creek (OR), 91
Cuthbert Amphitheater (OR), 96

cycling
    e-bikes, 5
    trail etiquette for, 4–5
    trail use icon for, 7

Dairy (OR), 86
Dave and Lynn Frohnmayer Bridge (OR), 96
Deep Creek (WA), 239
Deep Creek Trail (WA), 220
Delta Ponds (OR), 95
Denny Ashlock Memorial Bridge (WA), 239
Denny Park (WA), 182
Denny-Renton Clay & Coal Co. (WA), 131
Deschutes River Trail (OR)
    Bend, 48, 64–67
    Sherman County, 48, 68–71
Devil's Punchbowl (WA), 208
Dierkes Lake Park (ID), 18, 20
Dirksen Nature Park (OR), 74
Discovery Bay (WA), 206
Discovery Trail (WA), 112, 150–152
dogs, on trails, 5
Dorena Lake (OR), 91, 93
drinking water, map icons for, 3
Drummond (ID), 10, 12
Dungeness River Audubon Center (WA), 207
Dungeness River region (WA), 207
Duvall (WA), 232–235

Eagle (ID), 14, 15
East Bay Drive Trail (WA), 191
East Lake Sammamish Trail (WA), 112, 153–156, 227
East Uplands Trail (WA), 145
Echo Lake Park (WA), 180–182
Ellensburg (WA), 212, 214, 217
Elliott Bay Trail (WA), 112, 157–161
Elwha River Bridge (WA), 203 (photo), 207
Emerald Downs racetrack (WA), 185
Enloe Dam Powerhouse (WA), 229 (photo), 231
Enumclaw (WA), 169–171
etiquette, trail, 4–5
Everett (WA)
    Centennial Trail, 138–139
    Interurban Trail (North), 180–182
    Snoqualmie Valley Trail, 213, 233
Evergreen Campground (ID), 40, 43
Ewan (WA), 216
Expo '74 World's Fair, 241

Fairfax (WA), 170
Fairhaven (WA), 177, 237, 238
Fairhaven & Southern Railroad (WA), 177
Fall River (ID), 11, 12
Falls Park (ID), 28, 30
Fanno Creek (OR), 48, 74 (photo)
Fanno Creek Trail (OR), 72–75, 108
Ferry County Rail Trail (WA), 112, 162–164
Fidalgo Bay (WA), 243–245
Fife (WA), 183–185
Fish Lake Trail (WA), 112, 165–167
fishing, trail use icon for, 7
Five Mile Creek (OR), 86
flooding, on Cascade Trail (WA), 129–130
Foothills Trail (WA), 112, 168–171
Forest Park (WA), 108–111
Fort Dent Park (WA), 172–175, 183
Fragrance Lake (WA), 176–178
France (ID), 10, 12
Fred V. Habenicht Rotary Park (WA), 134
Freeman Loop/Park, Idaho Falls (ID), 21, 22
Fremont Cut waterway (WA), 127

Garden City (ID), 14, 15
Gas Works Park (WA), 126, 127
Gateway Regional Park (WA), 239
George Sellar Memorial Bridge (WA), 114, 116
Gibbon-Granger Shortline Railroad, 197
Gimlet Pegram Truss Railroad Bridge (ID), 46
Glacier Peak (WA), 135
Gladstone (OR), 80–83, 101–104
Gold Bar (WA), 199
Golden Gardens Park (WA), 127
Gonzaga University (WA), 239–241
Grainville (ID), 10, 12
Grand Ridge Park (WA), 188, 189
Grandview (WA), 196–198
Grass Valley (OR), 68
Great American Rail-Trail®
   project defined/explained, 1, 2–3
   trail profiles, 37, 124, 153, 187, 203, 211, 219, 225, 233
Great Northern Railway (WA), 129, 157, 163
Greater Yellowstone Ecosystem, 12–13
Green River Trail (WA), 112, 172–175
Green-to-Cedars River Trail (WA), 134
Gresham-Fairview Trail (OR), 97

Hailey (ID), 45
Hailey Native Plant Arboretum (ID), 46
Hall of Fame (RTC's) trail profiles, 33, 37, 97, 124
Hanthorn Cannery Museum, Astoria (OR), 52
Harrison (ID), 36, 37
Hells Canyon (ID/OR), 43
Heyburn State Park (ID), 36, 37
Higgins Point (ID), 28, 30
Historic Columbia River Highway State Trail (OR), 76–79
Hollywood Winery District, Woodinville (WA), 226, 227
horse trails, trail use icon for, 7
Hyak (WA), 213–214

I-205 Multi-Use Path (OR), 80–83
icons
   on maps, 3
   for trail use, 7
Idaho Falls Greenbelt (ID), 8, 21–24
Idaho State Vietnam Veterans Memorial, 20, 21
in-line skating, trail use icon for, 7
information kiosks, Crown Zellerbach Trail (OR), 61
Interurban Trail (WA)
   Bellingham, 112, 176–178
   North, 112, 179–182
   South, 112, 183–186
Iron Horse Trail (WA), 233
Issaquah (WA), 153–156
Issaquah-Preston Trail (WA), 112, 187–189

Jamestown S'Klallam Reservation (WA), 206
Johns Hole Boat Ramp (ID), 22, 23
Johnson Creek (OR), 97, 99

Karen Fraser Woodland Trail (WA), 112, 141, 190–192
Kellogg (ID), 36, 38
Kent (WA), 172–175, 184–1186
Ketchum (ID), 45
Kittitas (WA), 211, 214, 217
Klamath, 85–87
Klamath Falls (OR), 85–87
Klickitat Trail (WA), 112, 193–195
Klickitat Trail Conservancy (WA), 193
Kwayaylsh, Joe and Sarah, 199

Lacey (WA), 190–192
Lacey Depot (community space), 190–192
Lake Sammamish State Park (WA), 154, 155
Lake Wilderness Arboretum (WA), 134
Lamont (ID), 10, 12
Landsburg Park (WA), 131, 134
Lane County Covered Bridges Bikeway (OR), 91
Larrabee State Park (WA), 176–178
Larry Scott Trail (WA), 205–206
Latah Trail (ID), 8, 25–27, 123
Leach Botanical Garden (OR), 99
Leafline Trail Network
    Burke-Gilman Trail, 124–127
    Cedar River Trail, 131–134
    Cross Kirkland Corridor, 146–149
    East Lake Sammamish Trail, 153–156
    Foothills Trail, 168–171
    Green River Trail, 172–175
    Interurban Trail (South), 183–186
    Issaquah-Preston Trail, 187–189
    Preston-Snoqualmie Trail, 218–220
    Sammamish River Trail, 225–228
    Snoqualmie Valley Trail, 233–235
Lebam (WA), 248
Lewis and Clark Corps of Discovery/Expedition, 151, 193
Liberty Lake (WA), 119, 120, 239
Liberty Lake Stateline Trail (ID), 29, 239
Lighted Farm Implement Parade (WA), 197
Lind (WA), 214–215
Linnemann Station (OR), 99
Lithia & Driveway Fields (OR), 57–59
L.L. Stub Stewart State Park (OR), 55
Locks to Lakes Corridor, Seattle (WA), 125
Log Boom Park (WA), 126
Lookout Pass Ski Area (ID), 32, 35
Lower Yakima Valley Pathway (WA), 112, 196–198
Lucky Peak State Park (ID), 14, 15, 16
Lyle (WA), 183–185
Lynnwood (WA), 170–181

Macks Canyon Campground (OR), 69
Maple Valley (WA), 131–134
maps, 3. *See also individual trails*
March's Point (WA), 243–245
Marshall Creek (WA), 167
Marymoor Connector Trail (WA), 156, 225, 227
Marymoor Park (WA), 154, 156, 225–228
Marysville (ID), 10, 12

Matthews Beach Park (WA), 126
MAX light-rail service (OR), 82, 103
Maywood Park (OR), 80, 82
McCormick Park (WA), 232, 235
McDonald Creek, 207
McEuen Park (ID), 28, 30
McFee Tunnel (WA), 208
McIntosh/McIntosh Lake (WA), 254–256
Medimont (ID), 36, 38
Memorial Loop, Idaho Falls (ID), 24
Menlo (WA), 248
Midvale (ID), 40–43
Milton (WA), 183–184, 186
Milwaukee Road Corridor (WA). *See* Chicago, Milwaukee, St. Paul and Pacific Railroad
Milwaukie (OR), 97, 101–104
Milwaukie Bay Park (OR), 101–104
Mirabeau Point Park (WA), 239
Missing Link Trail (WA), 127
Monarch Sculpture Park and Art Center (WA), 141
Morrison Bridge (OR), 105 (photo)
Morse Creek, 73
Moscow (ID), 25–27, 121
Moscow-Arrow rail line, 25
Mosier Twin Tunnels (OR), 77–78
Mount Baker (WA), 135, 143
Mount Hood, view of, 97 (photo)
Mount Rainier (WA), 160 (photo), 169 (photo), 255
Mount Williams (OR), 108, 110
mountain biking, trail use icon for, 7
Mountlake Terrace (WA), 180–182
movie history, in Astoria (OR), 52
Mullan (ID), 36, 38
museums, 52
    historical, 228, 231
    maritime, 52
    railroad/railway, 219, 231, 234, 247, 254, 255 (photo), 256
Myrtle, Lake (WA), 251–252
Myrtle Edwards Park (WA), 157–161

Naches River (WA), 251–252
Naches Train Depot (WA), 251
Nakashima Heritage Barn (WA), 135, 137 (photo)
National Nordic Museum (WA), 127
The Nature Conservancy, 87
Neely-Soames Homestead, Kent (WA), 174

Nine Mile Falls Recreation Area (WA), 239–242
NorPac Trail (ID), 36, 38–39
North Clackamas Parks & Recreation District (OR), 101
North Head Lighthouse (WA), 150–152
North Idaho Centennial Trail (ID), 8, 28–31
North Idaho College, 28, 30
North Yakima & Valley Railway (WA), 143
Northern Pacific Railroad, 126, 147, 155, 157, 170, 189, 219–220, 234
Northwest Carriage Museum (WA), 247
Northwest Railway Museum (WA), 219, 234

OC&E Woods Line State Trail (OR), 84–87
Old Mill Reach (OR), 67
Old Mission State Park (ID), 26, 28
Old Oroville Railroad Depot Historical Society Museum and Log House (WA), 231
Old Railroad Grade (WA), 112, 199–201
Olene (OR), 84–87
Olmsted, John Charles, 97
Olympia (WA), 139–142, 190–192, 258
Olympian Hiawatha (passenger train), 34
Olympic Discovery Trail (WA), 6 (photo), 112, 202–209
  Blyn to Port Angeles, 206–207
  Lake Crescent to La Push, 208
  Port Angeles to Lake Crescent, 207–208
  Port Townsend to Blyn, 205–206
  Spruce Railroad Trail, 204, 206 (photo)
Olympic Mountains (WA), 202–209
Olympic National Park (WA), 204, 207, 208
Olympic Peninsula (WA), 202–209
Olympic Sculpture Park (WA), 157
Oregon, California and Eastern Railroad. *See* OC&E Woods Line State Trail (OR)
Oregon City Line streetcar route (OR), 101–104
Oregon Short Line (ID), 11
Oregon & Southeastern Railroad (O&SE), 91–93
Oroville (WA), 229–231
Orting (WA), 169–171
Othello (WA), 214

Pacific Flyway (WA), 235
Padden Creek (WA), 177
painted rock collection (WA), 197
Palouse to Cascades State Park Trail (WA), 112, 210–217
  Cedar Falls to Snoqualmie Tunnel, 213
  Columbia River to Idaho Border, 214–216
  Hyak to Columbia River, 213–214
Paradise Creek (WA), 121, 122, 123
Paradise Path (ID), 25–27
parking areas, 3. *See also individual trails*
Pe Ell (WA), 248
Pearson (ID), 33
Peninsula Trails Coalition, 204, 206
Perrine Bridge/Coulee (ID), 18, 19
Pillsbury Mills Elevator (ID), 10, 12
Pine City (WA), 216
Pine Flat (OR), 86
Pioneer Park (OR), 66
Pioneer Reach (OR), 66
Plummer (ID), 36, 37
Port Angeles (WA), 203–209
Port Townsend (WA), 202–209
Portland (OR)
  Banks-Vernonia State Trail, 48, 53–56
  I-205 Multi-Use Path, 48, 80–83
  Springwater Corridor, 48, 97–100
  Trolley Trail, 48, 102–104
  Vera Katz Eastbank Esplanade, 48, 105–107
  Westside Trail, 48, 108–111
Portland and Southwestern Railroad, 61
Post Falls (ID), 28, 30
Powell Butte Nature Park (OR), 99
Prairie Trail (ID), 28, 30
Preston (WA), 189, 220
Preston-Snoqualmie Trail (WA), 112, 113 (photo), 218–220
Prosser (WA), 198
Puget Sound (WA), 125–127. *See also* Leafline Trail Network
  Chehalis Western Trail, 139–142, 192, 256
  Elliott Bay Trail, 112, 157–161
  Interurban Trail, 112, 176–186
  Issaquah-Preston Trail, 112, 187–189
  Olympic Discovery Trail, 112, 202–209
Puget Sound Electric Railway, 183
Pullman (WA), 121
Pullman Loop Trail (WA), 123

Puyallup (WA), 169–171
Puyallup Indian Reservation, 184, 186
Queen Lucas Lake (WA), 165–167
Quileute people, 203

racetrack, 185
Raging River (WA), 219–220
Raging River ravine (WA), 113 (photo)
rail-trail, defined/described, 2
rail-with-trail, defined/described, 2
Railroad Bridge Park (WA), 207
railroads
    active, map icon for, 3
    museums, 219, 231, 234, 247, 255 (photo), 256
Rails to Trails Conservancy (RTC), iii, 265
    Great American Rail-Trail® project, 2–3
    Hall of Fame inductees, 2
Rainbow Falls State Park (WA), 248
Rainier (WA), 255–256
Rainier Trail (WA), 188, 189
Ralston (WA), 215
Rattlesnake Lake (WA), 233–234
Rattlesnake Lake Recreation Area (WA), 212, 222
Raymond (WA), 247–249
Red Bridge (ID), 16
Red Electric Trail (OR), 75
Redmond (WA), 125
Redmond Central Connector (WA), 149, 156, 227
Redmond Powerline Trail (WA), 149, 156, 227
Renton (WA), 131–134
restrooms, map icons for, 3
Ribbon of Jewels (Boise riverside parks), 15–16
Richland Riverfront Trail (WA), 112, 221–224
River Pointe Park (ID), 15–16
River Run Reach (OR), 66
Riverfront Park (WA), 241, 247
Riverside Park (ID), 15
Riverside State Park (WA), 239, 241–242
Robert Bush Memorial Park (WA), 247
Robin Hill Farm County Park (WA), 207
rock climbing, 20, 96
rock collection, painted (WA), 197
Rock Creek Trail (OR), 110
rock formations, Cowiche Canyon Trail (WA), 143

Rocky Mountains (ID), 45–46
Rogue River Greenway (OR), 88–90
Ron Regis Park (WA), 133
roughness rating, of trails, 3–4
Route of the Hiawatha (ID), 8, 32–35
Row River Trail (OR), 91–93
Ruby Carson Memorial Park (ID), 12
Ruth Bascom Riverbank Path System (OR), 94–96
Ryder Park, Idaho Falls (ID), 22, 24

safety guidelines. *See* travel precautions/preparations
Sammamish, Lake, 153–154, 153 (photo)
Sammamish Landing Park (WA), 154, 156
Sammamish people, 153, 187
Sammamish River Trail (WA), 112, 225–228
San Juan de Fuca (WA), Strait of, 202, 203, 206, 207
San Juan Islands (WA), 177
Sauk Mountain (WA), 129
Sawyer Park (OR), 64–67
sculptures/sculpture parks, 107, 127, 141, 149, 151, 157, 170, 174, 238, 247
Seabury Bridge (WA), 215 (photo)
Seattle (WA)
    Burke-Gilman Trail, 124–127
    Elliott Bay Trail, 112, 157–161
    Interurban Trail (North and South), 112, 180–186
Seattle, Lake Shore & Eastern Railway, 125, 137, 215
Seattle and Northern Company rail line, 243
Seattle Aquarium, 161
Seborne Hill Arboretum (WA), 236
Sedro-Woolley (WA), 128–130
Sellwood Bridge (OR), 99, 100
Sellwood Riverfront Park (OR), 99, 100
Sequim (WA), 202–209
Sequim Bay State Park (WA), 206–207
Sequim Lavender Festival, 207
Shoreline (WA), 180–182
Shoshone Falls (ID), 19 (photo), 20
Shoshone Falls Park (ID), 20
Silver Valley (ID), 38
Similkameen Trail (WA), 112, 229–231
Skagit River (WA), 29–30
skating, trail use icon for, 7
skiing, trail use icon for, 7

Skinner Butte Park (OR), 96
S'Klallam people, 203
S'Klallam Tribal Library, 206
Smith Cove Park (WA), 157, 161
Snake River, 18, 19, 21 (photo)
    Canyon Rim Trail, 18–20
    Idaho Falls Greenbelt, 21–24
Snoqualmie Falls (WA), 220
Snoqualmie Pass (WA), 213
Snoqualmie people, 153
Snoqualmie Valley Trail (WA), 112, 232–235
snowmobiling, trail use icon for, 7
Sontag Day Use Area (WA), 241
South Bay (WA), 139
South Bay Trail (WA), 112, 236–238
South Bend (WA), 247–249
South Canyon Reach (OR), 67
South Capital Park, Idaho Falls (ID), 22, 24
South Cle Elum Depot and Rail Yard (WA), 214
South Prairie (WA), 169–171
South Tourist Park, Idaho Falls (ID), 22, 24
Spokane (WA)
    Centennial State Park Trail, 112, 239–242
    Fish Lake Trail, 112, 165–167
Spokane, Portland & Seattle Railroad, 193
Spokane River, 29 (photo)
    North Idaho Centennial Trail, 28–31
    Spokane River Centennial State Park Trail, 28, 112, 239–242
Spokane River Centennial State Park Trail (WA), 28, 112, 239–242
Spokane Valley Mall (WA), 239
Sportsman Park, Idaho Falls (ID), 22, 24
Sprague River (OR), 85, 86, 87
Sprague River Valley (OR), 84, 86
Springwater Corridor (OR), 97–100
Spruce Railroad Trail (WA), 204–207
St. Joe River, 38 (photo)
St. Paul Pass Tunnel (ID), 32, 34
State Line Park (ID), 28, 29
Strait of San Juan de Fuca (WA), 202, 203, 206, 207
Stringfield Park (OR), 102, 104
Sun Valley (ID), 45
Sun Valley Trail (ID), 47
Sunnyside (OR), 80, 82
Sunnyside (WA), 196–198

Sunnyside Extension, Idaho Falls Greenbelt (ID), 22, 24
Swale Canyon (WA), 193, 195
Swede's Cut (OR), 86
Sycan Marsh (OR), 84–87

Tamarack lumber mill (ID), 40, 43
Tekoa (WA), 212, 216
Temple Loop, Idaho Falls (ID), 20, 23
Tenino Depot Museum (WA), 254, 255 (photo)
Tenino/Tenino City Park (WA), 256
Terminal 91 Bike Trail (WA), 157
Tetonia (ID), 10, 12
Three Friends Fishing Hole (WA), 172, 174
Tideman Johnson Park (OR), 99
Tigard (OR), 72–74, 75
Tiger Mountain (WA), 189
Tolt Pipeline Trail (WA), 228
Tolt River (WA), 234
Tommy Thompson Parkway (WA), 112, 243–245
trail(s)
    definitions, 2
    endpoints, 3
    general characteristics, 3–4
    Great American Rail-Trail® project, 1, 2–3
    hiking etiquette on, 4–5
    multiuse of, 6, 7
    in RTC Hall of Fame, 2
    travel precautions/preparations, 5, 6
    use icons, 7. *See also individual trails*
Trail of the Coeur d'Alenes (ID), 8, 36–39
TrailLink.com, 4, 7
travel precautions/preparations, 5, 6
    heavy metal contamination, 39
    wildlife, 6–7
trestles, historical
    Ashton-Tetonia Trail, 10–12
    Banks-Vernonia State Trail, 53–56
    Cascade Trail, 130
    Klickitat Trail, 195
    Mosby Park, 91 (photo)
    OC&E Woods Line State Trail, 87
    Olympic Discovery Trail, 207
    Palouse to Cascades State Park Trail, 216
    Raging River, 220
    Route of the Hiawatha, 33
    Row River Trail, 91 (photo)

Weiser River National Recreation
Trail, 41
Willapa Hills State Park Trail, 248
(photo)
Trolley Trail (OR), 48, 97, 101–104
Troy (ID), 25–27
Tukwila (WA), 172–175, 183–186
tunnels
    Route of the Hiawatha, 32, 34 (photo)
    Snoqualmie Valley Trail, 213
Twin Falls (ID), 8, 18–20
Twin Falls Visitor Center (ID), 18, 19

Union, Lake (WA), 126
Union Pacific Railroad, 39, 41, 45, 48, 99, 121, 165
University of Idaho, 121
University of Washington, 125, 126
Upper Yakima River Canyon (WA), 214, 215
U.S. Army Yakima Training Center (WA), 213, 214

Vancouver (WA), 81–83
Vancouver, George, 208
Vera Katz Eastbank Esplanade (OR), 48, 105–107
Vernonia Lake Park (OR), 53–56

walking, trail use icon for, 7
Wallace (ID), 36, 38
Wallace Falls (WA), 201
Wallace Falls Railway Trail (WA). See Old Railroad Grade (WA)
Wallace Falls State Park (WA), 199
Wallace Falls Timber Company (WA), 199
Wallace Lake (WA), 201
Warden (WA), 212, 214
Warren G. Magnuson Park (WA), 126
Washington, Lake, 125, 126, 131
Washington & Great Northern Railroad, 231
Washington State University (WA), 121
water for drinking, map icons for, 3

waterfalls
    Canyon Rim Trail, 19–20
    Historic Columbia River Highway State Trail, 78
    Idaho Falls Greenbelt, 23
    Old Railroad Grade, 199, 201
    Similkameen Trail, 229, 231
    Snoqualmie Valley Trail, 234
Weiser (ID), 40–43
Weiser River National Recreation Trail (ID), 8, 40–43
Wenatchee (WA), 114–117
Westside Trail (OR), 48, 108–111
Weyerhaeuser Timber Co. (WA), 139
Weyerhaeuser Woods line (OR), 86
wheelchair access, trail use icon for, 7
Whilamut Natural Area (OR), 96
White River (WA), 169, 170
Whitehorse Trail (WA), 136
Wild and Scenic Klickitat River (WA), 193–195, 193 (photo)
Wilderness Lake (WA), 134
wildlife, safety tips and, 6–7
Willamette River (OR), 96, 97–99, 101, 105, 107
Willapa Hills State Park Trail (WA), 112, 246–249
Winery Trail (WA), 145
Wood River Trail (ID), 8, 44–47
Woodard Bay Natural Resources Conservation Area (WA), 139
Woodland Creek Community Park (WA), 192
Woodland Trail Greenway (WA). See Karen Fraser Woodland Trail (WA)
Woody Trail (WA), 199–200201

Yakima (WA), 251–253
Yakima Area Arboretum (WA), 250, 252
Yakima Greenway (WA), 112, 250–253
Yelm–Rainier–Tenino Trail (WA), 112, 141–142, 254–256
Yelm/Yelm City Park (WA), 254–256

Support Rails to Trails Conservancy

Rails to Trails Conservancy (RTC) is a nonprofit organization working to build a nation connected by trails. We reimagine public spaces to create safe ways for everyone to walk, bike, and be active outdoors. Since 1986, RTC has worked from coast to coast, helping to transform unused rail corridors and other rights-of-way into vibrant public places, ensuring a better future for America made possible by trails and the connections they inspire.

We know trails improve lives, engage communities, create opportunities, and inspire movement. And we know these opportunities are possible only with the help of our passionate members and supporters across the country. Learn how you can support RTC, and discover the benefits of membership at **railstotrails.org/support.**

Rails to Trails Conservancy is a 501(c)(3) nonprofit organization, and contributions are tax-deductible.

Start your trail adventure with interactive maps on TrailLink.

Trail moments

Chelsea Murphy

Bree Corbin

Trail stories that inspire.

In neighborhoods across America, trails are essential—creating space for us to walk, bike and be active outside. Trails are places where we connect with friends and family, log daily steps, safely commute to the places we need to go or simply take some time for ourselves. The moments we make in these spaces are limitless, but across the board, **trail moments make our everyday moments better.**

View the Trail Moments collection or share your own story!
railstotrails.org/trailmoments

#TrailMoments

Our members make trails happen.

Join the movement! Become a member and help us build a nation connected by trails.

Give $18 or more to become a member. Your yearlong membership includes an exclusive member T-shirt, a subscription to our quarterly flagship magazine and reduced prices on trail guidebooks and gear!

Get even more benefits by becoming a monthly donor or auto-renewal member, or by joining the Trailblazer Society.

SUPPORT THE TRAILS YOU LOVE
railstotrails.org/membership